THE PERFECT $100,000 HOUSE

The Perfect

A TRIP ACROSS AMERICA AND BACK

$100,000 House

IN PURSUIT OF A PLACE TO CALL HOME

Karrie Jacobs

WITH ILLUSTRATIONS BY Gary Panter

VIKING

VIKING

Published by the Penguin Group

Penguin Group (USA) Inc., 375 Hudson Street, New York, New York 10014, U.S.A. · Penguin Group
(Canada), 90 Eglinton Avenue East, Suite 700, Toronto, Ontario, Canada M4P 2Y3 (a division of Pearson
Penguin Canada Inc.) · Penguin Books Ltd, 80 Strand, London WC2R 0RL, England · Penguin Ireland,
25 St. Stephen's Green, Dublin 2, Ireland (a division of Penguin Books Ltd) · Penguin Books Australia Ltd,
250 Camberwell Road, Camberwell, Victoria 3124, Australia (a division of Pearson Australia Group Pty Ltd) ·
Penguin Books India Pvt Ltd, 11 Community Centre, Panchsheel Park, New Delhi – 110 017, India · Penguin
Group (NZ), Cnr Airborne and Rosedale Roads, Albany, Auckland 1310, New Zealand (a division of Pearson
New Zealand Ltd) · Penguin Books (South Africa) (Pty) Ltd, 24 Sturdee Avenue, Rosebank, Johannesburg
2196, South Africa

Penguin Books Ltd, Registered Offices: 80 Strand, London WC2R 0RL, England

First published in 2006 by Viking Penguin, a member of Penguin Group (USA) Inc.

10   9   8   7   6   5   4   3   2   1

Artwork by Gary Panter

LIBRARY OF CONGRESS CATALOGING IN PUBLICATION DATA
Jacobs, Karrie, date.
    The perfect $100,000 house : a trip across America and back in pursuit of a place to call home /
  Karrie Jacobs.
      p. cm.
    Includes index.
    ISBN 0-670-03761-3
    1. Architecture, Domestic—United States—Themes, motives.   2. Architecture, Domestic—
Psychological aspects.   I. Title.   II. Title: Perfect one-hundred-thousand-dollar house.
  NA7208.2.J33 2006
  728' .370973—dc22   2006044741

Printed in the United States of America
Set in Bitstream Arrus
Designed by Amy Hill

In memory of David and Rose Jacobs,
who knew a thing or two about the concept of home

Acknowledgments

Endless thanks to my agent, Patricia van der Leun, for walking into my life at precisely the right moment; my editor at Viking, Rick Kot, for grasping the concept, letting me run with it, and then reining me in with precision and grace; and to Gary Panter for agreeing without hesitation to draw the pictures. I am also deeply grateful to the many architects, builders, and passersby who shared their ideas with me and took my project seriously, especially Brett Zamore, who was in this from the very beginning; Peter and Mark Anderson, who are this book's patron saints; and Bill Massie, who played the crucial cleanup position. Special thanks to my comrades in Prospect, Colorado—Mark Sofield, Kelly Feeney, and Kiki Wallace—for endless commiseration on the joys and sorrows of defying convention (and also for the gnocchi). And my friends Amelia Amon, Lynn Gordon, Jon Houston, Daisann McLane, and Victoria Milne for occasionally asking "How's the book going?" but not asking too often. Thanks also to Martin Pedersen, my editor at *Metropolis*, for asking that same question with alarming frequency, and to my column buddy Philip Nobel for demonstrating that it is possibly to actually finish writing a book; to Horace Havemeyer III and Susan Szenasy of *Metropolis*, Nancy Novogrod and Luke Barr of *Travel + Leisure*, and Sheila Glaser of the *New York Times Magazine*, all of whom have helped to insure that I still have no idea how to write a grant proposal. Thanks to my family—Alan, Alan, Ben, Frank, and Susan—for not really expecting me to remember birthdays . . . at least, not all the time. And also to the extended family of *Dwell* staffers and freelancers, past and present, without whom this book never would have happened.

Contents

THE PERFECT $100,000 HOUSE

Introduction

On the first of February 2003, the day the shuttle *Columbia* falls from the sky, I am in Houston, which likes to think of itself as "Space City." It's a Saturday, and I've gotten up early to go for a run around Memorial Park, a pancake of open land with a golf course at its center and a soft dirt running track around the perimeter. When I arrive the sun is just burning through a morning mist, and Houstonians are bundled up against what they imagine to be cold weather. I marvel at the woman wearing leopard-patterned fur gloves as she jogs. *Texas,* I think.

By the time I'm in my second lap the temperature is well into the 60s. There is a moment when the sun, still low in the sky, lights the beads of dew on the grass, turning the wet turf silver, and at that instant I tell myself that I could live in Houston. It is such little moments of pure euphoria that wed me to a place, that make me want to be there forever.

After my run I get back into my car—yes, one drives to run in Houston—and hear the voice on the radio. Scott Simon on NPR sounds so distraught that I know something is wrong, and when I realize that the space shuttle is lost, the first thing I think—maybe illogically—is terrorism. All jittery from exertion and fear, I drive my rented beige Taurus back toward the hotel, trying to navigate the maze of on-ramps, off-ramps, mall entrances, and parking garages, trying to pick up coffee at a Starbucks and get back to my hotel to shower in preparation for an early lunch date. During this second part of the morning, my exultation dissipated, I find myself hating Houston for its utter dysfunctionality. Suddenly, it is the last place I want to be, the last place I could possibly live.

I'll be honest: I am fickle. I fall in and out of love with places all the time. One minute I'm all transcendence and glow, and the next minute I'm ready to drive on. Earlier in the week, I'd had a similar moment in Galveston, 50 miles south and east. Part of it was the weather—70 and sunny—and part of it was the sight of a long stretch of beach, the feel of sand underfoot. But mostly I was smitten by the real estate. After a strange breakfast of an oyster po'boy and weak coffee, I sat down on some rocks by the water and wrote in my spiral-bound notebook:

I could just stop right here.

And I meant it. I did.

It is the perfect, funky, charming beach town with long expanses of waterfront esplanade, goofy motels. . . . There's an ugly 1960s hotel called The Flagship built on a pier, tacky souvenir shops, and houses that could easily be had for under $100,000. I could be a Texan.

I spent my afternoon in Galveston with a chain-smoking real estate lady named Shari. She was wizened and freckled and looked as if she'd been out in the sun and the wind forever. I imagined that forty years ago she had been a cowgirl or farmhand, someone who never spent the daylight hours indoors. But now she was working as a broker, coaxing listings from her computer. There was one on Thirteenth Street for $65,000, only 832 square feet, but cute as a button. Another, a little larger, was going for $82,500. We took a look.

The less expensive one was, on the outside, a perfectly restored cottage, with bright yellow paint and a new corrugated metal awning over its front door, but inside it was battered and mildew-scented. I just stared at the walls and envisioned the frayed wiring and wonky plumbing behind them. The more expensive house was plain as dough on the outside, a charmless white box, but inside it was spacious and well maintained. Neither had much land to speak of. But both were near the beach, on the Gulf side of the island, which, in Galveston, the scene of a devastating hurricane a hundred years ago, is considered something of a disadvantage. Still, they gave me confidence that not only was it possible to find a great $100,000 house but also I could have one on the beach for that price. I was sure that, if I spent a couple of days driving around with Shari, I would stumble on perfection.

I could just stop right here, I thought. And then I got in my car and drove on. I came to Galveston, as I came to Houston, on a quest: a search for the Perfect $100,000 House. I know that it is out here in America somewhere. I'm sure of it.

When I began my search I had owned only one piece of real estate in my life, a 720-square-foot co-op apartment at the corner of Third Avenue and Fourteenth Street in Manhattan. It was, when I bought it, a space with all the charm and character of a room at a Holiday Inn. But it had a view I liked of a particularly rakish streetscape: the Variety Photoplay Theater (which had gone from showing porn to being a respectable off-Broadway theater), the Faith and Hope Mission, and the Pitstop, a biker bar that eventually morphed into an NYU student hangout. My apartment had standard-issue parquet floors, a daffodil-yellow kitchen that I planned to someday paint and renovate, and lots of closets. On one of its completely featureless 8-foot-tall living room walls I had a furniture maker build a 17-foot-long shelving unit, which accommodated most of my books, my collection of oversized magazines, and my files. In the corner nearest the window, I had a desk that wrapped around and gave me a view of the ceaseless flow of traffic—so many fire engines, so many buses—careening (or crawling) down Third Avenue. This spot by the window, where I would sometimes sit all day, writing, making phone calls, thinking, this spot was as close as I've ever been to home.

I thought I would live there forever.

Back then, in 1999, I was a professional urbanist. I was the architecture critic for *New York* magazine, and my life was about exploring and understanding the city. I would look out my window as I'd begin my workday and nod to the Con Ed clock tower across Fourteenth Street or ride the elevator to the roof and take inventory, inspecting New York's skyline as if it were my job to make sure that each of the buildings was in its proper place (a chore that was then, happily, entirely unnecessary).

My greatest pleasure as a critic was gaining access to the secret or off-limits portions of big buildings: the attic of the Chrysler Building, the corporate dining rooms atop the Chase Manhattan tower, the roof of the still-under-construction Condé Nast headquarters in Times Square. One time I accepted an offer to climb the rigging to the very top of Grand Central Terminal when it was being cleaned and restored. As I stood on the scaffolding immediately below the station's starry ceiling, I rediscovered a long-dormant fear of heights. But even though my knees were shaking, I was happy to be up there, cultivating an intimacy with one of New York's signature buildings.

Then I was offered a job as the founding editor of *Dwell,* a new magazine about modern residential design. Taking the position would mean moving to San Francisco and devoting myself to thinking exclusively about small buildings, single-family homes. Instead of being led by architects and developers through their most ambitious creations, I would learn about building at a more personal scale, where homeowners and designers would point out the fabulous European showerhead, or the cleverly secreted storage space. I was making a headlong plunge into the nature and culture of domesticity.

In truth, I didn't have to lose my home but made a choice to do so. Because the price that the real estate agent told me I could get for my New York apartment in late 1999 was so much higher than what I had originally paid for it, I decided to sell. It made a certain amount of sense. I figured that the dot-com boom that was driving real estate prices higher couldn't last. I thought I might want to stay on the West Coast. I thought I might want ultimately to buy a place somewhere else and fantasized about a beach house somewhere in Marin County. It was all semi-rational.

What I didn't understand at the time about selling my home was how much *having* a home meant to me. The irony didn't escape me: I had sacrificed my own home to launch a magazine that was all about other people's homes.

Early in the process of developing *Dwell* we gave it a tagline: "At Home in the Modern World." Meanwhile, I was adrift in the modern world. I rented a large, elegant, art deco San Francisco apartment, overlooking the bay from a Pacific Heights hilltop. With its sunken bathtub and sun-filled living room, it was more beautiful than any apartment in which I'd ever lived, but it wasn't home. I missed the Variety Photoplay sign and the roar of Third Avenue.

All told, I lived for three years in a city in which I felt myself to be, in some deep, existential way, homeless.

During that period I dedicated myself to learning about every single architect, designer, developer, or homeowner in America who was doing something amazing with the economics, technology, or aesthetics of home. If my goal for the magazine was to showcase every new idea in residential design, my personal goal was to figure out how avant-garde architecture could be built for a price that any homebuyer could afford. Even me. *Especially* me.

What I quickly learned is that it was the commercial homebuilders—the companies that routinely bulldozed open desert and plopped down there a brand new subdivision of Spanish or Colonial or Tudor homes—that knew how to build cheap. One of their houses might, depending on the location, easily go for $100,000 or less. But custom homes, the kind of architect-designed places that a magazine generally publishes, almost always went for upwards of half a million dollars—and often much, much more. It occurred to me that there was no challenge in building an aesthetically perfect palace if you could spend a million dollars on it. The trick was getting results for a tenth of that price.

The other thing I came to believe was that the homeowners who took risks and the architects whom they hired were, in their own ways, more daring than the New York architects who built multimillion-dollar towers and their clients. They were experimenting with their own lives, testing how much architecture a typical suburban neighborhood would tolerate, jeopardizing their net worth to try something the lenders couldn't understand: a fabric roof, a lacquered concrete floor, walls that slid all the way open in summer.

I discovered a pair of architect/builder brothers in Seattle, the Andersons, who made prefabricated homes that were designed so that the components could be transported on the back of a flatbed truck or fitted into shipping containers for export to Japan. They were the architects of a house built for $86,000. I met an architecture professor in Bozeman, Montana, William Massie, who had devised a method of building $150,000 houses from concrete blocks shaped by an elaborate computer-driven modeling and milling process. I admired the $30,000 homes that the late Samuel Mockbee and his students built for poor rural clients in Alabama and the equally economical, galvanized aluminum house that a young Chilean architect based in Los Angeles, Rocio Romero, built for her mother. I came to understand that land prices and the condition of the land were very big factors in determining the final cost of a home, but I also realized that ingenuity and a creative spirit were critical, as well.

After nearly three years in San Francisco I began to think seriously about leaving. Why? The short answer is 9/11. The events of that day turned my homesickness for New York, my sense of displacement, into a fever, a condition that colored my waking thoughts and actions. The long answer is that the situation at my magazine became more complex and contentious, to the point that day-to-day life was beginning to require Machiavellian skills. I could stay in San Francisco and spend my life maneuvering and manipulating or I could go home. In the weeks before I finally gave notice I'd walk over Russian Hill, which separated my apartment from my office, and admire the terraced gardens of Vallejo Street or the pastel-tinted facades along Union Street at sunset. Or I would run along the Bay to Fort Point under the Golden Gate Bridge and try to keep pace with a swimming seal. Repeatedly I'd ask myself, How could I want so badly to leave a place this beautiful, how could I fail to love it? The answer was always the same: it's not home.

One evening, after a particularly long day at the office, I went to see the movie *Spider-Man.* Late in the film, there's a scene in which the villain, the Green Goblin, does battle with the hero in the airspace adjacent to the Queensboro Bridge. Just as the Green Goblin gains the upper hand, a group of ur–New Yorkers, who have congregated on the bridge, begin to throw bricks and stones at him. One of them yells something like, "Hey, Goblin! Leave Spiduh-Man alone! Yuh mess wid one New Yawkuh, yuh mess wid all of us."

The scene made me cry. I took this as a sign.

Later, when I told a friend about this moment, he labeled it "the *Spider-Man* epiphany." The next day, I walked out of a particularly aggravating meeting with the magazine's publisher. I walked out because I was angry. I'd been angry at plenty of meetings, but I'd never before actually gotten up and left. This was the end. I could no longer live in a beautiful city I didn't love and I couldn't spend my life being angry. I was going home.

Several months later, after the movers came and loaded up my belongings into a truck destined for a warehouse in New Jersey, after I handed off my cat temporarily to my regular cat-sitter's brother-in-law, a sad sack who lived in the Tenderloin, I felt completely and utterly drained. At that moment I had no place to live on either coast. I got in my car and drove to

Bolinas, a small town on the Point Reyes peninsula in Marin County that is regarded as one of the last bastions of the 1960s counterculture. Its small, seedy downtown is full of old hippies, young surfers, and the few tourists who find their way there despite the fact that the locals routinely remove the directional signs from Highway 1. It is a sort of ragtag Shangri-la with astronomical real estate values. In Bolinas I stayed for a few days in a borrowed house, resting up for the long drive back to the East Coast. The house belonged to an archetypal hippie couple, but a friend of mine, a New York graphic designer, had been living there for a few years.

The house was shaped like a half-moon, with a kitchen at one end of a long, curving room and a bathroom at the other; in between was a living room/studio and a sleeping area. The convex curve of the building was mostly glass, looking out over a patio, a flower garden, and, beyond, an uninterrupted vista of coastal meadows. The house was small, but it didn't feel that way, in part because of the daylight pouring in and in part because of the intimate connection between indoors and outdoors, a defining feature of California architecture. In this house in Bolinas I was happy for the first time in months, maybe in years. There I relaxed, I read, I thought. I pulled a novel off a shelf, *Bee Season,* and read it cover to cover without interruption. Friends came one day and cooked me an elaborate lunch. We sat outside, ate, and drank wine and watched the light change as the afternoon progressed.

Confronted with the long drive ahead of me and a return to a New York where I had no job and no apartment (aside from a dubious sublet), California felt pretty good. When I was packing up my San Francisco apartment, sorting through my clothing, I had come to a drawer in my dresser that I hadn't opened in months, my sock drawer. The pairs of socks there, all rolled into balls, looked to me like some sort of pupae. Did I ever wear these things? In California I didn't, and suddenly I began to have doubts about going back to my old, sock-wearing life. I dreaded returning to a place with winter. Now, I didn't want to leave Bolinas; to my surprise, this little house had suddenly come to represent everything I wanted in the world.

Reluctantly I began my drive east, stopping the first night in Tahoe City on the California-Nevada border. In the morning I filled my tank at a self-service gas pump. When the pump's LED display flashed a question that required a yes or no answer, I thought it was asking if I wanted a receipt, so I pushed "yes." Actually, it was selling me a car wash. I didn't want a car wash. I went inside to try and get a refund, and the girl behind the counter was rude and snotty. "You should learn to read," she told me. At that moment, all the anger that I'd accumulated in my last six months of Machiavellian fray and all the anxiety I had about returning to New York came bursting out. I began to yell at the girl and didn't stop yelling until some guy standing near the counter intervened, shouting, "Get the fuck out of here, you tourist!" I had two thoughts. *This is why it's a good thing I don't own a gun* and *He just might.* I quickly left.

Then, gradually, as I drove across the empty midsection of Nevada on Route 50, "the Loneliest Highway in America," where the scenery consists primarily of mirage lakes and dead cattle, I began to calm down. As I drove mile after mile, state after state, listening to the radio, visiting friends, seeing the sights, the anger leached out of me. I began to realize that long-distance driving was for me a form of meditation.

This book grew out of those two experiences, my stay in Bolinas and my San Francisco–to–New York drive. I realized that more than anything else at this point in my life, I wanted a place of my own where I would feel the way I did in that little half-moon house. Surely everything I had come to learn and everyone I had come to know during my years at *Dwell* could help me create such a place. And, if I had to embark on an epic road trip to accomplish my goal, so much the better.

As for the $100,000 figure, the simplest explanation is that it was the amount I had left over from the sale of my New York apartment. It's roughly what I had in the bank when I conceived this project. (Note that my $100,000 budget doesn't include land cost, in part because this is a book about building strategies rather than real estate per se and in part because land costs are such a wild card. I did, however, try to avoid parts of the country where the land prices were excessive, though a few of the houses I found—particularly in Texas—did include the cost of land acquisition in their selling price.)

But even more than that, it's what I decided that a house—my house—*should* cost: a thousand square feet, at a hundred bucks a square foot. This is not only not unreasonable, it's actually logical. The average American home today is 2,200 square feet (up from 1,400 in 1970), and the median home price (as of late 2005) is about $220,000, so my perfect house actually would cost the same per square foot as a typical American house. The complication, of course, is that I have no interest in the typical American house.

For starters, there is the issue of size. In truth, the single most radical thing about my ideal house is not the price tag but the square footage. Maybe I've lived too long in New York City, but I don't really understand what most people do with 3,000- or 4,000-square-foot homes. It's not as if the American family itself has gotten bigger. The average number of people per household was 3.14 in 1970 and had declined to 2.59 by the 2000 census. Honestly, I wish I could go into the sales office of some development and say, "I'll take the three-bedroom Tudor with the second-floor family room and the optional home office" and be done with it. But it doesn't work like that, not for me. It would be a little like finding true love on Match.com. The options are more finite than they appear.

This is, in part, a cultural preference: I would no more buy a McMansion than I would an SUV. But while import models offer a decent alternative to the giant cars that Detroit has been selling in recent years, the housing industry provides nothing comparable.

Fundamentally, my needs are not all that unconventional. My ideal house includes features that most ordinary people want: lots of sunlight; a tall, unbroken space containing the kind of kitchen that spills into the living room; an office; and a bedroom. There should be outdoor space of some sort, maybe just an urban patio or maybe some actual acreage. I can see myself with a garden. But the house in my head is modernist, maybe even minimalist in its architectural style, unornamented and lean. Someone once told me that he saw me as "ruthlessly pragmatic." And I think that's about right. What I love about modern design is not the high-gloss surfaces you now see in boutique hotels and noodle bars but the unadorned pragmatism of early modernism. The commercial homebuilders don't do that. Not yet, anyway.

So the $100,000 price tag is more than just a number. It's a divining rod that I hope will lead me to hidden reservoirs of the populist spirit that initially defined the modernist movement. The price tag is my way of getting past the modernist style per se and into the heart of the matter, to return to the moment when Bauhaus founder Walter Gropius talked about "simplicity in multiplicity," about making the kind of design that he saw as organic and innate "readily accessible to everyone."

Inexpensive, well-made housing used to be the Holy Grail . . . and not just at the Bauhaus. The search for a technique that was affordable, functionally sane, and aesthetically satisfying also drove—and defeated—such formidable players as Frank Lloyd Wright and R. Buckminster Fuller. The modernists tried to harness the power of industry while the hippie carpenters and New Age builders, who later took up the cause, went native (the yurt) or rediscovered primitive methods (rammed earth or straw bale construction).

The only identifiable success stories in this country, however, have emerged from the world of commercial builders, beginning with Levittown. The homebuilding industry routinely uses the most up-to-date construction methods (computer-controlled distribution of components, prefabricated walls and trusses) and materials (unsavory composites that simulate stone, synthetic stucco) to build houses that allude to a happy, preindustrial past, whether Tudor England, Colonial America, or the Spanish conquest of Mexico. Sadly, ironically, it's the homebuilding industry that has best lived up to the modernist dream of "economical utilization of space, material, time, and money." If you want a new house for a hundred grand or less, you'll have to buy it from a commercial homebuilder, preferably in a corner of the country with low land and labor costs. On the other hand, if you want a house that *looks* Bauhaus influenced, you'll have to spend a lot more. Houses designed by today's modernist architects are most often one-offs. They are custom designed and require highly skilled craftsmen to be built properly. They may embody modern style but they are antithetical to the modernist spirit. Clearly, my road trip would have to be a long one.

Before I began driving, I assembled a list of architects I had encountered while editing *Dwell* who at least dabbled in my price range. A few of them seemed like sure things. For instance, Adam Kalkin, a New Jersey architect who prefers to think of himself as a conceptual artist, had once approached me with a plan to build $99,999 houses from shipping containers. The Anderson brothers of Seattle used to have a section of their Web site about their philosophical interest in building a $100,000 house.

Others made it to my list simply because I wanted to meet them. For instance, there was John Ringel, a member of the legendary design/build team of the 1970s and 1980s, Jersey Devil. Although his career as a rene-gade is now twenty years in the past—today Ringel mostly rehabs expensive second homes in Bucks County, Pennsylvania, and in the more pastoral por-tions of New Jersey—I called him while I was preparing my itinerary and asked for advice. He doubted that a $100,000 house could be had, at least not in the Garden State: "A $100,000 kitchen, maybe," he suggested.

"Do you remember *The Millionaire*?" Ringel asked me. He wasn't refer-ring to one of the current crop of TV reality shows but to the 1950s series in which a guerrilla philanthropist hands out checks to needy strangers. "As I remember," Ringel continued, "he lived in a $100,000 'mansion' that looked like a major estate."

I took this as encouragement.

When I set out on my road trip in July 2003, the median American home price was $168,000. By the time I finished writing in July 2005, it had soared to $206,000. In late 2005 it had risen to $220,000. And those median prices sound like bargains. In New York City, the median is $750,000, and the average selling price broke a million dollars in 2004 and kept heading upward. The most recent market report from one of New York's leading real estate firms puts the average price per square foot for a Manhattan apartment at $984. Multiply that by a thousand, and you would get a rather different book than this one. When I tell people at cocktail parties that I'm writing a book about searching America for the Perfect $100,000 House, they generally think that I've left a zero off my title. But then, when they're done making fun of me, they ask with undisguised longing, "Well, did you find it? Where is it?"

The answer is yes; I found several. But this book isn't a reality TV show, where there is a winner rewarded in a stagey ceremony in which I hand out long-stemmed roses. Rather, it is my attempt to answer a question: Why is it that the typical American house can be cheap or it can be good but it can almost never be both?

In a way there is no "it." The thing I was looking for, the thing that this book represents, is a set of tools for upending the conventional wisdom about houses and housing in this country. It's a compendium of everything I learned about houses, about what they are and what they could be.

I have a little aphorism, a one-liner, that I've used a lot in recent years: The homebuilding industry in this country makes the auto industry look enlightened by comparison. This book is a reflection of my belief that the

American homebuilding industry is going to someday change, that it *has* to change. As the auto industry has, in recent years, been forced to rediscover the idea of fuel efficiency, a handful of homebuilders are dabbling in modern design by building subdivision houses they call "lofts." But mostly, that means they're gradually adding Modernist to their laundry list of historical styles. And style isn't the issue—not for me, anyway.

The modernism that I love, that I care about, isn't a historical movement that peaked in the mid-twentieth century and is currently enjoying a major revival but is rather a frame of mind. It's a way of thinking that involves an ongoing investigation of methods and materials. It's a design philosophy that values comfort but doesn't confuse it with excess. It's a strategy that views the most important elements of design as space, daylight, and the surfaces with which we routinely come into contact. Actually, I think that the term *functionalism,* which was used to describe the variety of modernism that emerged from the Czech city of Brno between the wars, comes closer to what I mean than the overused word *modern.* But if I were to label the movement that I have assembled by stringing together dots on a map, I'd call it the New Pragmatism. The practitioners I visited during my 14,520-mile road trip are all gifted at figuring out how to use (or misuse) all available technologies, methods, and materials to get the most architecture for the least money.

Occasionally, when I have expressed my views about housing, I've been accused of being Marxist or socialist, which is kind of strange, because what I think I'm being is American. The amalgam of innovation and egalitarianism that I admire is—or used to be—an essential part of the fabric of this country. Recently I was following a team of architects and planners who were helping to rebuild the Mississippi Gulf Coast in the wake of Hurricane Katrina. One of them, a Rhode Island–based planner named Bill Dennis, said to a gathering of small-town officials and residents, "Remember that the people who built this country weren't rich, yet they built great towns."

Dennis is by no means a modernist and his taste in architecture isn't mine. Still, I wanted to stand up and cheer.

So, I set out on a road trip in search of the great, cheap house, a place that I can afford, that satisfies my need for a home, my taste for innovative design, and my desire for a more enlightened approach to homebuilding. Unlike Walter Gropius, I wasn't looking for a way to house the masses. Honestly, I just wanted to buy a house for myself . . . and maybe a cat or two. But I do believe that my search for ways to build more sensibly, modestly, and beautifully is my personal contribution to the ongoing reinvention of the American dream.

The Primal Shed, Waitsfield, Vermont

Housebuilding Camp

1

*July 6, 2003   10:03 P.M.   **The White Horse Inn, Waitsfield, Vermont***

First there is the hard part, getting free of New York City's gravitational pull.

But on Sunday morning of the Fourth of July weekend even the most construction-riddled stretches of the Brooklyn-Queens Expressway don't back up, and suddenly, without delay, I find myself on the Tappan Zee Bridge admiring the beauty of the Hudson. Why do I want a house in the San Juan Islands, *I ask myself,* when there is all this majesty so close to home? *I can just stop the car and buy something.*

I think of myself as a smart girl, someone with a bit of depth, but as I set out on the first leg of a road trip that will take me 14,520 miles, from Brooklyn Heights counterclockwise around the United States and back, the thing that makes me happiest is the prospect of spending quality time with my car. I'd bought my midnight blue Volkswagen Cabrio during the three years I lived in California and haven't seen much of it since my return to New York City. Since I sold my Manhattan apartment, the car—okay, and my computer—are the only things of consequence that I own. Since I'd jettisoned my last real boyfriend in 2001 and my nineteen-year-old cat died in early 2003, the car is the one thing to which I feel any emotional attachment.

What I have with me is the stuff that's always in the car, a sort of time capsule of my former life in California: a roll-up bamboo mat, a beach towel, and a spare pair of running shoes. In the cupholder is one of those stainless steel traveler's coffee mugs, a welcome-to-California gift from a friend. The glove compartment holds a working flashlight and two tubes of sunscreen. My driving costume involves an olive drab baseball cap that I bought at a Target store in Colma, California, right after I bought the car—my first accessory—and a pair of Dolce & Gabbana sunglasses I picked up at the Neiman Marcus on the Strip in Las Vegas. (The saleswoman there informed me that the fact that I'd found sunglasses I liked meant that it was my lucky day.) I have my luggage: a neon blue ripstop nylon Patagonia suitcase full of summer clothing; a leopard-patterned plastic overnight bag stuffed with gear for running, hiking, and yoga; a tote bag full of cosmetics: and a knapsack with a padded compartment for my computer. I'm traveling with the tools of my own trade. In a wood-grain cardboard banker's box I packed a bunch of steno pads, a dozen pens, a package of Post-it notes, a little tape recorder, and a few legal pads.

I write the opening journal entry of my trip at the end of the first day of travel, while sitting on the faded floral bedspread in a room at the White Horse Inn in Waitsfield, Vermont, an undistinguished, no-frills lodge in the shadow of Sugarbush ski resort. In summer, the White Horse becomes the unofficial dormitory of Yestermorrow, a "design/build" school founded in 1980 as the outgrowth of a brand of renegade architecture that had flourished in the isolated mountain villages of Vermont, much as it had in Northern California, part of the 1960s back-to-the-land movement.

The mission of Yestermorrow—the name itself tells you much of what you need to know about the place—is to "empower people to unlock their creative spirit by teaching the integrated process of designing and making."

Specifically, what's taught at Yestermorrow is the design and building of homes. My idea is that I will start my quest in search of the Perfect $100,000

House by learning what I can about how to construct one myself. I've enrolled in a two-week workshop that promises to teach me everything I need to know about how to go from site analysis to orthographic drawings to three-dimensional models and even the fundamentals of construction. I tell all my friends I'm going to housebuilding camp, and they are all quite jealous.

I first heard about Yestermorrow through my contact with a trio of eccentric architects who, in the 1970s and early 1980s, worked together as "Jersey Devil." Steve Badanes, John Ringel, and Jim Adamson had met as architecture students at Princeton and rather than going on to practice the deadening corporate modernism of the period, chose to design and build homes that mixed a very 1970s take on ecology with a design sensibility that was deeply idiosyncratic and occasionally visionary. Jersey Devil was never exactly an architecture firm but more like a bunch of guys who got together periodically to build a series of houses. Still, among the architectural cognoscenti they were legendary.

Jersey Devil built strangely shaped houses—the Snail House, the Helmet House, the Silo House, the Airplane House—and used industrial materials like corrugated metal and poured concrete long before they were chic. They were innovators of green architectural techniques, wedding elements like solar power, earthen roofs, and sophisticated low-tech ventilation systems to their singular aesthetic. Their work was dramatic because it had little to do with the aesthetic of the moment—neither the mainstream corporate look nor the clunky antistyle of hippie architecture—and much of what they built looks current today. They were, once upon a time, rock stars. But now they have for the most part gone their separate ways: Adamson ensconced in an airy Jersey Devil–built cottage south of Miami, Badanes teaching at the University of Washington in Seattle and leading his architecture students on community building projects all over the world, and Ringel doing renovations and restorations close to his Lambertville, New Jersey, home.

Each summer, though, Adamson, Badanes, and Ringel reunite when they come to Vermont to teach. Adamson and Badanes often teach together. Along with a third instructor they run a course, intended for architecture students and assorted professionals, called "Community Building Through Design/Build" that begins late in July. Adamson isn't around during my stint at Yestermorrow, but Badanes, who spends his summers in Vermont, is a regular visitor to my class. I like watching what I think of as the John and Steve show, the two of them, Ringel and Badanes, channeling the remnants of a once close collaborative relationship into well-practiced banter. Badanes behaves as if he is the keeper of the Jersey Devil legacy, still posing as a rebel, still showing slides of the old work, while Ringel is content to focus on his less-glamorous present, a series of sun-filled additions to the old stone farmhouses of affluent Bucks County.

I have some history with Vermont, having spent my first year of college here. It was the mid-1970s, and I was attending Marlboro, which had a scant 200 students. The school was perched on top of a mountain and in winter became a study in cabin fever. My only escape was my cousin Linda, who'd changed her name to Verandah Porche, and her husband, former communards who still lived in the vicinity and would sometimes take me to a dinner or a party at the house of friends. This always involved a trip to some highly irregular cabin—like something copied from the set of *The Cabinet of Dr. Caligari*—way, way down a snow-covered dirt road. These places were inevitably in a state of partial completion; the bathroom wouldn't be done, or the floors would be raw, splintery plywood, but on one wall there would generally be a handcrafted stained glass window perfectly installed.

Warren, Vermont, may, in fact, be the birthplace of the design/build movement, the place where free-form hippie building practices cross-pollinated with professional architecture. In 1965, two Yale architecture graduates, Dave Sellers and Bill Rienecke, bought 450 acres in Warren and began, with a group of like-minded friends, to build unconventional houses and sell them as second homes to skiers. Eventually, Prickly Mountain, as the development was called, became a laboratory for disaffected architecture students turned off by the sterility of professional practice. Among them was Steve Badanes, who visited Prickly Mountain during his first year of architecture school at Princeton. "I saw these guys basically using architecture as a way to have a good life," he recalls. "They were having a fabulous time. That vision gave me the willingness to hang in there and finish school."

Sellers, meanwhile, went on to teach at Yale, and one of his students, John Connell, likewise inspired by Prickly Mountain, moved to Warren, established a design practice, and went on to found Yestermorrow, an institution that embodies that haphazard Vermont ethos. The main building, on which the school has spent what was left of its original endowment, is gradually being converted from an old Swiss-chalet-style ski resort into a collection of studios, workshops, offices, and dorm rooms. It is a place in mid-transition.

I arrive at the campus, a few miles from the White Horse, and am directed to a conference room where the students for two simultaneous two-week workshops are gathering for an orientation meeting and tour. My class is called "Home Design/Build." When an overtly jovial man walks in, I immediately mistake him for John Ringel, but he turns out to be a student in the other class, "Stone, Metal, Glass, and Wood." He announces that his young daughter thought he was going to spend two weeks in Vermont playing Rock, Paper, Scissors.

The vast majority of people in the room are schoolteachers or retired schoolteachers. Everyone eagerly exchanges information about where they're from. I, however, am suffering from a bad case of arrival malaise, a mood that I can usually pin on jet lag. This time it's more like cold feet: *Why* have I committed myself to spending two solid weeks in this program? "What is this pride we have in hometown?" I peevishly scrawled in my journal later that evening.

The campus tour is a stately promenade through fading light and thickening mosquitoes, past building projects in varying states of incompletion, as if we were sightseers at the ruins of some not-quite-dead civilization. Back in the woods is a cottage that has been constructed by the women's carpentry class, the roof held up by elaborate scissors trusses, as well as a relic of the hay bale construction class, its fat, lumpy walls daubed with pink stucco. It features a solar shower and a two-seat outhouse.

We all clamber into a large round tree house and linger there. While several of the men have a lengthy discussion about how the siding was made, I stand patiently, trying to intercept incoming mosquitoes, remembering the tree house in the woods behind Marlboro College. *It could be twenty-five years ago,* I think. *It could be twenty-five years hence.* In Vermont, time stands still.

The two classes have dinner outside: a chicken casserole, a tofu casserole, lemonade. No alcohol is served. I am almost ready to cry. Then the design/build class separates from the rock/paper/scissors class. Our teaching team introduces themselves: Ringel turns out to be a tall, broad-shouldered man with long dark hair, a full beard, and round wire-rim glasses, more or less how I'd expect a renegade hippie architect nearing sixty to look. He is teaching with Kathy Meyer, a Vermont architect who has spent most of her career attached to Yestermorrow. She is slight, with short brown hair and precise features. Tom Virant, the third member of the team, is a lanky, ponytailed North Carolina–based carpenter.

Our class gathers around a couple of picnic tables and plays a get-acquainted game of Architecture Pictionary. We divide into two teams, and each person picks a vaguely architectural phrase out of a bag and tries to draw it well enough to make it understood. The game goes on seemingly forever, taking advantage of the long northern summertime dusk. I am still irritable and wonder why the man who is given the task of depicting a "big box store" draws a rectangle with—of all things—windows and doesn't even think to add a parking lot. Has he never seen a Wal-Mart? By the end, I am grateful when one of my teammates, Caitlin, a young Olympic athlete in training, figures out that my wonky-looking toilets connected by a wiggly set of lines indicate a "plumbing system." I guess this is the point: team building has, to some extent, occurred.

July 7, 2003   The White Horse Inn

Got up at 5:30 A.M. Ran. Ate breakfast at 7 or so. Began the day at Yestermorrow at 8. Finished at 11. What is that, a fifteen-hour workday? Jeez Louise. Did I know that this was what I was signing up for?

The high points: I learned how to use a circular saw. We are building a shed for a flatbread pizza company down the road from Yestermorrow. It will house the company's sauce cauldron and its office. As someone, maybe Jane, pointed out, it's not often you get to build something that involves a cauldron.

Each morning we assemble in the Yestermorrow studio, a long, windowed room full of drafting tables, newly remodeled and completed the day we arrive for school. Some days, there's a well-defined break for lunch. Other times we eat our sandwiches on the run as we caravan to a house under construction for an educational or inspirational tour. In the afternoons we work on-site, building a 10 × 16 shed on the property of the American Flatbread (which is indistinguishable from pizza) Company. For years its cooks had been preparing their sauces in an outdoor vessel of the sort associated with witches, but the Vermont health department had recently noticed this infraction and required them to build a shed. There is always a dinner break followed by more lectures or studio time.

Ringel has been teaching at Yestermorrow since 1990 and, while he revs a little higher than your typical Vermont-based hippie architect, he aptly embodies the spirit of the place. Dressed in a brown-and-beige-checked, long-sleeve shirt and gray work pants, he delivers his first morning lecture pacing from easel to whiteboard and back.

His mission this morning is to explain the meaning of design/build, "a philosophical approach to making things which involves the whole process of designing and building." Ringel cites Leonard Bernstein, who once said, apparently, that jazz was about finding the note that comes between two keys on the piano. Ringel asserts that the magic of design/build is embedded in that slash between the two words.

"What we're doing is magic, literally magic. We're pulling a rabbit out of the hat. We start with nothing. We start in the dream realm," Ringel continues. And I'm totally with him. I can be very metaphysical first thing in the morning.

He then draws a series of boxes on the whiteboard and labels them: "Dream. Decided. Develop. Document. Decipher. Define. Do. Done."

It's his theory of process. Although the editor in me rejects alliteration, I try not to let my wince show.

Soon we progress from the theory of design/build to our drafting lesson. And it turns out to be one of those things that is, in fact, magical about Yestermorrow: a semester's worth of skills are compressed into an hour's worth of instruction. We all gather around a drafting table where Kathy shows us how our new set of drafting tools work: how to sharpen a lead, how to use the different scales on our architect's rule, how to correct tiny errors by erasing through a sort of screen. Ringel starts measuring the room and calls out measurements to Kathy. With a wonderful precision, she translates those measurements into lines, and the lines effortlessly cohere into an elevation drawing of one of the room's long walls.

After lunch we get a lecture about power tool safety; are assigned tool belts stocked with a hammer, a tape measure, a pencil, and a piece of bubble gum; and carpool to the work site where we learn the basics of circular saws. Those of us who clearly don't know what we're doing are closely supervised,

Ringel making sure that both our hands are firmly positioned on the saw, that our legs and torsos are safely off to the side in case the saw kicks back, and that we follow the pencil line drawn on the board we're working. He talks us through each cut: "Keep going. Keep going. Faster. You've got it."

So we saw-novices cut 2x4s into 13¾-inch lengths to be used as shims between floor joists. Cool using a power tool. Hard to make it go straight.

After our dinner break we return to the studio and once again divide into teams. Caitlin, a woman named Cindy, and I are assigned the task of measuring the kitchen and lounge. On top of the fifteen-hour-a-day class schedule, Caitlin is doing twenty hours a week of training—running or roller skiing on the hilly roads in preparation for the 2006 Olympics. She writes down measurements as Cindy and I call them out, just as Kathy had done when John called them out that morning. Only Caitlin is so exhausted that she can't quite remember which set of numbers is connected to which wall, or door frame, or alcove. Then we each draw our own elevations and sections from the long, incoherent list of measurements. I suddenly understand how much experience lies behind Kathy's effortless precision.

And so it goes: a morning of lectures and design time, an afternoon of building (if it doesn't rain), and an evening spent either listening to a guest lecture or designing, or both.

Over the years Ringel has adopted and refined a method of teaching design to non-designers first elaborated by the school's founding architect, John Connell. Much of its aim is to demystify the language of architecture. Ringel kicks off the second morning with a lecture about "programming." "That's the technical name, just so you know that jargon, for dreaming about it," Ringel explains. "It's not a list of rooms. It might be a list of functions."

"Architects talk about spaces," he continues. "They have a physical reality but they also have some sort of mood to them."

Ringel offers another little nugget of Yestermorrow wisdom. He says the process of design is like alchemy: "The lead never becomes gold, but the process changes the person who does it."

Okay, fine, I think, still resisting the touchy-feely nature of Ringel's remarks, but objecting less strenuously. I cheerfully set about my task for the morning, making a program for my house. The surprising thing is that I know exactly what I want. I draw up a long list of requirements and some unresolved questions:

Permanent home for books and papers

Space to work

Space to entertain, read

Outdoor space

Double-height main room w/kitchen, dining, living, and work areas

Public vs. private

1,000 square feet

Master bedroom, guest room

Two areas upstairs

Bedroom/work area

Garage or no garage?

Antisocial quality of a garage vs. value of elevated deck

Raised deck

Deck as private space

Solar—passive

Hot water—photovoltaic roof tiles

Double-height book wall w/ library shelves, ladders, cat walk? (Morgan Library)

Shelving on concrete block

Lofted second floor

Guest bed with own bathroom in back

Closets

Built-ins

Shelving

House as archive

Don't want a lot of square footage but don't want a house that reads small

I am working from a photograph of a house by Mark and Peter Anderson, two brothers who have a design/build firm based in Seattle and Berkeley. They built a home in the late 1990s on Fox Island, outside Tacoma, for about $86,000. It has the double-height front room I am after, a front deck, and a rounded roof that rolls back to front. I've often thought of it as my perfect house. Although now, as a newly minted designer/builder, I study the photos with a more critical eye and begin to see things about the detailing—the construction of the steps, the kitchen finishes, the siding—that I could surely improve.

I also have another picture in my head, the magnificent library that J. P. Morgan built for himself at East Thirty-sixth Street and Madison in Manhattan. I'm not after the classical architecture by McKim, Mead, and White or the opulence of its Renaissance-inspired ceiling. Rather there is something about the proportions of the room, surrounded by three levels of handsome shelves accessible from a series of catwalks, that I've always found moving. It seems like a very sincere expression of Morgan's passion for the books he collected. That room transformed the archetypal robber baron into a sympathetic character, someone I could imagine liking. For that reason the home of one of the richest men on earth becomes an inspiration for my austere program.

The next day we all make presentations of our programs, sites, and budgets. Steve and Betty, a couple from San Luis Obispo, California, who have bought, renovated, and sold several houses, now own a 350-square-foot cottage near the beach. Their plan is to build an addition out back, and like me they are working from photos torn from magazines. I recognize houses that had appeared in *Dwell,* in stories I'd edited. It makes me feel as if I have been the carrier of an architectural virus. It's a strange feeling.

There's a man named John who missed the first night's dinner and Pictionary game. He hasn't had a real chance to introduce himself to everyone. Based on his demeanor, I stereotype him: *Gay. San Francisco. Interior decorator.* In fact, he turns out to be a priest who's working on the design for a small monastery to be built near his central Pennsylvania church.

Mark, from Knoxville, Tennessee, is renovating a ranch house that he'd bought as an investment and plans to sell. Miguel, from suburban Boston, intends to rehab a house he'd seen in a real estate ad, which he's been dreaming of as a new home for him and his son. Jane, a retired schoolteacher in her seventies, has purchased a 120-acre spread on Prince Edward Island that she will someday leave to her grandchildren. Meanwhile, she wants to build herself a retreat. And Caitlin, who grew up down the road from Yestermorrow, wants to somehow replace the house her mother sold while she was away at college in Michigan.

Most ambitious are Phil and Cindy, a couple who both teach at a private school in New Hampshire. They are one of two couples in the class, and I noticed on the first day that they had deliberately taken drafting tables at opposite ends of the studio. Both of them project a steady intelligence and reliability developed, I assume, in working with their students and as leaders of outdoor expeditions. On the first day of construction on our cauldron shed, I admiringly watch Cindy, slim, curly-haired, comfortable in her tool belt and work boots. If I had to describe her, the first word that would come to mind is *healthy.*

Phil and Cindy had bought a seventy-two-acre tract along the Vermont-Massachusetts border, and want to build a house that would serve as their home and also as a showplace of environmentally sensitive design, the basis of an educational foundation they hope to organize. They explain that they're motivated by the fact that Cindy, at age twenty-nine, had been diagnosed with breast cancer but is now in remission. They feel compelled to play out their most idealistic dreams.

As the days pass, I get better at suspending judgment. For instance, when we go to look at a hilltop house under construction as an example of traditional timber framing, I try not to be too vocal in my objections to its grand size or the fact that an exposed timber frame—as much an aesthetic as a structural device—is supporting a house with an exterior fashioned from a high-tech, prefabricated panel system. The house is sealed inside a sandwich of Sheetrock on the inside, dense Styrofoam insulation, and some sort of cement panels on the outside. I keep thinking about the irony of the traditional-looking beams (which were probably made with a computerized milling system) supporting a house with walls like a picnic cooler. I don't say too much about it until I'm back in my car, when I try explaining how weird I find the house to my regular passenger, Ringel, who has taken a shine to my convertible.

The thing that bothers me is not the use of the prefabricated panels, but the conceit that the house is handcrafted and old-fashioned when, in fact, it isn't. Ringel, however, doesn't share my objection. He is, after all, no longer a renegade but a more pragmatic guy, who is now in the business of making quaint old houses more energy efficient . . . exactly the point of the Styrofoam sandwich.

The next morning, after breakfast at the White Horse, we all line up to make sandwiches for our brown-bag lunches, a daily ritual. Ringel asks me if I've seen his lunch bag. He had, in fact, left a greasy, crumpled brown paper bag in my car the previous day, and I'd thrown it away when we got back to the inn that evening.

"Where did you throw it?" Ringel demands so anxiously that I begin to wonder what, exactly, he left in it.

I think about it for a moment and reply: "The little garbage can upstairs in the lounge."

Ringel dashes up the steps and comes back carefully uncrumpling and smoothing out the much-used bag. He explains that he and a few of the other instructors at Yestermorrow have a competition to see who can reuse a lunch bag the most times. This particular lunch bag is left over from last year. It clearly has talismanic significance.

I am trying to just let myself sink into the sweet-natured Yestermorrow culture. But I don't always succeed.

Later that same morning, I have to remind myself to stay open-minded as Ringel explains the art of "bubble diagramming." A bubble diagram, it turns out, is a form of design by free association based on a series of questions you answer about your project. What are the functions that you'd like in your house, and how do they relate to one another, not spatially but conceptually? How do you prioritize the things that you do in your daily life? What holds center stage?

And so I begin drawing bubbles. In my diagram sunlight gets a giant bubble front and center. I don't have to think too much about that; addiction to sunlight is a legacy from my California years. Then percolating back from that central bubble are a series of smaller ones. Close in are things like "yoga," "deck," "cats" (in a tiny bubble), "coffee on the deck," "thinking," "writing," "reading," "friends." The next tier of bubbles includes "music" "books and papers," "eating," "cooking." Then in subsequent tiers that trail off to the edges of the paper are "guests," "closet space," "sex," "laundry," "bathing," "coffee in bed," "TV," and "sleep."

How, I asked myself, did "sex" get crammed in there between "closet space" and "laundry"? Do I really mean that? What's going on in my life?

Then in circles that are not attached to the main cluster are a few other concepts: "front door," "beach," "bicycle and miscellaneous gear," "parking," "walking distance to store," "restaurant," "bars."

The front door turns out to be one of the hardest problems for me to solve. I easily map out a floor plan that has everything I want in a concrete block box built atop a garage, but finding a place to put the front door proves almost impossible.

The bubble diagram, while it initially gave me the willies, turns out to be profoundly revealing. I mean, how many years of therapy would it have taken to discover that having a spot for the welcome mat is not a very high priority in my life?

July 11, 2003   The morning lecture at Yestermorrow

It's pouring out. The sky is relentlessly gray. It's freezing in the studio and I'm having a hard time keeping my eyes open.

The discussion has gone from strength of materials to foundations, footings, and moisture seals to something about roofing.

I feel like I did in high school, counting the minutes until lunch.

Maybe this was the day that Caitlin comes in from her morning run, eats her big bowl of cereal, fruit, and yogurt, and nods out on the drafting table. I think I'm the only one who sees her. Given her training routine, I'm surprised it didn't happen more often.

The best thing today is that Tom made some good suggestions about how to give my house an entrance.

The interesting thing is that—and maybe this is the fatigue—I am beginning to believe in the potential existence of this house. I can see it.

Each afternoon, we troop to the work site and saw or hammer or squirt long streams of industrial glue on the edges of 2×4s to hold the floorboards in place. Gradually, I develop an understanding of the relationship between the abstraction of the house I'm designing in the studio, methodically working out a floor plan line by line on translucent paper, and the shed I'm physically building in the afternoon. Even though our construction project is much simpler than any of the houses we drafted—it was merely a box with a sloping roof, which I came to think of as the "Primal Shed"—it has illuminated a connection between design and material that I knew all about in theory but had never experienced before. The physical act of shaping pieces of rough-sawn lumber into walls, floors, and siding informs the more complex structure that I'm drawing. And my drawing, in turn, which compels me to think about my house not simply as a set of conceptual bubbles but as a structure defined by specific lengths and densities, as something with materiality and texture, helps me understand the process of building.

We've been working from a set of construction drawings supplied by Tom, the real carpenter on our teaching team. He isn't always the most articulate person in the classroom, but on-site he solves problems with patience and grace. Tom's working drawings are so simple—just 2×4s and 2×8s of different lengths configured into walls—that they could have been painted by Mondrian. But it isn't until well into week two, when I somehow find myself in charge of making sure that the saw crews are supplying the correct lengths of lumber to those of us who are assembling the wall, that I truly understand what the drawings mean. Finally, I am able to look at the pieces of wood, already set in place, about to be nailed together, and see that one piece indicated on the drawings is missing. I have finally formed some crucial connection between the abstraction of the drawing and the reality of the unfinished shed wall in front of me.

The next day, in the studio, I finally get to the point where I'm able to take the detailed renderings of my house, the drawn-to-scale elevations of each side of the building, and fashion a cardboard model. The way I do this feels like cheating. I photocopy my renderings and reduce them on the copier over and over until they're the right size for a model. I then glue them onto cardboard, cut around the borders, and make my boxy house into a houselike box. Ringel gets into the spirit of the enterprise, fabricating railings for my deck out of strips of corrugated boxes cut so that the baffles inside the cardboard look like high modernist detailing. "These are your aesthetic," he says, handing me a pile of dollhouse-sized architectural details.

Miraculously, over the course of two days, I've progressed from thinking in two dimensions to thinking in three. All the reservations I had at the beginning of the class evaporate as Ringel keeps adding miniature cardboard railings to the growing pile on my drafting table. It occurs to me that I am having fun.

I am completely infatuated with the way my drawings look, reduced and assembled into a model. But I'm far from the most fetishistic student. Mark makes an exquisite model in blue clay of his ranch house with an insanely complex new roofline. For days he carries the model around with him, using a leather Filofax as a platform, bearing it in front of him as carefully as if it were a reliquary.

Caitlin, meanwhile, decides to build a model of her traditional Vermont stone house by gathering pebbles and erecting the walls, course by course, with a glue gun instead of mortar. After days of this labor she encloses the little building with a roof of Seasoned Ry Krisp.

One evening, Steve, Betty, Jane, and I drive back to the White Horse together and stop at the local gas station convenience store to pick up some wine. Jane says that she feels as though she's in a foreign country. "I showed Tom my drawings for the front hall of my house, and he said I need a soffit. A soffit?" We explain to Jane that a soffit is something pretty mundane, a little box projecting from the ceiling that might hide plumbing or cables. But Jane doesn't really want a definition as much as she wants to bask in the exoticism of the word. I realize, at this moment, that I am in love with the whole Yestermorrow scene.

Then there is Miguel, who spends a whole afternoon nailing up roof rafters specifically to conquer his fear of heights. And Katy, a red-haired, freckle-faced intern who holds her hammer with the nonchalance another girl might exhibit wielding a cell phone or a purse. And Amy, the lost soul, whose strongest design statement is a giant question mark she presents to the class. The group has gelled into a crazy sitcom family—*my* crazy sitcom family—and I am loath to leave them behind.

There is a moment during one of the final days of construction when I am standing on our homemade scaffolding with Caitlin, nailing the last rows of siding to the shed. All around us is green Vermont landscape and blue skies full of fluffy clouds. There could be no better spot on earth. While we are waiting for the saw team to deliver another piece of lumber, we somehow wind up talking about leg shaving. Caitlin hasn't been shaving hers for the past few weeks because she's living in a tent on the Yestermorrow grounds and she thinks the young guys who hang around the school will bother her less if she doesn't. She has a boyfriend, another Olympic athlete, to whom she's being faithful. I explain that when I was her age, I didn't shave my legs at all because it was a feminist statement, and the first time I did it, I was in my early twenties and borrowed my boyfriend's razor and shaving cream. I didn't know that shaving cream wasn't really necessary. Caitlin is astonished.

From the perspective of this perch ten feet off the ground in the backyard of the flatbread company, it now seems as if time has not stood still. The fact that Caitlin, the champion cross-country skier, has evolved so far beyond the need for feminist gestures makes me feel for one delirious moment as if I'm living, not in Vermont's hippie past, but in a much-improved version of the present.

Our last day of construction is Thursday. Because we were slowed down by a couple of rainy days, we're not quite done with the shed. Yestermorrow interns will come and finish the roofing after we've gone. But the rafters are up, and so Ringel climbs up holding a big pine branch and, as he ritualistically nails it to the highest point on the building, he makes a crazed speech about pagan ritual and the mystical power of trees. For a moment I see the

Jersey Devil up there on the cauldron shed roof, fearless countercultural hero, instead of the king of Bucks County passive solar retrofits. Down on the grass, where I am—unlike Miguel, I have no compulsion to conquer my fear of heights this time around—the owner of the American Flatbread Company, our client, is sitting cross-legged nearby, methodically peeling cloves of garlic and dropping them into a bowl. When Ringel's speech ends, the Flatbread Man stands up and goes on for a bit about the value of good food and the sanctity of the Earth. By this point, I am beyond wincing.

On the last day we have to present our designs to outside critics. After more than fifteen years of writing about design, this is my debut as a designer. It's been a strange experience. I try to explain it to Ringel on one of our drives from the White Horse to the school. When I write, I have a set of moves that are mine and are as familiar to me as breathing. I know who I am as a writer. But while I may know more about the language of design than most designers, it's not a language I know from the inside. My design for the house accordingly feels as if it's been made from a kit of parts, gestures that I picked up over years of looking at design, that don't feel as if they're my own.

I started with the Anderson brothers' Fox Island house and kept their odd rounded roof. I haven't been able to figure out a way to accurately calculate the curve of the roof, so I traced the line of a banana I happened to have on my drafting table. (I later learned that, in spirit at least, this isn't too far from how the Andersons made their curve.) I decided to make my walls, exterior and interior, out of concrete block because I have a favorite house by a San Diego firm, Public, built of exquisite-looking polished concrete block.

My dimensions were pretty arbitrary, 24 × 40. I initially set out with the idea that my office would be front and center, in the best, sunniest spot on the ground floor, next to a double-height wall of books. Then I wondered whether the most private place in my home, my office, my sanctuary, should be in the most public spot on the floor plan. So I moved it upstairs. My main floor now consisted of 20 feet of double-height space containing living and dining quarters. The back half of the house, beneath the lofted upstairs, held the kitchen, a guest bedroom, a bathroom, and some closet space. Stairs running from the garage level entrance through the house to the loft level were at the very back, as was a back door.

On the 24 × 20 loft upstairs I placed a bedroom and an office overlooking the main floor. The double-height bookshelves continued along the office wall on the loft level. There was closet and storage space and a bathroom.

The most complex thing in the plan was a catwalk projecting from the loft level, designed to give access to the higher levels of the bookshelves. I couldn't figure out how to attach it and finally solved the problem by suspending it from the ceiling.

Tom prompted the most interesting departure from the Anderson house. Instead of a deck running the width of the house, he suggested breaking the box by making a deck that projected from one corner and intruded 10 feet into the living room area, so a portion of the living room shifted from being interior to covered exterior space.

The truth is I have no idea what this house would actually cost to build— especially in my theoretical location, on Orcas Island in the San Juans, where real estate is not impossibly expensive (if you don't want waterfront property), but where supplies would have to be brought in by ferry and the labor market is tight. I suspect that the hanging catwalk will be the first thing to disappear, the first bubble to pop.

Two weeks at Yestermorrow have brought me to the point where I am ready to think about specific variables like the labor market and the insulating qualities of different types of concrete blocks. What I end up with, I think, is a remarkably pragmatic fantasy.

All done with Yestermorrow. Yesterday we did crits all day. The guest critics in the morning were someone named Wendy Cox and another architect, Art Schaller. Both teach at the architecture school in Norwich, adjacent to a military academy.

They were both very enthusiastic about my box-shaped house. What this suggested to me was that I had designed something that was recognizably architecture, that they could relate to it.

Wendy thought I might be interested in the work of Herzog and de Meuron, suggesting them without having any sense that I might already have heard of them. Then she said that my entry arrangement, such as it is, brought to mind the Villa Savoye. It's the first time I have ever been compared to Corbu.

Art had a very good suggestion for the house: to take the wall of shelves and extend it back, all the way through the house, through all three levels, through the back bedroom and bathrooms. It's an idea I really love.

What I have gotten out of this experience, besides an understanding of how complicated it is to build even the simplest little shed, is a new tolerance for other people's ideas about what a home is and how one should look. I'd spent years crafting a Manichean aesthetic universe: modernism good; traditionalism bad. And after Yestermorrow, my universe is somewhat less black and white.

One morning in class, Kathy told the story of how she designed her own house. She started with the image that was most powerful for her, the standard child's drawing of house with peaked roof and smoking chimney. She played with that simple idea for a while and came up with a house that had a chimney right in the middle and stairs that wound around it. On a Saturday, halfway through the class, we spent the day driving around the surrounding area, touring the houses of Yestermorrow-affiliated architects. Each was the expression of some conceit or whimsy. Each was as pure an expression of the owner's personality as it was possible for a house to be. I came away thinking that Kathy's house, a quiet little meditation on tradition, was my favorite.

At the opposite end of the spectrum was a sprawling home belonging to a family in which both the husband and wife were architects. It consisted of a series of shake-clad, metal-roofed, oddly shaped buildings, topped with the occasional turret, connected by peculiar passageways and strangely configured staircases. It looked like the perfect hybrid of Vermont hippie architecture and the postmodern movement: a bit M. C. Escher, a bit Sir John Soane's Museum, a bit early Frank Gehry.

No one was home when the class arrived, and we all wandered around the house, gaping as if we were in a museum. If there was a feature any of us liked, our teachers encouraged us to take note of it and measure it—we were supposed to be carrying tape measures at all times. I measured the living room because it felt like the right shape and size for my place, a particularly well-proportioned rectangle.

Outside I ran into the owner, architect Jim Sanford. He had been wandering around with a chain saw, cutting wood. He kept shaking off compliments about his house, arguing that because it so perfectly expressed his architectural thinking of a decade ago, when he built it, he simply couldn't bear it anymore. Sanford, in his orange woodcutting jumpsuit, saw in hand, ear protectors wrapped around his neck, was either a madman or an oracle. More tormented than a man living on a lush Vermont mountaintop spread has any right to be, he lamented, "I'm living in a ten-year-old idea."

The good thing about being a writer, not an architect, is that all my ten-year-old ideas are confined to paper and stored on shelves or in boxes. I don't have to confront things that once seemed true every time I wake up in the morning. I don't have to inhabit my stylistic choices quite so literally. To me, Sanford represents a powerful argument against the whole Yester-morrow philosophy. Maybe it isn't such a good idea to live in a house of your own design.

The Road to Nowhere

July 22, 2003   9 A.M.   The Treadway Inn, Owego, New York

The morning after my first real day on the road. Vermont was a cocoon. Now I am traveling. At this moment I am sitting on the edge of the cement pad that constitutes my patio. In front of me is the river, the banks lined with willow trees. Beyond the river is the highway, just roaring.

I book an extra night at the White Horse because I can't imagine packing up the day after Yestermorrow graduation, a giddy affair involving large quantities of red wine, and setting out for points west. For one thing, I am too tired—physically, emotionally, intellectually. I feel as if I am weeks behind on sleep, as if I am made of lead. I'm just not ready to leave. Also, I have an appointment farther north, outside Burlington, with a New Jersey architect, Adam Kalkin, who spends his summers in Vermont.

Kalkin is from a part of New Jersey that I don't think I knew existed when I grew up—a leafy, semirural place that, even today, is beyond the amorphous spread of ochre ink that, in the Rand McNally road atlas, indicates the New York metropolitan area. He's someone who has turned up in my life at odd moments. We first met in the early 1990s, when I was working on Benetton's magazine, *Colors,* and he was collaborating on an ambitious conceptual art installation with a Dutch artist and wanted, I guess,

The Collector's House by architect Adam Kalkin, Shelburne, Vermont

publicity or attention. Then, a few years ago he turned up again, this time in the guise of an architect. He had an idea for a $99,000 house that he'd make with the help of a company called Butler. I found the notion exciting.

Butler Manufacturing, based in Kansas City, Missouri, bills itself as "the world's leading producer of pre-engineered metal building systems." If you come across a corrugated metal warehouse or factory, chances are that it was made by Butler. The company, which was founded in 1901, actually partnered with R. Buckminster Fuller during World War II to produce round prefab housing based on Butler's galvanized steel grain silos. The Dymaxion Deployment Unit, as Fuller called it, was originally commissioned by the British War Relief Organization as a form of emergency housing for England's bomb-damaged cities. Steel, however, was in short supply, so relatively few of the units were ever made. This had been Butler's one significant brush with residential construction, and the official corporate history records it as a watershed moment: "Through its connections with Mr. Fuller, Butler Manufacturing Company gained the confidence to take the rigid frame design to the limit, and to lead the growth of pre-engineered buildings into worldwide acceptance and favor."

What Kalkin would like to do is take Butler back into housing. It remains to be seen whether a self-described "anarchist" from New Jersey can accomplish what Buckminster Fuller couldn't. I had initially gotten together with Kalkin about the project in early 2002, when we met in the Upper East Side offices of interior decorator Albert Hadley. In an environment that felt traditional to the point of being frumpy, we chatted about his idea for this house, but I got the impression then that he didn't really mean to build it, that it was just a clever conceit that he was batting around, hoping, once again, for attention.

But before I left for Yestermorrow, I'd met with Kalkin again, this time at his home in Bernardsville, New Jersey. I'd seen pictures of the house, Kalkin's first experiment with Butler components, in a generous spread in the Sunday *New York Times Magazine.* But I had shrugged it off as a gimmick, conceptual art gone a little too far.

Finding Kalkin's place hadn't been easy, and involved negotiating a dirt drive off a well-camouflaged road a couple of miles outside Bernardsville's quaint downtown. The house stands on land that was once part of the Pfizer estate, as in Pfizer pharmaceuticals, and was originally a modest 1890s cottage, with a roof that slopes from front to back. It had belonged to the Pfizer family's Japanese gardener.

Instead of building an addition, Kalkin surrounded the little house with a 3,000-square-foot (at ground level), four-story-tall Butler building, a massive construct with the feel of an airplane hangar. At one end of the Butler building is the cottage and at the other is an austere three-story concrete block structure that contains bedrooms for Kalkin and his wife, and their two children, plus offices for the adults and a classroom for homeschooling the kids. The old cottage houses the kitchen, a formal-looking library, and a couple of auxiliary bedrooms. In between the two houses is a formal living room by interior decorator Hadley, a plush, conservatively appointed room—all beige upholstery and antiques—in the midst of this vast, industrial space. On the balmy June day that I visited—I was on pre-road-trip reconnaissance mission—the Butler building's giant garage doors were open and the living room seemed more a feature of the surrounding greenery than a proper indoor place. Despite the fact that his living room had no walls, Kalkin liked entering it through a conventional door that led to the back porch of the original cottage.

It was strange. And quite beautiful. I kept telling Kalkin that his house was what I imagined the future to look like, but I couldn't quite explain what I meant. It wasn't until months later, when I was at the Metropolitan Museum of Art and I meandered into the vast glass and steel space that encloses the Temple of Dendur, that I understood what Kalkin had done. He'd turned his little cottage into a museum piece, treating it as if he had been looking at the gardener's old house as an artifact from some long-dead civilization.

But in conversation, as we lounged in the overstuffed, very traditional sofas and armchairs in his open-air living room, Kalkin was unable or unwilling to offer a detailed explanation for why he chose to enlarge his home in this jolting, eccentric way, except to say that he has long had a fascination with corrugated metal.

Kalkin told me that while he'd gotten lots of inquiries about his theoretical $99,000 house after it was mentioned in a builders' magazine, none of them really panned out. The catch, as it turned out, was that banks are reluctant to loan money for something so unconventional. Because lenders don't have a fascination with corrugated metal, a prospective client would have to have the money to pay for the house up front. In other words, to afford Kalkin's bargain-priced home, you had to be pretty flush.

"I am so bummed," he complained. His one client was an IBM exec who had been so badly shaken by the dot-com bust, that he lost his appetite for adventure.

"I really have technically designed a great house that is inexpensive," Kalkin said. "The problem is that the house has balls, a real presence. People need to get comfortable with it."

The pivotal moment for his prospective client had come when he was warned by Sotheby's real estate division, "You have zero percent chance of reselling this in two years if you have to."

Kalkin had encountered the strongest force that keeps the American housing market timid and conservative: resale value. People buy homes as an investment. Very few of them expect to live in one for twenty years—the average period of home ownership is eight years or less—and so they buy with an eye on the home's value as a commodity. If you build an odd-ball house, you risk being stuck with it. My gut feeling on that June day was that Kalkin was a theory boy, someone with good ideas who had been leading far too comfortable a life to go into the homebuilding trade. He wasn't hungry enough, metaphorically or literally. As pleasant as it was sitting in his yard, eating sandwiches from a local gourmet shop, staring at the big Butler building on the lawn, the machine in the garden, I was convinced for a second time that whatever Kalkin had to offer was not for me. I drove away from Bernardsville puzzled by my encounter with him.

Then I got trapped in a traffic nightmare—the radio promised two-hour delays in crossing the George Washington Bridge, the Lincoln Tunnel, and the Holland Tunnel back into the city, and, rather than sit in my car, I elected to kill some time in northern New Jersey. I had learned the landscape there—plain, used up, and uninspiring—during my first sixteen years. It is hardwired into my system. It's my native language. Without thinking, I took the exit off Interstate 80 that leads to my childhood home, stopped at the Carvel where my father used to take us for soft serve, and drove slowly down Broad Avenue to Palisades Park.

The house I grew up in was still there, with its yellow aluminum siding, flagstone walkway, and one touch of grandeur, the sparkly granite wall that marked the front of the house. Gone were all the details that had once made the house distinctive. The semicircular attic window and the shutters with the crescent moons cut into them had vanished when my parents had the aluminum siding installed. After my mother sold the place in early 1993 (and died several months later), the new owner converted the front garage to an additional room, complete with picture window, and the old wooden garage doors that swung outward like barn doors had disappeared. All the foliage—the massive oak tree in back, the blue spruce in front that was taller than the house, and the two giant forsythia bushes—was gone. But the house, at least, was still there.

Across the street, most of the houses I knew, an eclectic line-up of vernacular styles that no one had bothered to name, had given way to the two-family anonymous brick things that were now the norm in this part of New

Jersey. It's funny, but when I go looking for a way to explain what kind of house I grew up in, I can't find it in any of my architectural reference books. It was sort of colonial in form, with its main part under a gabled roof that sloped from side to side and one upstairs bedroom, the kitchen, and the garage under a secondary pitched roof that sloped front to back. It seems to fit in a category that the authors of *A Field Guide to American Houses* call "Minimal Traditional": "With the economic Depression of the 1930s came this compromise style which reflects the form of traditional Eclectic houses, but lacks their decorative detailing."

The house my parents bought, postwar by a couple of years, was an example of compromise style. In fact, the entire block I grew up on was a string of compromises, although, unlike newer suburbs, its houses were idiosyncratic, mismatched. Not just my flawed memory but period photographs tell me that First Street in Palisades Park wasn't such a bad place forty or fifty years ago. But now the block has been taken over by a new set of compromises.

As I walked the length of my old block, it looked so naked, so defoliated, so charmless. On a sunny June Saturday, the street was devoid of human life. Where were the kids? Where were the adults? Compared to Kalkin's genteel, pastoral slice of New Jersey, the street was a desert. How did I ever find my way out? How did I grow up to be someone with an appreciation for design, with something that resembles taste?

Part of the answer has to do with my parents' best friends, the Ehrlichs. When the Ehrlichs came into money, they sold their two-family brick house up the hill from ours and moved into a three-bedroom apartment in Horizon House, the brand new 1960s modern apartment towers atop the Palisades in nearby Fort Lee, overlooking the Hudson River and Manhattan. Driving to visit the Ehrlichs, a distance that was hardly more than a mile, was a journey into an environment free of compromise.

The Ehrlichs furnished their place with George Nelson wall units, Breuer dining chairs, a Saarinen womb chair, a Noguchi coffee table, and Danish rugs—not that I knew any of those names at the time. This was my introduction to modern design, and it's conceivable that my future career path began at Horizon House (as did my strange affection for parquet floors). I have no recollection of anyone's discussing the elements that made the Ehrlichs' new home different from their old home, or from our house. I just knew that I was happier in this sophisticated environment than I was in my parents' house. I spent as much time there as I could, curled up in the womb chair or perched on the balcony, gazing at New York City across the Hudson through binoculars.

So, in late July, after two exhausting, inspiring weeks at Yestermorrow, I drive up to Shelburne, a little town on Lake Champlain, just south of Burlington, to see Adam Kalkin again and another one of his corrugated metal houses. This one is an exhibition in a museum village.

The Shelburne Museum was the creation of Electra Havemeyer Webb, daughter of H. O. Havemeyer, who made a sizable fortune in the sugar trade. Webb and her husband, who had been raised in Shelburne, established a museum village, rescuing abandoned historic buildings from sites in New England and upstate New York and transporting them to a 45-acre plot. The collection of orphaned buildings eventually came to include a Lake Champlain lighthouse and the steamboat *Ticonderoga,* which was moved two miles along a set of rails from Lake Champlain to a grassy berth adjacent to an old post and beam barn and a re-creation of a Vermont painter's studio.

When I arrive I feel as though I've stepped into a through-the-looking-glass version of Yestermorrow. Here, too, the grounds are dotted with an eccentric assortment of buildings, but instead of the remnants of years of carpentry lessons and old ski chalets, these are impeccably restored examples of every sort of traditional architecture that New England has produced. The visitors' center is in a round barn, and as I stop to look at the way the siding curves and how the building's frame has a central hub, like a wheel, I consider how one might go about constructing such a building. After two weeks of housebuilding camp, I am beginning to look at the world as my father, who was in the garment business, used to look at ski jackets, as the sum of their component parts and fabrication techniques.

I wander through the museum village in a daze, past the blacksmith shop and meeting house, through a wedding ceremony, and over the covered bridge. Eventually I loop back to Kalkin's Collector's House, which stands at a remove from everything else, a lone representative of the present moment in architecture. It's another big Butler building with giant glass garage doors, an open kitchen and living area in the middle, and private spaces like bedrooms and bathrooms formed by a stack of shipping containers at either end. Essentially, it's the Bernardsville house minus the old cottage.

As I approach the house, I pass a couple who have just inspected it:

She: "There's a part of me that it appeals to because of how easy it would be to clean it."

He: "Just take a fire hose."

Kalkin materializes, lanky, tanned, laconic, ambling across the green in his khaki shorts, looking like the leisure class personified. He shows me around the interior of the house, which keeps to the Bernardsville formula—traditional interior décor with aggressively industrial architecture—at, perhaps, half the size. The floors are concrete, the walls corrugated steel. There are second-floor exterior balconies at either end, one of which is a long stretch of steel cantilevered off the back of the building. "I love the idea that this is a diving board," says Kalkin as we pace the length of the balcony.

We sit down on a bench outside the house and stare at it. I ask Kalkin to pretend I'm a client looking for a low-end version of the Collector's House. He thumbs through his self-published booklet, "The Butler Variations," and finds a simple, computer-generated rendering of something called the "20 Triple Stack." The book, in which the houses are ordered by cost, states that this one will go for $79,000. He lists the materials: 33' × 40' Butler building, three 20' transoceanic shipping containers, two aluminum garage doors. The schematic drawings show a corrugated metal building with a stack of three containers in the middle.

More interesting to me is the "Three-Room House," priced at $82,000. It involves one Butler building and four huge garage doors. Two of the garage doors open to the outside, and two of them are used to divide the space inside the giant shed. According to the book, the Collector's House itself would go for only $125,000. Presumably, that cost doesn't include the services of Hadley, the interior decorator, or the powder blue upholstered chairs. But it's also not clear whether the costs cover niceties like insulation or plumbing.

At this juncture, Kalkin, playing the artist, doesn't have the patience for matters he considers trivial. He's bored with people asking him about insulation. He's even bored with Butler buildings.

"Emotionally, I've exhausted this whole line of thinking," he says. "Everything I do, I'm so ambivalent about."

I walk away thinking that, although he has probably done the most finely crafted version of the industrial house, audacious and brilliant, I'm not sure I'd choose Kalkin as my architect. I'm not convinced he's serious about the buildings. It seems like he's more involved in making a Duchampian statement about the transformation of found objects than in creating genuine living spaces.

I drive up the road to Burlington and spend a pleasant evening shopping, dining, strolling the Lake Champlain waterfront, and thinking about houses. Kalkin's Collector's House feels so much less resonant to me than the funky shed I had a hand in building. I think it's a matter of sincerity. It's Kalkin's use of the word *ambivalent* that disturbs me. I have just spent two weeks in a place where there simply isn't time in the schedule for ambivalence, where every waking hour is spent trying to learn how to implement your dreams. On that Saturday in late July, ambivalence seems criminal. But I also wonder whether some little bit of the Yestermorrow aesthetic—the shaggy, hippie traditionalism for which I initially had so much contempt—has gotten under my skin. After all, who knows where taste comes from? Perhaps in twenty or thirty years I'll regard Yestermorrow the way I currently regard the Ehrlichs' Saarinen womb chair, a warm, comfortable environment that somehow influenced my worldview.

As I drive out of Burlington that evening, the sun setting behind me, I realize that I am actually going to miss John Ringel. I want to talk to him about round barns. I want to talk to him about sunlight. In New York, the light in the hour before sunset always seems to glow pink, but outside Burlington, the last light of day is yellow, like sunlight in a crayon drawing.

I started thinking about quality of light versus quantity of light. Most of what Ringel had said in the previous two weeks had been about quantity of sunlight, while architecture, good architecture, and many other things that make a difference have to do with quality of light. And one of the great, universal problems is that the quantitative thinkers and the qualitative thinkers are never in the same room. I urgently wanted to find Ringel and discuss this with him.

But the next morning, before I leave the White Horse, I run into Ringel, and we have an awkward, unexpectedly emotional farewell. During the course of our conversation, I realize that subjects like the quality of sunlight are better to sort out in my own head as I'm driving than as the topic of an actual conversation. Ringel can teach the secret of how to make a little shed square and true, but when it comes to the metaphysical stuff, I am still on my own.

———

I don't think I planned this, not consciously anyway, but the process of looking for a new home requires me to stop off and visit all my previous homes. The first place I lived after I left my parents' house in New Jersey was the ugliest dormitory—it looked a lot like a motel—at Marlboro. The school is more or less on my way to Ann Arbor, Michigan, my next real destination, so I drive up the familiar Route 9, west out of Brattleboro, then up the narrow road that passes through the perfect little whitewashed village of Marlboro, then to the college itself.

July 21, 2003   2:40 P.M.

Sitting on the steps of the Marlboro College dining hall. As if I never left. Inside, a string quartet rehearses. Over in Dalrymple, the classroom building where Audry Gorton once terrorized me, a piano and vocalist rehearse.

It is still a little bit of heaven. A heaven I once bailed out of, a heaven I couldn't handle.

I was sixteen when I arrived for my freshman year at Marlboro, I'd graduated high school early, and my experience of the world was limited. I understood suburbia and I knew my way around New York City. But Vermont was very exotic. My first question to my adviser there was whether there were other towns on our mountaintop. I had no concept of a place where towns were not butted up next to one another without breathing room in between.

Back then I learned that winter on a mountaintop in Vermont is a hostile environment for an insecure seventeen-year-old who doesn't know the first thing about skiing. At the time, I did the reasonable freshman thing; I kept myself well supplied with 48-ounce bottles of Narragansett beer and boxes of Freihofer's chocolate chip cookies.

I sit for a while on the steps of the dining hall, trying to figure out how the better part of thirty years had passed. From my vantage point, it could still be 1974. Nothing much at Marlboro has changed. I try for a minute or two to pretend that I haven't changed. Time, I decide, is strange, elastic. *What,* I ask myself, *would Einstein say?*

Under darkening skies I drive west, from cozy, civilized Vermont to the wilds of New York's southern tier. Once you get beyond the reach of the New York City metropolitan area, upstate New York is large and strangely empty. As I drive, I appraise abandoned barns along the interstate, admiring the ones with barrel-vaulted roofs, the curve rolling from side to side, not from back to front. I make a note to myself to try redrawing the roof of my Yestermorrow house with a side-to-side roll.

Then the rain begins, and I can't see anything at all, not even the road ahead of me. I just join a slow-moving caravan of cars, all of us with our flashers flashing. I don't think to question how the lead driver, wherever he is, can see any better than I can. I guess getting off the road would be sensible, but the storm is so intense, so cataclysmic, that I'm afraid the surrounding towns will be underwater. The highway, at least, feels like high ground.

The storm eventually ends and, as sunset approaches, I pull off the road in a town called Owego, somewhere between Binghamton and Elmira. I ignore the usual strip of motels just off the interstate and head into town. It is a handsome Victorian downtown with no hotels or motels that I can find. Everywhere there are fire engines, police cars, and utility company trucks inspecting the damage where trees or branches had fallen in the storm. Power is out in much of downtown, so I make my way back toward the interstate and check into a Treadway Inn, a strangely lavish place with a formal dining room. Front and center is an electronic player piano broadcasting an old Billy Joel song to a sea of clean white tablecloths. I find it suspicious that the keys don't move.

In the morning, I learn from the TV news that investigators are trying to substantiate reports of a tornado during the storm. I sit on the edge of the concrete pad that forms my patio and drink motel room coffee while watching the Susquehanna River flow by and, beyond the river, the traffic on the highway.

I revisit downtown Owego, and discover that the banks are all on the side of the street that still has no power, so the ATMs aren't working. I check out the real estate office and discover that $86,600 will buy me a 1930s saltbox house on nine acres with "carpet and vinyl floors." I keep going.

I try to find people I might want to talk to in downtown Owego and look for a café where I might strike up a conversation. But all I turn up is an antiques store that also sells fussy sandwiches. I wind up having tuna salad on a croissant for breakfast. At the occupied tables around me, a few local women lunch, but I can't find an entry point into their conversations.

In Owego, I am forced to confront a question fundamental to my search: which nowheres are good nowheres? In upstate New York, the farther you stray from the banks of the Hudson River, the less expensive it gets, but also the less like somewhere I'd want to be. What would be the point, I wonder, of building an uncompromising house in a place where I don't actually want to live?

What you're paying for, I recognize, when you pay top dollar for real estate is not the land or the house on it, but proximity. Location, location, location. You're paying to be near people like yourself, who have similiar values, interests, and tastes, who have already driven the prices up. The trick, of course, is to pick a town that's a little beyond your known orbit, a town with unexploited charm and undiscovered potential, buy or build a place, and invite your friends. I'm not sure, however, that I have the wherewithal to both build an unconventional house and to establish a hipster outpost in uncharted territory. I will have to give the matter some thought.

Still, compared to the territory that follows, upstate New York practically oozes potential. There is obvious beauty in its emptiness. The next day, as I drive across the modest nub of Pennsylvania that abuts the edge of Lake Erie, I can almost see the potential leaching out of the landscape. The topography evens out and there's less to look at.

July 23, 2003   In a Burger King parking lot outside Cleveland
Ohio is like New Jersey without the benefit of ocean, New York City, or Philadelphia. It is just too normal.

I have it in my head that I should stop for the night in Ashtabula. I like the way it sounds and its position on the map, at the edge of Lake Erie, suggests an idyllic spot. I imagine a 1950s lakefront resort with pretty little hotels serving drinks on their terraces. I don't know where I think I am. The south of France, maybe? Miami Beach? I follow a small highway, the one closest to the lake, and noodle my way to the water's edge. I stumble onto a little resort town called Geneva-on-the-Lake that does, in fact, have the cotton candy sheen of 1950s America. Families drive down the main street in slow-moving pedal cars. Midway-style games and restaurants featuring hot dogs and beer light up the street. I desperately want to spend the night here. One motel manager gives me the keys to two rooms. One is small and horrible; the other one faces the lake, but it hasn't been cleaned and is full of dirty laundry and ashtrays. Other motels have signs that say "bikers welcome." Reluctantly, I drive on.

Away from the lake is nothing but dull-looking neighborhoods. There's a shortage of topography, and all the houses are "compromise style." Every time I spot the contours of a modern building, I get excited. It always turns out to be a church.

Ultimately, I find myself a Red Roof Inn off I-90, somewhere east of

Cleveland. I eat dinner at a chain restaurant called the Roadhouse, which features sports on big-screen TVs and oversized drinks. I feel like a foreign tourist. I feel defeated by Ohio. I want to go home.

Fortunately, the next day I reach Ann Arbor, and in Ann Arbor, I learn my first lesson about place: if you are hungry for a sense of place, go to a college town. This is an obvious one, that any form of intellectual or cultural life will attract interesting people, and it is people who create a sense of place.

It's upon that simple truth that consultants like Richard Florida have built an empire. Florida, the author of *The Rise of the Creative Class,* goes around the country explaining to city fathers that the care and feeding of creative professionals is the path to sustainable economic development. Nowhere is the logic of this formula more apparent than in the Midwest, where university towns like Ann Arbor are oases.

I drive Ann Arbor's vibrant Main Street from south to north, staring longingly at all the crowded sidewalk cafés. Eventually, I cross under a railroad bridge. In an industrial zone on the other side of the tracks, I find a simple concrete block building painted a stylish black, part of a series of buildings that includes one in corrugated metal and a strange, wedge-shaped office building.

This is the turf of PLY Architecture, a young firm headed by partners Craig Borum and Karl Daubmann, both of whom teach at the University of Michigan. They initially came together to collaborate on architectural competitions, and these informal collaborations eventually grew into a formal partnership. Karl, tall and lean with a close-cropped head of hair and architect's glasses, went to MIT and considers himself the tech guy. Craig, a little stouter with a round face and pointy beard, says his expertise is "cultural context within the history of architecture."

What has drawn me to PLY is the fact that they won a competition sponsored by a Cleveland art gallery, Space, to design a low-cost modern house. Craig and Karl took the competition very seriously. Actually, I get the feeling that they take pretty much *everything* seriously.

They came up with a plan for a house that could be built in phases, depending on the client's financial means and needs. For $130,000 they proposed a ground floor consisting of a series of rooms configured around a small interior courtyard. For an additional $80,000 they would add a second story, consisting of three prefabricated "lofts," discrete undefined living spaces, one of which could serve as a rental apartment.

The computer-generated images they produced for the competition show generous, open rooms with pale wooden floors, lots of glass, and shelves and cabinets, which always make my heart beat faster. One of the upstairs lofts seems to be nothing but an enormous bathroom, reflecting the concept, popular in the homebuilding industry these days, of the master bathroom as a private spa, an indoor theme park for grown-ups.

What was ingenious about the plan was that it combined a frugal, efficient, site-built ground floor—concrete block walls on a concrete slab—with an optional prefabricated second floor. The second-story "lofts" would be trucked in from a manufacturer, the sort of company that makes the ugly double-wides you often see rolling down the highway on the back of a truck. Except that the PLY architects discovered something that a lot of young architects around the country have just begun to realize: if you meet with the manufacturers, you might find out that they're willing to customize. And by combining a site-built ground floor with a manufactured second floor the architects hoped to avoid one of the pitfalls of manufactured housing. "There's always a negative aspect," Karl tells me. Modular houses often look like "they don't belong to the site, like they just dropped there."

Sadly, the Cleveland case study house doesn't exist. The premise of the competition was that the winner would actually get built. But that never happened. "They never had any clients," Karl says of the competition organizers. "And they weren't brave enough to build it without clients. All we got out of it was $700."

Nevertheless PLY's research has brought them together with a couple of local developers. Peter Allen, a real estate professor for whom PLY built the jaunty corrugated metal building up the block, and Jim Lamb, an auto body shop owner, are interested in the idea of adding manufactured modular apartments to existing Ann Arbor buildings, a practice that is commonplace in Sweden but is relatively new in this country.

Craig points out that three-quarters of the town is supported by the University of Michigan or Pfizer. "There's a demand for a high level of housing. Real estate is expensive here."

Given that, my best shot at a $100,000 house in Ann Arbor is the subdivision of a dozen or so houses Lamb wants to build on his property. Lamb is a casual, tanned, Hawaiian shirt-wearing kind of guy. He originally hired PLY to rehab his tract house, to convert it into a modernist bachelor pad. They built him a kitchen that has dozens of drawers—so many drawers that he will put something in one and never be able to find it again—and encased the old house in a bold new angular shell. Lamb intends to set up a house factory in the stables on his property. With his background in the auto business he is infatuated with the automobile assembly-line fantasy of mass-produced housing. "A house," he muses. "What a perfect thing to do over and over again. Over and over again, slightly different."

Lamb, like everyone who argues that if we can mass produce cars we can mass produce houses, forgets one crucial thing: the modern, moving automobile assembly line was invented almost a hundred years ago, and made efficient by Henry Ford in 1913. Since that time, the business of building cars has been refined and capitalized by some of the world's largest and most powerful corporations. Ford's goal was to transform "as complicated a mechanism as the motorcar from a luxury article into one of common use, and of bringing its price within reach of the average man." A real, mass-production housing industry will require a similar investment of time, money, and ingenuity. But that may never happen, because America's largest homebuilders turn out between 27,000 and 44,000 houses a year. A manufacturer like General Motors cranks out millions of cars. Until the Henry Ford of housing comes along, manufactured housing in this country continues to consist of conventional houses—an assemblage of 2×4s and Sheetrock—built indoors. Jim Lamb's stable is as good a place as any for that kind of "manufacturing."

As for my $100,000 house, Craig says, "I think we could do that easily. But you have to be willing to be creative about how you use the space."

Karl is more skeptical. "A house for $100,000? A house costs $170 a square foot at the low end. Or $200 a square foot." For one thing, labor costs are high in Ann Arbor, and a large part of a house's cost per square foot is labor. "So something has to change."

Unfortunately, the "something" might be labor costs. Some "manufactured home" companies pay their labor far less than what a union carpenter would make. (Henry Ford initially paid his assembly line workers five dollars a day, double the going rate at the time.) And a house built in the construction industry's version of a sweatshop is not what I have in mind. The "something" might also be geography; wages are typically higher in the industrial North than in the South and Southwest.

I have dinner with Karl, Craig, and Craig's wife, Kathy. I desperately want to go to one of those lively sidewalk cafés in downtown Ann Arbor and imagine a vodka martini and something involving fresh vegetables. But dinner with architects is never just dinner. The PLY boys decided to take me to a restaurant they designed in East Lansing, a ninety-minute drive away.

East Lansing is also a university town, but it's the home of Michigan State, a less prestigious institution than the University of Michigan, Ann Arbor. I've been there before because it's an ex-boyfriend's hometown where

I once spent a very bleak Christmas. But the architects take me to a wonderfully chic little sushi joint where undulating blue walls give the place an underwater feel. It is so perfectly stylish, and the owners are so engaging, bringing us more food than we could possibly eat, that I can almost forget that I'm in East Lansing, that there is no liquor license, and that central Michigan is not the best place in the world for sushi. I realize that a little bit of architectural ingenuity can make a nowhere kind of place feel like it's somewhere.

Rocio Romero and the Extraordinary Ordinary

3

July 27, 2003   Columbus Inn, Columbus, Indiana

So now I am in Columbus, Indiana. A small town, home of serious architecture. Sort of fun. Sort of disappointing. Most of it is from some bad moment—1970s, 1980s—and there's a lot of Roche-Dinkeloo. Actually, the post office is perhaps the best Kevin Roche building I've ever seen, brown concrete block pillars supporting steel beams. Very elemental. But my question is: Where is all the modern housing?

My original plan after leaving Ann Arbor is to backtrack, driving east to Dearborn, Michigan, outside Detroit, to visit the Henry Ford Museum. And not just because I want to meditate on the power of the assembly line. Sometime in the years since my last visit, the museum has acquired one of Buckminster Fuller's Dymaxion Houses, which I very badly want to see. But I want a beach more. So I drive west instead, to the shores of Lake Michigan. I get off the interstate in Benton Harbor, find a road that follows the contours of the lake, and, at an arbitrary intersection, hang a right and wind my way down to The Ideal Beach. The sand is so white, the water so blue and calm and warm that I feel as if I'm on some Caribbean island. Of

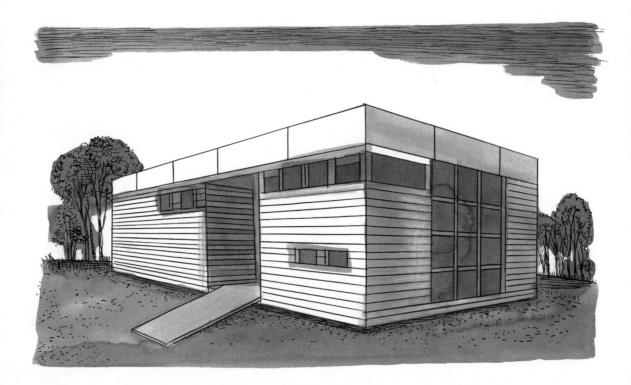

The LV Home by architect Rocio Romero, Perryville, Missouri

course, when I swim out into the lake and see the cooling towers of a nuclear plant just to the north, the illusion is spoiled. But no matter. This is heaven. I doze in the sun as the trim, young Midwestern mothers all around me tend their well-behaved children and trade notes on which local church has the best Sunday school.

Relaxed, happy, I spend the next three hours driving the 50 miles into Chicago. I haven't exactly forgotten about rush hour, but I have forgotten that the time zone will change when I cross into Illinois. I imagine I'll be hitting town between six and seven, but instead I creep in between five and six. Although there is still sand in my hair, that placid beach feeling has long since evaporated by the time I maneuver my way onto Lake Shore Drive.

Chicago has always been like that for me. Everything is a little bit off. I have stopped here mostly to report a story for the *New York Times.* Michael Heltzer, furniture designer and manufacturer, had bought an old boatyard, intending to turn it into a factory. Along the way, he fell in love with the boat business and wound up obsessively refitting an old, steel-hulled Cris Craft, a Roamer, into a showcase for his brand of style. I have been expecting a boat ride up the Chicago River, but by the time I arrive, Michael has discovered a soft spot in the boat's hull and has hauled it out of the water. Whacked-out from lack of sleep—he's been up all night working on the boat—he talks nonstop. "It was an *Apocalypse Now* experience," he says, describing the scene as he and his crew ground away the corroded metal. "We were in a Boston Whaler underneath the Roamer with rats swimming all around. There were 40 tons overhead, with one guy keeping rats off the boat."

I make a few tentative pokes at finding a $100,000 house in Chicago, but I don't really see the potential. One developer of low-cost housing who is working on blocks of townhouses that will replace some of the city's most notorious projects thinks that there might be something for $155,000, but

I would have to have a low enough income and I would have to be disabled. I say no thanks.

I do, however, have a phone conversation with the Waukegan, Illinois, yacht broker who sold Michael Heltzer his Cris Craft, a man named Harvey Caplin. He tells me that I could get a used Roamer. "It's a lot of home for $100,000," he claims. I consider driving north to take a look, but I am pretty sure that the curving walls of a boat interior won't accommodate my bookshelves, and a Roamer, by definition, will not cure my rootless condition.

After Chicago, the road once again gets lonely. I drive through another nightmarish rainstorm in Indiana. The radio keeps reeling off names of counties where tornadoes have been spotted, but I have no idea what county I'm in. All I can do is keep a wary eye on the horizon, looking for black patches or funnel clouds. I can't really say what Indiana looks like. The secondary highway I choose appears to have more strip malls than the population can support. Eventually, the stores give way to fields. They might have been cornfields, but everything is a rain-soaked blur. Somewhere along the way, I stop at a gas-station-themed café—old license plates and gas pump signage nailed to the walls—where everyone around me is eating a Sunday supper of fried chicken and mashed potatoes. I try to make small talk with the waitress, but she is not the talkative type. I go for the hamburger, thinking it is what they'll do best.

Columbus, Indiana, is an anomaly, a town where, since the 1940s, Cummins Inc., an engine company, and the foundation it sponsors have promoted and underwritten progressive architecture. As a result, the small city is full of churches, schools, and government and office buildings designed by prominent architects. Modern houses, however, are conspicuous by their absence.

The highlight of my visit is the 1967 firehouse by Robert Venturi and John Rauch, a boxy little building famous as an early attempt by Venturi to incorporate vernacular signage—in this case, a giant number 4. I've seen it lots of times in photos, and it's never really done much for me, but in person, with the fire engine inside and lawn chairs—metal ones with scalloped backs—out front, I find it moving.

Writing about that firehouse ten years after its completion, Venturi (together with Denise Scott Brown and Steven Izenour) described it as "ugly" and "ordinary," qualities he considered virtues. Citing its flagpole, standard roll-up garage doors, and big "Fire Station 4" sign, he argues that these elements "are not merely ordinary but represent ordinariness symbolically and stylistically."

What Venturi meant, I guess, was that his firehouse was self-consciously ordinary. That's its appeal; it's *especially* ordinary. But standing across the street looking at it as cars whizz by, I'm not conscious of all those layers of meaning. At this moment, the building possesses the same innocence I have sometimes witnessed in early modernist buildings, especially the obscure ones that are tucked away in quiet residential neighborhoods in Eastern European countries. But that innocence, like Venturi's ordinariness, is an illusion, the product of a gifted architect's experience and calculated effort. So, while Columbus, Indiana, yields nothing in the way of houses, it does provide a lesson about what it is that I'm looking for. What I want is a house that, like this landmark fire station, isn't truly ordinary, but one that speaks the language of the ordinary with extraordinary eloquence.

After consulting a map I decide to spend the next night in Chester, Illinois, forgetting that most Midwestern river towns are built as far away from the water as possible, to protect them from floods. The only thing anywhere near the river is a monument to Chester's favorite son, cartoonist Elzie Segar: a 6-foot-tall bronze rendition of Segar's most famous character, Popeye. Popeye looks like a balloon animal on steroids and, while I generally like pop culture shrines, this one gives me the creeps.

I meet Rocio Romero in the parking lot of Buchheit, a lumber wholesaler in Biehle, Missouri, just across the river, the following afternoon. She leads me to her office, a quiet little corner inside the main building of the lumberyard where she has a computer, a shelf full of architecture and building books, and two chairs. A nearby vending machine supplies coffee. And Rocio has her cell phone. Every time it rings—loudly, frequently—she apologizes.

Rocio was born in Chile, but her family left the country soon afterward, when Salvador Allende's government was toppled by Augusto Pinochet in 1973, and settled in San Diego. And that's how she looks: all American, with a sturdy frame; straight dark hair, loosely tied back; a few freckles.

Rocio, now thirty-one, may seem perfectly average, but she is doing something I find amazing. She is taking the house she built for her mother in Chile on a $30,000 budget, a sea view glass and galvanized aluminum box, and she is re-creating it as a kit, a shipping container full of components that when reassembled—preferably by an experienced contractor—will turn into a dazzling modern house.

She had originally wanted to outsource the project, to find other people to figure out all the problems in her design and manufacture it. But the professionals she contacted didn't quite understand her goals. Los Angeles contractors said they could reproduce the house there for $190,000, when her aim was to sell the kit for between $35,000 and $40,000. Manufacturers wouldn't talk to her unless she walked in the door with a hundred orders. After a number of frustrating meetings, her husband suggested it might be better if she did it herself and offered to back her.

At first she hired a company in Louisiana to help her assemble her kit, but that didn't work. "My builders there were total flakes," she explains.

Through her husband's business connections—his family is well established in the health-care field there—she found her way to the Southeastern Missouri planning and economic development board, which introduced her to Buchheit. What the lumber company provides, besides a small office, is economy of scale. With the help of Buchheit she can purchase lumber and other components at the reduced prices big builders pay and, she says, "radically drop material costs."

"Here in Perryville," she adds, "there are a lot of hardworking carpenters."

Today's event is that the 8-foot-tall wall panels (designed to fit perfectly inside a shipping container) are supposed to be completed, ready to be picked up, and delivered to the property where Rocio is building a prototype LV Home (named for Laguna Verde, the stretch of beach in Chile where the original house was erected).

"It's a very difficult process," she says of reformulating her house in this country. She explains that she had a California structural engineer figure out the requirements for the house. It is four feet wider than the house she built for her mother in Chile, more American in scale. And it's reengineered to meet California's stringent building codes, including Los Angeles County's seismic codes. "I tried to make it work in the worst scenarios." The house is engineered to withstand 100-mph winds for hurricane season but only 50 pounds per square foot of load on the roof. That's not enough for a flat roof in areas with heavy snowfall, like Vermont.

Certain key things are not included in the sale price. "The plumbing and electrical codes vary the most," Rocio explains. "So we just sell the exterior package, provide exterior finishes, the metal cladding. Everything is precut."

"It comes with a videotape," she notes. She hopes that watching someone build the house on a video will answer any questions that the plans don't address.

At the time of my visit, Rocio hasn't produced the LV video yet, but she has prepared one for a smaller house, a simple shed on stilts that she calls the Fish Camp. "My husband is a huge fisherman," she explains. The video that documents the construction of a one-room, zinc and aluminum-clad cabin with a pale yellow interior and a generous deck is not exactly *This Old House*. It features a shirtless carpenter at work, and his supersized belly, rather than his technique, winds up being the focus of every scene.

Rocio's phone rings. "I just got a call from Buchheit. They're on the way over."

We walk to a barnlike structure to check out Rocio's assembly line. It doesn't look like much. There are piles of lumber and perhaps a dozen of the prototype panels consisting of pine 2×6s and sheets of plywood formed into sturdy 4 × 8 panels. These are the exterior walls of the LV Home. They are stunningly low-tech.

I am reminded of the moment when you open a box from IKEA and realize that the shiny piece of furniture you saw in the store is now just a box full of particleboard. Before I can even begin to tell Rocio how strange it is to go from the picture in my head, the gleaming, efficient, high-tech instant house, to this sawdust-covered pile of wood, a flatbed truck that says BUCHHEIT in big letters behind the cab arrives. A team of young guys dressed in jeans and white T-shirts starts picking up the panels. They look more like bed frames from The Futon Store than elements of the house of the future.

Rocio and I get into her Subaru Forester and drive north to her property, 68 acres of an old chicken farm along a smallmouth bass fishing stream. As we drive through the beautiful countryside of Southeastern Missouri on quiet back roads that trace the ripples of little hills, Rocio tells me about how she and her husband, an old high school sweetheart, found each other again. At *Dwell,* a freelancer wrote a short article about the original LV Home. The writer interviewed Rocio by e-mail, as did the fact-checker, whose job it is to make sure each article is accurate. Both assumed that the architect with whom they were communicating was a man. The fact-checker never thought to inquire about the architect's gender, which seemed obvious. It wasn't until after the magazine came out that we learned of the mistake. I was embarrassed by it and especially annoyed that we'd blown an opportunity to properly promote the work of a female architect. Naturally, we printed a correction in the next issue. Rocio's old boyfriend, who hadn't read the original story, saw the correction, and tracked her down. Their romance was reignited, and they got married.

Rocio takes me to look at the Fish Camp, and I instantly fall in love with the little cabin she and her husband have built on the low-lying land by the stream. It speaks to what has become one of my road trip obsessions: the Primal Shed. It started, of course, in Vermont, where I spent every afternoon helping to build a rectilinear building with a slanted roof. And then, on the road, I'd see a building that I liked, and it would be some industrial building or a muffler shop and it would have this same form. As the pitched roof is the symbol of traditional architecture and the flat roof is the symbol of modernism, the slanted shed roof has become the symbol of the thing I am seeking out, a simple, elemental American approach to architecture. Unornamented. Nondoctrinaire. At once without pretension and as elegant as a minimalist sculpture. Extraordinarily ordinary.

And here it is again. The Fish Camp is a single room of perhaps 200 square feet built atop a simple 24 × 24 platform. Its exterior is covered with galvanized aluminum, the ridges running horizontally. Facing a large deck occupied by a single cot are a pair of translucent barn-style sliding doors, and above the deck is an overhang so elemental that it looks like a mistake, as if someone forgot to shear the end of the roof off where it meets the wall. The whole structure sits astride fat, plug-shaped concrete piers so sturdy in appearance that it would likely require a flood of biblical proportions to dislodge them. Inside, the shed's yellowy walls seem to radiate light. A clerestory window, just covered with screening, no glass, creates a strip of brightness just below the roofline. The only furniture is an orange, modern, Scandinavian-style woodstove in a corner. If it had a kitchen and a bathroom, I would gladly move in. But the Fish Camp, as the name implies, isn't intended as a real, year-round residence.

"It's for dove-hunting season," Rocio explains. "Spring is for bass. Fall is for doves."

We drive uphill to the main part of the property, past fields that the couple is thinking of planting with sunflowers and soybeans, past the old chicken house and a series of barns, where there's a foundation for a 48 × 24 house, approximately 1,200 square feet, all told. It's just there, standing in the middle of a patch of cleared land looking like a giant waffle. The floor has been framed, the Simpson metal connectors are there to hold the wall panels in place, as are the metal anchor bolts. The floor is supported by laminated 4 × 6 girders.

"Our beams are mega monstrous," Rocio boasts.

The Buchheit truck shows up, and Rocio supervises as the guys move the panels into one of the barns for storage, to keep them safe and dry until construction commences. I watch, waiting for something revelatory to happen, but all I see are a bunch of amiable, hardworking men moving lumber.

What I keep thinking—and maybe this is the revelatory part—is that the fantasy of prefab housing is so different from the reality.

That fantasy, a very fashionable one at the moment, is fed by the idea that you can generate convincing computer renderings of just about anything. And if you can also use the computer to specify the shape and size of manufactured objects, you can magically extrude a house or spit one out of your office printer. But houses are complicated. Even the Primal Shed, as I learned at Yestermorrow, requires endless component parts, all measured and cut properly, all assembled with focus and precision.

Rocio, talking about the simplicity of the Fish Camp, says, "Essentially you build a 24 × 24 deck. It's common knowledge." But embedded in that phrase is a whole set of assumptions. What is common knowledge for a contractor isn't necessarily common knowledge for a homebuyer. The most basic process, such as building a deck so that it's level and true, requires skill. Joining two pieces of wood so that they form a right angle is not something you can do in Quark or Photoshop. Not yet, anyway.

Even Rocio's own sales materials tell two different stories. In a detailed set of questions and answers on the LV Home Web site, Rocio takes on the deal-breaker, the sticking point that could sink her entire enterprise:

"How do I overcome the objection of my banker that it is prefab and thus does not qualify for a traditional mortgage?"

The answer, she reassures prospective buyers, is that the LV Home, despite appearances, is really quite traditional. "The LV Home qualifies as new construction. The LV Home is a kit of parts, which is a type of prefabricated methodology. It is different from manufactured and/or modular housing. It is erected on-site as opposed to off-site; this allows the home to qualify as new construction and therefore your home can qualify for a traditional mortgage and your building inspector can inspect throughout all the build phases like a normal stick-built home.

"Since most of the LV Home is actually constructed using traditional methods and on-site, properly constructed, your foundation will be of traditional reinforced concrete, constructed by a local foundation contractor, compliant with state and local codes. Your prefabricated open wall panels are assembled employing traditional construction techniques. . . ."

Traditional. Traditional. Traditional. That's one message. What Rocio has not done is change the way homebuilders function. Her revolution is of a different nature. Rather, she has changed the way architects sell their services. Instead of working like an artist who prepares a uniquely commissioned work for each patron, she's retailing her services.

"They're buying the design and buying the fact that it's been built before," she says. And she's saving her buyer from one of the routine expenses of custom construction, the midcourse corrections that contractors charge extra for. "No change orders," Rocio adds.

The photos of the prototype house she eventually completed on her property in Perryville tell a somewhat different story. They show a seamless, galvanized aluminum box with generous windows that, inside and out, speaks of a high-tech modernity. The interiors feature stainless steel appliances, minimalist furniture, and spare, stylish bathroom fixtures. It is the perfect showroom for the fantasy of the prefab house, the ultimate modernist dream. But just beneath its sleek surface, the LV Home is lumber, as handmade as any Vermont hippie homestead, as traditional as the farmhouse up the road or the chicken barn where Rocio stores her prefabricated components.

Rocio Romero has taken the prefabricated idea as far as it can go without the capital to build a factory and work at a mass-market scale. And, in doing so, she's presented me with my first real option.

The prototype of the LV Home that Rocio built in Perryville cost $98.19 a square foot, for a total of $113,315. A minimal version of the same house with less expensive finishes would cost about $82,315.

The kit itself, which includes plans and instructions, structural materials such as beams and joists, interior and exterior wall panels, the Zincalume or Galvalume cladding, costs $31,050. Rocio estimates that shipping costs across the country are about $2,800. The kit doesn't include window glass or the services of a glazier. She estimates that buying and installing windows will cost $9,500. Her costs for the Perryville model include $12,440 worth of site preparation, including excavation, a foundation, and a septic tank. She purchased a commercial air conditioner, installed two full bathrooms, and put in a backup generator, a built in audiovisual system, and a burglar alarm. Her mechanical and electrical systems cost $19,000, but she estimates that a one-bathroom, efficiency kitchen version of the LV with a residential HVAC unit and fewer electronic systems would cost about $11,000.

Her finishes included Pergo wood flooring, a drop ceiling, and built-in stainless steel cabinets. Her finishes cost $19,800, but she estimates that by using less expensive finishes and standard cabinets, the tab could drop to $10,100.

On paper, at least, it all seems pretty reasonable. If I had a level site in a part of the country where it doesn't snow too much and where labor costs were relatively low, I could build myself an LV Home.

Rocio takes me for lunch in Perryville to a place off the highway where the specialty of the house is fried okra. We split an order and each have a Reuben sandwich. We talk about the fact that her life is dominated by "the devil in the details," about trying to understand exactly how to take one simple house apart and put it together again. She tells me about studying homebuilder videos on TV to figure out how exactly houses are made. "It's a level of complexity," she sighs. "Always. Always."

Before I leave Rocio back in the Buchheit's parking lot, we discuss Missouri, where the scenic parts are, where I should try and spend the night. She hasn't lived in the state long but she thinks that maybe the Lake of the Ozarks is nice.

So I find a promising name on the map—Osage Beach—and drive the back roads in that general direction. I imagine a quiet resort town where I can go for a swim or a run along a deserted lakeshore road. When I get there, I realize that I've made a terrible mistake. The narrow road I'm on opens up to a four-lane stretch of chain motels, fast-food restaurants, monster trucks towing monster boats. And my attempts to do what I did so well back in Michigan, to instinctively wend my way to the water's edge, all lead to clusters of resort homes with meandering roads that end in cul-de-sacs rather than beaches.

Finally, as the sun is beginning to set, I stop in a bar perched on an outcropping of land high above one tendril of the man-made lake and ask the bartender for advice. The customers suggest a few resorts. I make a couple of phone calls and secure a room for the night at the pastoral sounding Red Oak. It turns out to be the Red Oak RV Park and Resort. I stay in one of their little vinyl-sided condominium cottages.

July 30, 2003   The Red Oak RV Park and Resort

This place is an agglomeration of Bad Decisions. I've never seen so much vinyl siding in my life. Everything here is the wrong size or the wrong shape or badly oriented or cheaply made.

I try to figure out the culture of the place. As best I can tell, the Lake of the Ozarks exists for people who like to fish off pontoons that resemble floating RVs. Further down the road, someone tells me that Midwestern lake culture, such as it is, is an invention of the Army Corps of Engineers, and that it's always a little strange.

I end my day with renewed appreciation for Rocio Romero's vision. Knowing that her LV Home and her Fish Camp exist makes it a little easier for me to spend the night here. I don't know whether to be annoyed with Rocio for being so naïve about the true nature of the Lake of the Ozarks or be grateful to her for sending me someplace that makes me truly respect her talent and her dedication. All I know is that the Red Oak RV Park and Resort is a prime example of the ordinary. Not Robert Venturi's ordinary—there's no symbolism or style here—but the ordinary ordinary.

Flatter Than a Pancake

4

July 31, 2003   Lawrence, Kansas

The Eldridge Hotel: it's an old, sort of elegant, sort of seedy nineteenth-century hotel in downtown Lawrence. Really, it's the perfect thing. I should make a point of seeking them out rather than look just for motels.

As I drive, I keep hearing a story on the radio about some scientists who decided to figure out whether Kansas really is as flat as a pancake. They determined that, because of irregularities in the surface of a sample pancake purchased at an IHOP, Kansas is actually flatter. Maybe there's some sort of shortage of human interest stories—no children trapped in wells, no dogs playing hero—but this report is all over the airwaves.

Well, Kansas *is* flat. But it's interesting. And Lawrence, where I spend a couple of nights, not only turns out to have an actual hill but also is the first place, maybe since Vermont, where I actively fantasize about settling down.

Lawrence has a great main street—Massachusetts Avenue—full of unusual stores, restaurants, and life. I buy a pair of royal blue Converse high-tops. I eat stir-fried vegetables with tofu. I sit on a downtown bench and watch the people of Lawrence stroll by, licking cones from a local ice cream store. The town has actively resisted the incursion of malls and Wal-Marts, and guarded the vitality of its central business district. There is, of course, a university

1718 Atherton Court by Studio 804, Lawrence, Kansas

and beautiful, leafy neighborhoods, and a fascinating abolitionist history. The Eldridge Hotel, where I'm staying, originally called the Free State, was twice burned down by pro-slavery raiders.

But the thing that is make-or-break for me, as it turns out, is whether there's someplace good to run. Flat is an advantage when it comes to running. Lawrence has a levee that protects the farms east of town from the Kansas River. And the top of the levee is very flat. I'm out there early one morning, before the temperature has had a chance to climb, trotting alongside cornfields, grain elevators, and train tracks. Flocks of yellow-bellied birds zip across my path every now and then. Maybe it's the endorphins, but by the end of my run, I'm ready to settle down.

The reason I've stopped in Lawrence is to visit an architect named Dan Rockhill, who teaches at the university and runs a program called Studio 804. Every year Rockhill and a group of architecture students design and build a house in Lawrence that is sold to a low-income family through a program called Tenants to Homeowners. And I have a fantasy that the methodology that Rockhill's students apply to designing and building these houses might be applicable to my own quest. It's a nice fantasy.

Dan did me the favor of making a reservation for me at the Eldridge Hotel, the first in a series of old downtown hotels that I come to treasure on this trip. My room—a suite, really—is full of furniture that is old without being too precious. While everything is basically clean, I notice that there is a seepage situation behind the toilet that causes mushrooms to grow. Even in the rain-soaked Pacific Northwest, I've never seen mushrooms sprouting behind a toilet before.

But despite the mushrooms, or maybe because of them, I like this spot. Compared to my vinyl-sided cabin at Lake of the Ozarks, the Eldridge is deluxe. My room is at the corner of the building, several flights above Massachusetts Avenue, which means I can watch the traffic and the pedestrians go by and the customers drift in and out of the variety store across the

street. When a big storm rolls in, I am high enough up, by Kansas standards, that I can see it from a distance and be grateful that I'm here in this
solid old hotel instead of out in my car.

Maybe I'm a bad modernist to love an eighty-year-old hotel so much,
but it's as much about the place as it is about the style of architecture. I feel
like Lawrence is the first real town I've visited since Columbus, Indiana, or
maybe Chicago.

And part of what's interesting about Dan Rockhill's Studio 804 is that it
is so much a part of Lawrence. I meet Rockhill at a restaurant housed in
what was once a bank on Massachusetts, the kind of restaurant where the
waitress introduces herself and then describes each element of the meal,
down to the grains and herbs that distinguish each variety of dinner roll.
Each year Rockhill starts out in January with a new group of students, who
finish building their project by the time school lets out in the spring. It's an
ambitious schedule, especially because the designs for the houses seem to
get more sophisticated with each successive class. Maybe too sophisticated.
Studio 804 has left the ordinary behind. According to Rockhill, the program is creating houses that are so good they don't fit anyone's criteria for
affordable housing.

"I think we're maxed out," he says, and tells me a story:

Because the Studio 804 houses are sold to low-income families as part of
a federally funded program, they are subject to an energy audit. The problem is that, even though the structures use passive solar energy, strategic
daylighting, and sophisticated insulation techniques, the federal inspectors
focused on the recycled industrial steel window frames. "They permit thermal wicking," which, as Rockhill explains, means that heat and cold pass
too easily from inside to outside or vice versa through the steel. The inspectors ignored the fact that the windows were automatically covered at night
for insulation purposes. "We get caught up in this bizarre world where common sense is lost. We don't seem to fit within guidelines."

After dinner Rockhill drives me around town telling me the history of Lawrence, the birthplace of Kansas, a town that has been politically liberal from its inception, and showing me houses he's built commercially and houses his class has built. "They're not affordable houses, in that we put more into them than we would if you gave us $70–80,000," he notes.

Still, the houses are impressive. One of them, 1603 Random Road, is 1,500 square feet covered in rust-colored Corten steel, with windows shaded by louvers made from heartwood salvaged from an old water tower. This particular house, a dramatic trapezoid with an angled roof sloping downward from a two-story bedroom wing to a single-story garage, looks especially astonishing because it abuts an entire subdivision constructed by Habitat for Humanity, conventional single-story homes dominated by their two-car garages.

Kent Spreckelmeyer, another University of Kansas architecture professor and Dan Rockhill's collaborator at Studio 804, spends a few hours with me the next day and takes me to visit the most recent Studio 804 house, 1718 Atherton Court, built on a $95,000 budget. It's a stunner—a pair of simple, corrugated steel-clad boxes topped by these crazy, ellipsoidal roofs made out of a new plastic roofing system. Below the slanting wings of the roofline are generous clerestory windows that flood the house with daylight. I walk into this light-filled wonder and it makes me thankful that I'm no longer a shelter magazine editor. Because here is the perfect piece of architecture owned by an extremely appreciative working-class family that fills the minimalist rooms with its mundane, messy, comfortable possessions. I imagine doing a shoot that shows it exactly as it is lived in and having the ad sales department go batshit because there are no high-end, name brand designer products in sight.

But as stunning as Studio 804's houses are, as much as they seem to satisfy my desires, they aren't available to me. According to Rockhill, the buildings cost something like $70,000 in materials and include another $30,000 or $40,000 in donated materials like LEXAN from GE Plastics. One company gives them as much steel as they can cart away. And student labor is free labor. The completed structures are ultimately sold to whatever family is next on the waiting list on a five-year lease-to-buy plan. The family might pay 60 to 80 percent of the house's official purchase price, $95,000, and after five years own a home that is easily worth $200,000.

But Spreckelmeyer tells me there's no way for a private individual to come in and purchase the services of Studio 804 or to get the benefits of student labor and donated goods. You can't muscle your way to the head of the Tenants to Homeowners' waiting list. And he adds, as we drive away from Atherton Court, that the local press has been critical of the premise "that low-income housing should be innovative." In part, conservative critics don't believe that poor people deserve fancy architecture, but more galling to them is the fact that owners can eventually sell the houses at a significant profit: "Why put poor people in a house with a high equity stake?"

So I go on another field trip, reluctantly leaving the comfort of Lawrence for Kansas City, Missouri, about half an hour due east, to visit a firm called El Dorado that employs several Studio 804 graduates. I want to see what they can do for me.

What they do, initially, is give me a hard time.

El Dorado's offices are in a warehouse building in a part of Kansas City that looks as if it had been painted into existence by Charles Sheeler. The streets are lined with Midwestern industrial buildings that shimmer in the harsh summer sun. Most of them have been converted into design studios or art galleries, but because the conversions are relatively fresh, typically having happened within the last five years, the neighborhood still looks as if it could be warehousing corn or grain. El Dorado's offices were formerly a brick industrial building that has been refitted into a design office, a metalworking shop, and a gallery. I meet with three of the firm's partners, young, clean-cut architects who have a little bit more attitude than your average Midwesterner.

Partner Dave Dowell says to me, "It seems like your magic $100,000 house can't be bigger than 400 square feet."

This is based on the only $100,000 house the firm has designed, a tiny backyard office they refer to as "The Barker Pod." To me it's yet another version of the Primal Shed, with a sloped roof and built-in furniture—perfect, but way too small. I'm beginning to learn something about architectural math: the smaller the building is, the more it costs per square foot. The Barker Pod runs $250 a square foot, which is way too much.

The El Doradans are giving me the usual complaints about clients who don't appreciate how much work goes into what they do, while not subtly bad-mouthing Studio 804: "There's no student labor in our projects," says Dave. "It's all market rate."

Then Josh Shelton makes me an offier. "I could put you in one of these for $100,000."

"One of these" is a manufactured home built by a company in Osage City, Kansas. El Dorado is on to the trick of having a standard manufactured housing mill turn out the structure of a home and trick it out in Polygal, a translucent polycarbonate that, when used as siding, allows houses to glow like a lantern. The idea in this case is to design the homes for a developer in Topeka who wants to build a quality low-income subdivision.

"We went to Osage City and visited the plant," says Josh. The level of quality is much higher, he insists, than you'd get with standard stick-built construction, because these units are built to survive the trip down the interstate.

I can't say that I'm interested. I am, at best, lukewarm about the idea of double-wides decked out in fashionable new clothes, in part because I believe that one reason manufactured housing is relatively inexpensive is that the labor costs are lower. In theory, carpenters get paid more when they work outdoors than when they work indoors, but really the issue is union vs. nonunion and, sometimes, more pointedly, documented workers vs. illegal aliens. While the average carpenter's wage in this country is about $16 an hour, and experienced carpenters earn upward of $24 an hour, I've read reports of undocumented workers in Texas building houses for $6 an hour, which is part of the reason why new home prices are low in that state.

I drove away from Kansas City and back to my temporary hometown of Lawrence, thinking that as much as I admired El Dorado's aesthetic and craftsmanship, I hadn't turned up any good options. All that was really available to me was a 400-square-foot pod or a gussied-up double-wide. Oh, or I could go the *This Old House* route. "I bought a house for $40,000," Dowell tells me. "A bungalow. I spent $40,000 rehabbing it."

Josh Shelton, however, does keep in touch. His e-mails and renderings began turning up in my computer's in-box.

"A funny thing happened the day after your visit," he writes. "Diane Alpert (the developer determined to make the affordable housing development in Topeka a reality) called me to discuss her desire to create an actual prototype . . . 'floor model'. . . to have up and running at the site during the overall development's design phase. And her words exactly . . . 'I want to do this to see if Topeka is ready and willing to purchase something as progressive as this house, but I don't want to spend more than $100,000 testing the market. Even better would be to pre-sell the prototype at a floor-model price, and once it has served its purpose, ship it to the buyer.'"

A floor model? The wheels started spinning. Okay, it would be a manufactured house, but, like a demo model on an auto showroom's sales floor, the Topeka sales model would likely be the nicest manufactured house anyone had ever built. Josh has my attention.

"Of course, the reference to $100,000 led my brain right back to you and your quest," he continues. "I was suddenly intrigued by the idea of the function of this floor model—your 'one-off' serving the higher cause of helping a progressive modular approach to an actual, affordable housing project development become feasible. With regard to your quest, it could be a house for a hundred large, showing up to your site with a good deed already under its belt."

God, I could have my $100,000 house *and* serve a "higher cause." Suddenly, my stop in Kansas City is beginning to seem very fruitful indeed.

Shelton's drawings show a small community of factory-built modules. Multifamily clusters, long rectangles surrounding courtyards, take up one side of the proposed Topeka site, while on the other are rows of single-family homes. In the site plan rendering, there are so many sloping roofs that the development looks like a highly evolved skateboard park. The single-family homes, at least as they appear in computer renderings, are disarmingly lovely. In one image, a pair of low, rectangular buildings face each other, linked by an outdoor deck and an indoor corridor. The roofs of the two modules slope in opposite directions, so the house has a butterfly shape, and clerestory windows fill the space between the slanting roofline and the top of the single-story wall. It looks a lot like a house I might want.

A smaller variation features a single module with sloped roof, a deck, and a parking structure in the back. Larger units use stacked modules to make two- and three-story homes. But the minimal, one-story version looks just about right to me, like a less overtly fashionable cousin to Rocio Romero's LV Home. I imagine myself buying a piece of farmland outside Lawrence and waiting for the truck to pull up with my house, completely assembled. No IKEA effect.

Eventually, I get back to Josh, ready to discuss how I could become the proud, practically philanthropic, owner of the Topeka prototype, especially if it could be delivered to me anywhere in America. He, however, has a sad story to tell.

"We've come to a pausing point," Josh confesses.

The developer, Diane Alpert, had paid for a complete site plan and sent the El Dorado architects on an R & D trip to California to look at innovative low-income housing in the Bay Area. They went to study the funding mechanisms as much as the architectural methods. "We came back," Josh says, "did some case studies. And we started to talk to the city of Topeka." But the city lacked the political will to advance the project. "We were asking them to participate in the development of new infrastructure for the homeowner sites." Not much had to be done: some drainage, some grading for streets. But in Topeka, unlike progressive Lawrence, turning low-income people into homeowners was not a high priority, and so the developer backed off. At least for now.

What Alpert did wind up building in Topeka about a year later was a mini-storage facility. It's a low rectangle topped by a giant, almost heroic, sloping roof. It was the primal shed writ large. Shelton took the El Dorado approach and turned it inside out or, at least, sideways. Instead of applying industrial materials like Polygal or corrugated metal to a residential project, Shelton applied those same materials to an industrial project with the kind of obsessive attention to detail that he would have employed for a residential one. "The structure and roof come from the VP Buildings catalog," he tells me. In other words, it's prefab. To the standard-issue frame he's added a big expanse of translucent Polygal to bring daylight into the facility, corrugated steel walls, and corrugated garage doors in four rich, subtle colors. "Uniclad has always been my favorite corrugated," Shelton notes. "It's got curves to it, not crimped at all." And then there are the details, such as the strip of light hidden in the soffit above the doors, the squishy neoprene that seals the edges of the corrugated walls, and the cedar on the roof overhangs. "The cedar was a little extravagant," he admits.

He put all the energy and thought into a mini-storage facility that he might have put into a house, the demo model, my house. It breaks my heart. There's nothing for me to buy. All I can do is rent a 10 × 10 storage unit with the prettiest corrugated metal detailing I've ever seen.

I visit Josh Shelton's Topeka mini-storage on a subsequent trip to Kansas. On the same trip, I discover that Studio 804, squeezed out of Lawrence by a lack of inexpensive building lots, has established a new partnership with City Vision Ministries in Kansas City, a religious nonprofit with a history of developing affordable housing. The 2004 class project, a modular house constructed in a Lawrence warehouse and assembled on a lot in Kansas City, was sold for roughly $140,000 to a hip, twenty-something curator named Hesse McGraw. It's an extraordinarily lovely, simple, rectangular house clad in a reddish Brazilian hardwood. It was built in five pieces that were trucked to the site, a sleepy, largely African American neighborhood called Rosedale, and assembled in a single day. Unlike the families who purchased Studio 804 houses in Lawrence, McGraw and his girlfriend have furnished the house in impeccable style.

And while McGraw is certainly a first-time home buyer and he met the income requirements, I hear that his purchase of the house caused jealousy and resentment, particularly among the Studio 804 students, who didn't like it that someone so close to them in age and sensibility—as opposed to a more conventionally needy family—was awarded the house.

"I didn't get that sense," Rockhill tells me. "But I'm in a different world than Hesse is. I never thought that we would be selling these houses to people who are financially disadvantaged. We are looking for opportunities to bring new life to neighborhoods that no one has looked at in forty or fifty years, and if it takes urban hipsters to make that happen, then so be it."

Rockhill is so impressed with the response the house has gotten that he's considering taking his own commercial architecture practice into modular homebuilding. "I wouldn't mind finding a warehouse where we could crank these things out on a regular basis." He acknowledges, however, that he doesn't quite have the financial wherewithal to set up a true homebuilding factory. "To really get something under way where you can show a profit and produce a house under $200,000 on a regular basis, you've got up-front investment you've got to cover . . ." says Rockhill, trailing off as he begins to think seriously about capital. He's not quite ready to be Henry Ford. Not yet, anyway.

The Z-Bar Motel, Buffalo, Wyoming

Land of 500,000 Bikers

5

August 2, 2003   Yankton, South Dakota

I got a speeding ticket about ten miles out of town last night. The limit was 60, and I was going over 70. The interesting thing was that the cop was coming toward me when he caught me speeding. He was able to measure my speed while we were moving toward each other. Or it certainly seemed that way.

My plan is to drive state and county highways west for a bit and then north for a bit. Here in the deepest Midwest, the highway system works like a street grid in the simplest of cities. You make a right somewhere; you make a left somewhere. It hardly seems to matter which highway you take. Eventually you reach your destination, assuming you have one. I'm heading for Yankton, South Dakota. Why? Because according to a 2003 survey by the real estate company Coldwell Banker, Yankton has the lowest home prices in America.

In between Lawrence and Yankton are roughly 300 of the least memorable miles in America. Generally, I resent people who write off the Midwest as flyover country. In the past I've had great experiences in Kansas, Nebraska, and South Dakota. In fact, at this point in my trip, I miss Lawrence the way I missed Vermont a couple of weeks earlier.

But on this particular day everything I encounter is irritating, from the convenience store not far out of Lawrence where I stop for gas and snacks to the blinding sunlight to the Nebraska state trooper. He approaches my car with the hard stare and swagger that policemen learn from the movies and, with his wide-brimmed hat, dark sunglasses, and fixed expression, he looks like trouble. Someone I later meet in Yankton theorizes that he stopped me not for speeding but for having out-of-state plates, that he assumed I was running methamphetamines. Why anyone would drive all the way from New York to Nebraska to deal the kind of drugs that the locals can cook up in their garages is, however, beyond me.

The trooper does ask me a lot of questions about where I am going and what I am doing. When I tell him I am looking for the Perfect $100,000 House, his expression instantly changes. All of a sudden he drops the badass demeanor and becomes all genial. We chat about real estate. Prices in Yankton, he tells me, are going up. He then shaves a few miles per hour off my alleged speed and writes me a ticket. I drive slowly and carefully across the border to South Dakota.

Now I'm in a Super 8 Motel on the outskirts of town. There were two motel strips: A newer, flashier one north of town by the shopping malls and the Wal-Mart. And this one, east of town in an area that seems to be more rural.

My smelly "smoking" room is made tolerable by the fact that the window opens onto what looks like a soybean field. Fresh air and bird songs go a long way toward alleviating the chain motel nastiness of the room.

My last visit to Yankton was in the mid-1990s, when I was writing about how electronic technology had changed the old meatpacking hubs of Omaha, which had refashioned itself as the telemarketing capital of America, and Sioux Falls, which had become Citibank's credit card payment center. With a little extra time on my hands, I made a field trip to the Corn Palace, the exposition building in Mitchell, South Dakota, where the walls are covered with murals made of corn, wild oats, rye, and other grains. I had planned to drive on all the way to Mount Rushmore but realized I'd never make my flight back to New York the next day. So I turned south and east and found myself in Yankton, in the corner of the state, right on the Missouri River.

I assumed I'd have lunch in downtown Yankton, where a major local event, the Yankton sidewalk sale, was in progress. Lots of Christmas ornaments from seasons past and fussy, hard-to-identify, crocheted items were laid out on tables outside stores, but there were no shoppers and no places to eat.

I didn't know whether it was in honor of the sale or whether it was always this way in Yankton, but there was ambient music seeping out of speakers mounted on the utility poles all over downtown. It made me feel as if I had stumbled on an abandoned attempt to re-create Disneyland's Main Street, U.S.A., a small town that somehow died trying to make itself into a theme-park version of a small town.

During that visit I eventually gave up on downtown Yankton and found a restaurant on the local highway retail strip, a family-style coffee shop like a Denny's, but not part of any chain I'd ever heard of. All the tables were booths designed to hold no fewer than eight large adults, and as I sat by myself at an endless plateau surrounded by unused place settings and eating the Jell-O based concoctions that dominated the salad bar, I felt a bit like Miss Havisham, awaiting the arrival of an imaginary husband and several strapping children.

Now I'm back, and the big surprise is that the downtown area has improved. It's Saturday morning and a farmers' market is in progress on the main drag, mostly kids selling small quantities of tomatoes and zucchini, but it is likable and friendly. At least there are people walking around, and the ghostly ambient music is gone. Even Yankton is not immune to the trend I've seen in other parts of the country, the rejuvenation of urban downtowns and main streets. This time, I even find a place to eat. I stumbled on The Pantry, a self-styled gourmet gift shop, the kind of place where you might buy a soufflé dish or a trivet. In the back of the shop is a coffee bar where I sit down and have a cup of coffee and an amazingly rich rhubarb muffin. I chat with an attractive young couple whose two children roam in and out of the store. When I explain why I'm in Yankton, they say, "Oh, you must have read the article."

The article in question ran in the *San Francisco Chronicle* in January 2003. It was illustrated with a map that showed that a 2,200-square-foot, four-bedroom house with a two-car garage would cost $1.26 million in Palo Alto and $101,000 in Yankton, "less than anywhere else in the nation."

"Yankton is a lonely speck of Midwestern America," reported the *Chronicle,* "nestled on the banks of the Missouri River in the southeast corner of South Dakota, more than 1,700 road miles from the pampered San Francisco suburb of Palo Alto.

"But Palo Alto, best known for Stanford University and Hewlett-Packard, and Yankton, best known as the hometown Tom Brokaw left, share distinct places of honor at either end of a national housing survey."

The article went on to compare the lifestyles and cultures of the two places: lower grocery prices in Yankton, but no Whole Foods Market; very little crime in Yankton, but not much excitement, either. The upshot of the story was, "Despite its charms, Yankton is in South Dakota."

But despite the article's mean little digs, Yanktonians seem flattered by the attention. The couple next to me moved here from Sioux Falls because the schools are good and jobs are plentiful. It is a place where life hews to a comfortable medium, where the middle class still exists.

But nothing they have to say about the quality of their lives or the housing market is as important as the advice they offer about the road ahead: "You know about the Sturgis rally?" the man asks me.

As it turns out, a few days hence some 500,000 bikers will converge on the town of Sturgis in the Black Hills. It's really a scene, the man tells me, and I should make sure to get a motel room early in the day if I'm heading in that direction.

I finish my muffin, take a second cup of coffee with me, and pay a visit to the local Coldwell Banker office, a wood-paneled storefront sporting a "Just Say NO to Drugs" wall clock. There I meet Stan and Emma, a couple of real estate agents who, on a Saturday morning, seem to have nothing better to do than talk to me.

"The real estate is higher here than in the small towns," Emma tells me. "In small towns you can't give the stuff away." Yankton, with its 13,500 residents, is the area's population center and shopping hub. In Yankton, according to Stan, "a three-bedroom ranch with one and a half baths . . ." He snaps his fingers. "It's gone."

Emma explains the geographical hierarchy of the town: Whiting Drive, a bit north and east of downtown, is "lower Budville," whereas Grandview, near the golf course, is the high end of the market.

I take a few choice listings with me and set out, soon pulling up in front of a little white Craftsman bungalow on Sixth Street West, an old neighborhood with mature trees near downtown. "Original woodwork, screened porch, hardwood floors." It's the perfect $65,000 house, sweet as pie. In some high-end, New Urbanist community an imitation of this house would fetch half a million, easy. And I could have this one for next to nothing. Yankton, I remind myself, is in South Dakota.

I drive to the north end of town, up near the new Wal-Mart, where a cul-de-sac subdivision is rising out of the adjacent fields, and check out an open house advertised in the *Yankton Daily Press and Dakotan:* 2904 Lakeview Drive. "Stop by and look at this new construction . . . Split-level with two bedrooms on main and more planned for the lower level. $130,000 with allowances available."

I pull up in front of a generic beige tract house. There is something about the way it's proportioned—maybe the stubby basement windows—that makes it look like the top half of a taller house that has accidentally been buried. It seems incomplete or badly proportioned, and its one stab at distinction is a boxy projection coming off the front that extends the living room a foot or so. In a more ambitious house, it might hold a bay window.

As I stand outside playing one of my favorite games, What's Wrong with This Tract House?, I'm greeted by Century 21 salesman Tom Goddard, who informs me that the great virtue of this house is its affordability: "In Sioux Falls this would be $160,000." He adds that it's 2 × 6 construction rather than 2 × 4, "so it'll be solid when storms come through."

Goddard points out the back windows at the hay fields, which are rapidly giving way to more streets lined with more beige houses. "We're pushing in from where the power lines come through. We'll probably put in ten foundations before winter hits."

I drive away wondering why I feel compelled to visit new subdivisions. I think it's misplaced optimism, as if I expect them at some point to get better, as if the homebuilding industry will have had a breakthrough that will completely transform what they build. I expect that one day I'll drive into a seemingly ordinary subdivision and find that the Age of Enlightenment has begun. Or, more realistically, I periodically need to check out the kind of house I don't want as a way of reminding myself of what I do want.

On that trip to Omaha in the mid-1990s I had spent an afternoon at a new development on the western fringe of the city, out by Boys Town, in what had once been open prairie. It was my first exposure to the McMansion phenomenon. After driving slowly around the loopy streets, staring at the cathedral-style entryways that were de rigueur at that moment in subdivision history, I got out of the car to look at an enormous new house that was just being completed. It bore a passing resemblance to Blenheim Palace. Out front, there were massive columns. I touched one and was shocked to realize that it wasn't marble or stone but some sort of synthetic, a lightweight composite.

Since then, every so often I visit new subdivisions and touch things: the siding, the walls, the flooring. And I am almost always repelled, not just by how these houses look, but how they feel. I imagine that I can feel the difference between genuine stucco and the synthetic stuff called EIFS that commercial homebuilders prefer. As in fashion, where the quality of a garment can be judged by its "hand," architecture is not just about appearances. It's about how a building treats your body, how it feels physically to be in a space. I stand in rooms and try them on like I'd try on a dress. And it is amazing to me how bad a very simple house can feel.

I finally drive on, west toward the hills. As the day progresses, I am joined on the road by more and more Harleys. Gas stations, few and far between in central South Dakota, begin to have lines. Flyover country, a section of America that should by rights be empty, is suddenly quite, quite full.

Heeding the advice of the man at the coffee bar, I check into the Interior, South Dakota, Budget Host Motel in late afternoon. Out front there's an aboveground swimming pool and a petting zoo with a pair of sleepy buffalo. I buy a couple of beers at the motel store and sit on the balcony outside my room and watch the parking lot fill up with bikes. I begin to notice that these bikers are not what I've imagined. They are, for one thing, resolutely middle aged. They are polite, door-holding guys—shy guys, not shitkickers. Brief conversations reveal them to be accountants and dentists. One man from the Seattle area tells me that while he's biking alone with his friends to Sturgis, he'll take his wife to the Harley hundredth anniversary celebration in Milwaukee later in the summer. They'll drive there in a camper, towing the Harley in a special bike trailer.

I walk around Interior, a place that looks like it's been beaten by the wind for way too long and should have blown away by now, and notice that its gas stations have been transformed into biker bars. Striped party tents have popped up on the asphalt and they are quickly filling with beer-drinking bikers, guys who, despite the leather and the bandanas, would look more at home astride their riding lawnmowers than on their Harleys.

In what must be the civic center of Interior, on the edge of a battered-looking playground, there's a sign that pretty much sums up the history and the culture of the place. The words are burned into four raw boards, one of which is lying on the ground resting against the sturdy beams that hold the sign up.

> *"I was born of wagons west. The oldest town in the Badlands. I've known drought and winter's fierce storms. Three times fire has swept my streets. Yet my rodeos were known throughout the west. Yakima Knute—Stroud—Earl Thode. Champions all have ridden my arenas. The great Jim Thorpe has played my fields. The early music of Lawrence Welk has sounded in my nights. This is a land that bred great Indian chiefs and mighty warriors. Now it is a land of neighbors. WELCOME TRAVELER."*

Almost on cue a local bar owner—I'd seen him minutes earlier putting the finishing touches on his big "Bikers Welcome" sign—pulls up in a pickup truck accompanied by a dog and two sidekicks. He yells, "Do you like to party?" "Depends on the party," I reply. He tells me I should come to his bar that night and he'll buy me a drink.

It is one of those times that I wish I had a traveling companion. I don't really want to go into a bar full of bikers—even if they are all middle-aged suburbanites (*especially* if they're all middle-aged suburbanites) by myself. At that moment I feel like Thelma with no Louise.

Instead of partying I turn in early and go hiking in the Badlands the next morning before the sun gets too hot. As I weave my way through the crazy rock formations, I make up a new rule: I have to live in a town where it feels comfortable for a woman to go into a bar by herself.

And then, in what may be the strangest leg of the trip, I head west and south to Mount Rushmore, accompanied along the way by a swarm of bikers that grows thicker as I get closer to the monument until, on the final approach road, I feel like a float in a parade. In my Volkswagen, I am the only nonbiker in a stream miles long. I pull into a concrete parking garage that works like a woofer, amplifying the thrum of thousands of unmuffled engines.

Outside, Washington, Jefferson, Teddy Roosevelt, and Lincoln look on impassively at a plaza filled with black-leather-vest-wearing family groups, Leathernecks Corpsman and Leathernecks Wife, patrons of Morrie's Place and fans of George Strait. *What would Thomas Jefferson make of this scene?* I wonder, as I search his stone face for any sign that he regrets penning that thing about the pursuit of happiness.

The Kennedy residence by Anderson Anderson Architecture,
Fox Island, Washington

The Perfect House

6

August 8, 2003 Downtown Seattle, Washington

The Union Street steps, a recently completed urban amenity. I am just downhill from the art museum on my cell phone trying to play office. Too many tourists. Too much ambient noise. It's interesting how the new, improved Seattle feels like the old, unimproved Seattle, except that the trappings of my life aren't here. I could see how they might be, though.

Flat as a pancake might be good for running, but it's topography that makes me happy. By the time I arrive in Buffalo, Wyoming, I am positively giddy. Drawn by a sign that advertises "modern log cabins," I spend the night at the Z Bar Motel in a one-room cabin that looks as if it were made with Lincoln Logs. It is a toy house, cute and elemental, its own logs painted brown and their round ends, protruding at the corners, a decorative forest green. I wish I could put it in my glove compartment and take it with me, but I settle for tucking a couple of postcards into my notebook.

Even this far west my neighbors at the Z Bar are all bikers heading east to Sturgis. I talk to a couple of guys at a local restaurant and ask them what they do when they get there. "Do?" one asks. He tells me they set up camp on the outskirts of town. They wander around, reveling in the pleasure of being surrounded by so many other Harley owners. They party. "Do" is irrelevant.

In the morning I run on a trail beside a stream that meanders its way through cow pastures and continues up into the foothills of the Big Horn Mountains. If I took it in the opposite direction, it would lead me all the way into that part of town dominated by the interstate highway and all the ancillary services. I love Buffalo for bothering to push a footpath deep into an area mostly owned by drivers. I eat breakfast in the best diner I've found on the whole trip. I buy a T-shirt to ensure that I'll remember the town and study a copy of the "Buffalo Home Guide."

I do yoga in Bozeman and watch the low riders cruise the streets of Coeur d'Alene. I make my way up and down countless mountain passes. By the time I arrive in Seattle, I'm ecstatic. My drive through the Cascade Mountains, east of the city, reminds me how much I miss this part of the country, how glad I am to be someplace that was, for seven or eight years, my home.

During my freshman year of college, I discovered that Marlboro, Vermont, was not as far from New Jersey as I had initially believed. Two hundred miles was not, at that point in my life, enough distance between my "compromise style" family home and me. Also, I was deeply unhappy during my one winter on a Vermont mountaintop. I began researching other colleges and other climates. My criteria: I wanted a school with an experimental approach to curricula, no grades, and no competitive sports. A temperate climate would be a plus. The Evergreen State College, a newly established institution in the state of Washington, perfectly met my needs, and the fact that it was as far from New Jersey as it was possible to go, without leaving the contiguous United States, sealed the deal. The day before I left for Washington, my mother walked into my New Jersey bedroom and informed me that her mother had left Poland at the age of eighteen—my age—and never saw her family again. I don't remember what, if anything, I said in response.

I spent the rest of my college years at Evergreen, about 60 miles south of

Seattle in the state capital, Olympia. And this was the spot where I had my second meaningful encounter with modernism, and where I became truly aware of it, although I don't think I began to understand it until years later.

I first arrived in Olympia, Washington, in 1975 by Greyhound. Before this trip, I'd never been farther west than Ohio. Somehow I expected that a small city isolated in the far northwest corner of the country would be quaint in exactly the way a small Vermont town is quaint. I got off the bus and stared at the undistinguished assortment of boxy buildings, mostly constructed in the 1950s and 1960s. At the time, I didn't know enough to assign them dates or styles, as I didn't have a language to describe architecture or urban design to myself. All I could deduce was that this place was, in some loosely defined way, "western." I wanted very badly to like it, but I didn't know how.

I took a taxi from the Greyhound station to campus, which turned out to be miles from town on a small peninsula projecting into Puget Sound. When I arrived at the main entrance I was astonished by what I saw: a vast brick plaza, Red Square, surrounded by poured concrete buildings so rudimentary in form that they looked like someone's idea of a joke. This was Washington State college architecture of the early 1970s—perversely, almost every campus in the state had a Red Square—and it frightened me. I desperately wanted to be back in my little whitewashed village in the Green Mountains.

All the school's major buildings had a wood-grain pattern pressed into their concrete. The students, myself included, naturally assumed that this pattern was a stab at decoration, a cynical attempt on the part of whoever designed this monstrous place to acknowledge the natural surroundings, the wooded splendor of the Olympic peninsula. We all made fun of the wood-grained concrete, but none of us understood it for what it was: the imprint left by the wooden forms into which the concrete was poured, a mark of the architecture's functionalist roots. I remember reading an art history book by Nicholas Pevsner for a class at Evergreen and joking about the fact that he described the design of an early twentieth-century mantelpiece as functionalist because the bricks were arranged vertically, supposedly encouraging the movement of smoke up the chimney, but no one ever pointed out that the functionalism to which Pevsner alluded was all around us.

Years later, in the early 1990s, I spent months exploring and writing about Eastern Germany and developed a strange affection for the Plattenbau, the homely apartment houses the GDR built on the cheap from prefabricated concrete components. These were buildings so frugally constructed that they were sited so that two towers could be erected using only one crane and, in the completed buildings, elevators only stopped on every other floor.

My fondness for something so ugly made no sense until I returned to my old college campus more than twenty years after I'd graduated and realized that the dorm where I spent my sophomore year was made of prefab concrete, that the whole Evergreen campus was an example of Plattenbau construction. I'd spent my happiest college years in a Plattenbau cocoon.

While it would have been tempting for me to return to Seattle and do nothing but wallow in nostalgia for the city where I spent my early twenties, where I helped found a rock'n'roll magazine, where I never ran out of opportunities to be in love, I remind myself that I am here to think about my future. I have come to Seattle to meet with a couple of architects, Peter and Mark Anderson, the designers of the house that, more than any other piece of architeture, has inspired this journey.

The house in question stands on Fox Island, a community across the water from Tacoma. It was built for a young woman named Melissa Kennedy, a firefighter, whose parents had earlier commissioned a more conventional house from Anderson Anderson Architects. The original budget for the Fox Island house was $65,000. The finished house cost somewhere in the neighborhood of $86,000; Kennedy's family pitched in on the labor to keep the costs low.

Originally I discovered the Andersons when I was fishing the Internet, trying to make the various search engines cough up a decent modern house in Tacoma, Washington. At the time I was planning a magazine issue about unsung, unloved American cities. The Fox Island house was wrong for that issue—I thought it was too rural—but I ran it on the cover of *Dwell*'s first prefab issue a few months later. The building fascinated me because it was resolutely modern but followed no particular formula that I knew of. It didn't look like the slick revivals of midcentury style that were becoming increasingly popular. Instead, it was its own icon, a shed with a roof that rolled from front to back, with zebra-striped siding, a big front window placed off center and a deck surrounded by a yellow metal railing. The house was built into a hill that had been landscaped as a terraced garden, the terraces held in place not by conventional retaining walls but by stacks of old tires. The magazine shoot took place on a typically drizzly Puget Sound day, and the house was completely surrounded by foliage in a shade of deep green peculiar to the rain forest climate of the Pacific Northwest. I looked at the photo and I could smell the moist air. Somewhere, buried deep in this image, were my late teens and early twenties. I looked at the photo and saw nostalgia, but it felt like love. This, I decided, was my house. I had set out on this trip to lay my claim on it.

When I first started talking with Peter Anderson, the younger and more communicative of the Andersons, in 2000, he and his brother Mark were leading the most amazing lives. They divided their time between their Seattle-based architectural practice, teaching in Hawaii, and clients in Japan, where they built houses from modular components. They would do much of the fabrication in the States and ship the panels they'd built in containers to Japan for construction.

This was the hallmark of their method, building houses from prefabricated components that could be easily transported. The Kennedy house had been built from pieces that could all fit on the back of a flatbed truck. Panelized construction, the practice of constructing a house from a prebuilt set of wooden wall sections or panels, is not the Andersons' invention. One history of innovative approaches to housing cites an example of panelized housing from 1624, when components for houses were shipped from England to Cape Ann, Massachusetts, as temporary housing for the fishing fleet. Most contemporary art historians like to attribute the idea to Walter Gropius and other Bauhaus-related architects who experimented during the 1910s and 1920s with a variety of systematic approaches for building low-cost housing.

By the time I reach Seattle in the summer of 2003, the Andersons have a new arrangement. Mark is now teaching at the University of California, Berkeley, so the brothers have set up an office in San Francisco, while continuing to maintain their Seattle office near Pioneer Square.

As I walk along Western Avenue on an atypically sunny day, I think about the ways the city has changed since I lived here. Western had then been a forgotten place, home to low-rent businesses that needed access to the waterfront a block away. It was a dark street that always stank of cheap wine and urine. The original production facility for *The Rocket,* my old music magazine, was just off Western, and I'd spent many late nights in the area. Now it's lined with pricey condos and designer furniture showrooms.

The Andersons had moved from a space directly on Western to a loft on Columbia Street, just around the corner. Peter, a slight, precise-looking man in his early forties with short, sparse blond hair, greets me and gives me a tour of the office while we wait for Mark. He shows me a model of a house they're building in the mountains east of Seattle, a 2,000-square-foot home with a planted roof, glass walls to show off the view, and a shower that is magically cantilevered into space. At $300,000, it's well over my budget, but by normal standards it's an inexpensive mountain retreat.

Then we come to a workshop project that he and his brother are developing for the UC Berkeley campus. Situated within the courtyard of an existing building, it will be constructed from folded sheets of high-tech polycarbonate panels. It looks like an especially complex Chinese lantern, and in essence, that's what it is. "The strength comes from the shape," Peter explains, "from the geometry of folding."

And then there's a house that will be built on the Olympic Peninsula. The idea here is that most of the square footage will be outdoors. Even the kitchen and dining room will have open walls; only the bedrooms and home offices will be completely enclosed and climate controlled. The whole house will sit on a 4,000-square-foot deck, covered with a translucent LEXAN roof. The deck will be supported by wooden columns custom fabricated by an Austrian-made, computer-controlled timber milling machine of the type that is now used to economically fashion the components of the more "traditional" timber-framed houses I visited during my stay at Yestermorrow. "A high-tech timber frame," is what Peter calls it. It's a reminder to me that the real difference between a house that advertises its technological sophistication and one that hides its provenance beneath a veneer of traditionalism is the intention of the architect or builder. You could, in theory, build two completely different houses from the same kit of parts.

The Andersons' version of a timber frame involves columns that stand upright and others that lean in a way that suggests instability, even though they actually add to the strength of the building. "It's slightly structurally perverse," Peter acknowledges. He then expounds on the notion that "wood can be a very high-tech material." If, for instance, you manipulate wood fibers the way the scientists at DuPont do with the fibers in composite materials, you understand that a piece of wood has different properties and strengths, depending on the way the grain is oriented.

As Peter leads me from model to model, I feel as if I'm being teased. I'm not here for all these other projects, as intriguing as they are. I'm here for the house I love. Still, I begin to understand more about why I fell for the Fox Island house in the first place. It's not just the low cost or the lush green setting or longing for my misspent youth. It is also the message the house telegraphs about its makers. It isn't a slick assemblage of stylistic moves, for in truth there is nothing slick about it. Rather, it speaks to me of architects who behave like mad scientists operating a rogue R & D facility. The most successful example of the architect as Mad Scientist is, of course, Frank Gehry, whose famous mutant forms are generated not by a computer but by the architect tinkering like a kindergartner with boxes and pieces of wood. Gehry's staff then translates his idiosyncratic forms into computerized drawings, objects that can only be built with the latest materials and methods.

The Anderson brothers are like quiet Gehrys, fearlessly reinventing how things are built and what they are built with. They are like little boys with an Erector Set, except that they insist on creating the Erector Set from scratch again and again.

Lunchtime comes, and Mark still hasn't shown up, so Peter and I walk over to a Thai restaurant on Western Avenue. He tells me the story of how he and his brother got into architecture. As teenagers, they worked for a man named Ted Litzenberger, from whom the Andersons' parents had bought a log cabin. Litzenberger had come up with a method of building with a waste product of the plywood industry. Plywood is made by peeling away the outermost layers of a tree, in much the same way that an old-fashioned, rotating apple peeler removes the outer layers of an apple. Litzenberger's company was called Log Systems. Peter explains, "It started out being a good thing because there were these eight-inch cores that no one was using. They were turning them into firewood after peeling off the outer part. Initially, they were pretty good-sized chunks of wood and they made sense as a building system. Then as the wood industry realized they were chucking out a lot of valuable wood, they improved their machines so that they turned them down to six-inch cores."

Litzenberger adjusted. "He then came up with a new system that used smaller logs with an insulation core in the middle. So it became a more hybrid system. As the industry developed further and they began peeling them down even smaller, the company shifted to making climbing toys for children, playground equipment."

Litzenberger, who died in 2004, was a renegade and he taught the Andersons the potential of using unconventional materials or using conventional materials in unconventional ways. He was also an entrepreneur. "He wasn't a theoretical person who'd imagine how things could be," Peter recalls. "If he had an idea, he would find a project to try it on. His own house was kind of a laboratory for him."

I return to Anderson Anderson the next day, and this time Mark, two years older than Peter, actually shows up. He's softer looking, a little bit heavier, scruffy and boyish. He's slower to speak, less glib, but what he says always seems carefully thought through and occasionally profound. He has the demeanor of a techie, the sort of guy who inhabits the hallways of a very cloistered building at Stanford or MIT.

The Andersons and I sit down at the conference table, and I try to get them to tell me what they'd do if I came to them wanting a $100,000 house. They tell me that it's a request they got a lot these days. "A lot from New York," Peter says. "We try to prepare people for the fact that it's not an easy number to achieve." He cautions that to make it worthwhile for the architects, they'll need to take "an unsual approach." The vision of the Perfect $100,000 House is as alluring to them as it is to me, but because they won't make any money on it, they have to get something else out of their efforts. It has to be a project that teaches them something new about design or the potential of materials. They will take on a client who is willing to experiment, who, as Peter says, "is interested in going along for that ride."

Mark points out that "people interested in a $100,000 house have unconventional property." "Unconventional" means added cost. It could be a hillside considered unbuildable or a property that is simply remote, completely off the grid. And while installing necessities like a septic system, power, or a road wouldn't be "a significant part of a larger budget," Mark explains, $30,000 for infrastructure would put a big dent in a bare-bones budget. The lesson, if you want to build cheap, is to have a level lot that is already connected to utilities. Of course, such lots generally come with neighbors, and neighbors don't always appreciate it when an unconventional house goes in next door. And litigation could cost more than bulldozing a road or digging a cesspool.

Then there's the other factor, the architect's time. "Doing something where you're really trying to stretch a budget is a lot more work," Peter explains. "You have to value engineer all the way through." *Value engineering.* The term is usually used as a euphemism for what happens toward the end of a major project that has gone significantly over budget: luxuries like skylights or bamboo flooring suddenly disappear from the plans.

The upshot is that they will agree to do a $100,000 house only if "there was the ambition for it to be an interesting piece of architecture." There's another condition. It has to be something, Mark insists, "that could be done as a multiple."

"We have a whole body of research into smaller, lower-cost houses," Peter adds. "It would have to be thought of as a series."

At this point, I want to jump up and shout, like a worshipper at a revival meeting. A truly perfect $100,000 house isn't one that simply meets my needs but one that could be replicated, one that could replace the miserable beige tract house I toured in Yankton, one that could replace miserable beige tract houses all across America. Amen, brother Mark. Amen, brother Peter.

Then Mark interrupts my happy reverie. He suggests that the whole notion of an inexpensive experiment might simply be wrong. "The least expensive way of building," Mark points out, "is the most conventional." He argues that the whole process of wood framing is so standardized, so familiar to building inspectors, that doing things the ordinary way is, in fact, "a virtue."

Not that the Andersons operate in an ordinary way. The Fox Island house is a case in point. "The trick was to avoid any type of material that was expensive," Peter says, explaining the strategies the brothers used to build within the original $65,000 budget.

The Andersons devised their system of panelized construction to compensate for the fact that the Fox Island site was so steeply sloped that there was no room for staging the work. The panels could be assembled nearby, with a roof overhead to keep the rain out, and trucked to the site; eight feet wide, they were sized to fit on the back of a flatbed truck to avoid incurring the additional expense of transporting a wide load. Once on the site, the panels took only a day to assemble.

The house is only 18 feet wide, because that's the width that could be spanned with off-the-shelf materials. The roof, for instance, isn't supported by beams. There's no steel. There aren't even any glue-lams, the strong, relatively inexpensive, engineered wood product that has become a standard tool in the low-cost kit of parts. "It's just 2×12s spanning across. It's mostly standard things from the lumberyard."

The Andersons also took advantage of whatever free labor was available. "Melissa's father was an Alaska ferry pilot, trained as a welder," Peter continues. The steel railings on the deck were his handiwork. "He'd work on the house in between ferry runs."

The distinguishing features that define the look of the house all grew out of the need for economy rather than aesthetic decisions. The staircase seems peculiar because it's built like a shelving system. Each step is a thick plank resting on a pair of 2×4s that are in turn held in place by wooden braces that are, in turn, connected to the steel pipes that the architects substituted for the I-beams that ordinarily support floors.

The distinctive striped siding is actually $300 worth of roofing material installed by Kennedy and her family, a project that Peter describes as "fairly labor intensive." Melissa Kennedy described it this way in an interview: "All I remember is standing, my brother-in-law, dad, myself, and a friend of my brother-in-law, nailing away."

In the Anderson Anderson monograph, published in 2001, the brothers devote several paragraphs to the striped siding: "Ever since one of our first roofing jobs, we have wanted to build a house sided with stripes of asphalt roll roofing. On a hot roof, doing a dull, tedious job, your mind sometimes drifts to thoughts of vandalism." They go on to explain that there were two colors of roofing material available because they were leftovers from other jobs. They weren't sure which to use, so they used both. "Ever since then we have thought that stripes are an honorable mark of indecision—and indecision, or at least a decision maximally postponed, has always been our most fiercely preserved operating method."

The roof was a sheet of corrugated metal nailed into place over 8-foot panels of plywood bent on-site to follow the curve. To plot the curve of the roof, they rented a warehouse and drew it, using a giant compass they fashioned. When I find that out, I don't feel so bad about having used a banana to calculate the curve of the roof for my imitation Anderson Anderson house at Yestermorrow.

Still, inventing the inexpensive strategies they used for the Fox Island project used up endless amounts of the architects' time. "I'm sure we lost a considerable amount of money on this house," Peter confesses. Nonetheless, he thinks it could be replicated today for about $100 a square foot, or $100,000. Perfect.

By the end of our conversation, I'm more convinced than ever that the Andersons are the right architects, the ones who should build my house. The question is whether I could get them to do it, whether I could come up with a way to make it worth their while. I begin to fantasize about building more than one house, about developing a parcel somewhere with ten or twenty Fox Island houses. Mark offers me a piece of Japanese candy from a bag on the conference table, and I pop it in my mouth without thinking, as if to demonstrate my willingness to experiment. The Andersons think my reaction to the strange, salty plum flavor is pretty funny.

Then, as I am desperately searching for a discreet way to spit the candy out, Peter and Mark offer to show me the Kennedy house the next day, as well as the house they built for their parents, and, more to the point, a large shedlike structure they built so their parents could have a place to live while the real house was under construction. I leave the Andersons' office still trying to get the strange taste out of my mouth. But I am very, very happy. I am finally going to see the house I've been dreaming of for years.

My stay in Seattle is a very dense, emotionally complex montage of my present and my past. I walk out of the Andersons' office, where it is very much 2003, and find myself again in the Seattle I called home from the summer of 1978 to the fall of 1982. It was before grunge emerged as a fashion or a lifestyle, before Nirvana burst onto the scene, before Microsoft created a city full of ridiculously affluent twenty-five-year-olds. During my five or so years in the city, I lived in seven different apartments and, true to the spirit of this trip, I walk past most of them.

To my surprise, the buildings are all still standing. One, on Lower Queen Anne Hill across the street from the Space Needle, has become a low-end boutique hotel. I am amazed to see another little building, 123 Bell—formerly an SRO hotel—where I once shared a sprawling apartment with several roommates. One night in 1982 someone set fire to the siding; flames raced up the wall and damaged the apartment, leaving us all homeless. And while condo towers have replaced many of the area's low-rise buildings, 123 Bell has been repaired and is still there, as is the building that formerly housed *The Rocket.*

Back in the *Rocket* era, one of our advertisers, a local radio station, started a campaign to build a memorial to Jimi Hendrix, who had grown up in Seattle. Somehow, all the promotion—which involved dragging Jimi's dad to endless events—produced only enough money to build a very small memorial, a heated boulder at the Woodland Park Zoo. Decades later, Microsoft billionaire Paul Allen decided to commemorate Hendrix with a music museum, the Frank Gehry–designed Experience Music Project.

Casting nostalgia aside, thinking not of my rock 'n' roll youth but of my architecture critic adulthood, I visit the building. From the outside, it is Gehry's most ungainly creation. The rationale for this crumpled mass of parti-colored steel is that it's supposed to resemble a smashed guitar. I am prepared to hate it until I realize that it is situated in Seattle Center's amusement area, the Fun Forest. And somehow the messy, garish building looks right at home next door to the log flume ride.

But the biggest perspective-bender is inside. In the first-floor gallery is a show called "Paper Scissors ROCK," which chronicles the history of Seattle punk posters. It opens with a wall of posters and flyers from the late 1970s and early 1980s, all for shows I attended, all designed and made by people I once knew. I feel that as long as I remain in Seattle, I will occupy a very permeable place, liable to slip from the 1980s to the 2000s, backward and forward, at any moment without warning. I am having a "total experience" of my own.

August 9, 2003   Gig Harbor and Fox Island, Washington
I ran on the waterfront in Seattle and thought serious thoughts about what it might take to live here again, how quickly I'd get bored or broke, whether I would be the ideal outdoorswoman in my second Seattle life. I'd like to imagine that I would.

On Saturday morning, I follow a map that Peter has drawn so carefully that every traffic light along the way is indicated on it—an architect's map—to the Anderson family home in Gig Harbor, a tranquil waterfront enclave east of Tacoma.

Mr. and Mrs. Anderson give me a tour of their home, a very warm, comfortable, light-filled place facing Puget Sound, very Scandinavian in feel. The 1993 house, which includes a book-filled study for Mr. Anderson, a retired chemistry professor, is one of those contemporary designs that seems from the outside to have no particular form. In actuality, it was designed to respect the topography of the narrow site and to spare as many of the existing trees as possible. From the inside it is clear that the intention is to maximize the daylight and water views available to every room. At the top of the house, up a spiral staircase, is a guest bedroom, where Mark is currently camping out.

While young architects often build their first houses for their parents, most of those projects speak more loudly of the architect's ambition than of the parents' desires. The parents become guinea pigs, testing whatever theory was in vogue when their architect offspring graduated from school. But this early Anderson Anderson project is primarily a testament to the conviviality and intelligence of the parents. It is less a portfolio piece than a heartfelt gift.

Eventually, Mark and Peter arrive at their parents' house and, from Gig Harbor, we drive across a bridge to Fox Island to visit Melissa Kennedy's place. Seeing it in person is a bit like meeting a celebrity whom I've worshipped from afar. As Peter drives us there, I brace myself for disillusionment. It's a house I've studied in photographs for years and fallen in and out of love with a dozen times. When we finally arrive, I'm amazed by the fact that it actually stands just off an extremely busy road. It is not the isolated island retreat I'd imagined it to be.

Once we get past the barking dogs at the gate to the driveway, I can see that the landscaping has grown up around the house. The terraces are now planted with tall flowering plants that hide the tiers of tires from view, and the zebra stripes on the house have faded and become discolored over time so the black is less black and the white is more like gray.

The house also looks smaller than it does in the photos. It is, in fact, quite modest, only 18 feet across and 50 feet deep, but the vivid graphical quality of the cheap siding, the unusual back-to-front curve of the roof, and its position atop a hill all make it read large. It is modest, but appears monumental—exactly the qualities I said I wanted in a house back at Yestermorrow.

And it is wildly, wonderfully imperfect, which somehow makes it more perfect. Standing before it, I can see that there is a rightness to the things that looked wrong in the photos, like the awkward way the front deck is half hung from piping and half supported by a narrow I-beam. It is a beguiling combination of a trained architect's rationalism and a design/build firm's improvisatory approach. Peter and Mark haven't been back to see the house themselves in a few years and they're fascinated by the way it's aged. "I like the rusted nail heads," observes Peter, closely examining the siding. "You can still see the blue chalk lines."

While the barking dogs calm down once we are inside the gate, the house itself is guarded by a screeching parrot. The bird produces the decibel level and pitch of a smoke alarm and it does not shut up for a moment. So here I am inside my perfect house, moving slowly from room to room, examining every detail: the extraordinary grace of the curved roof from the inside; the way Melissa's office sits at the front of the loft level, exactly where my office would sit if it were my house; the way that each design decision can be read by looking at the structure; the fact that despite its narrow dimensions the house feels spacious inside.

Even the things that I never liked in the photos—such as the fact that the big windows are broken up by 2×4s, a by-product of the Andersons' panelized method—make sense to me in situ. Peter points out that the picture window on the front wall of the house is actually a stack of the cheapest, off-the-shelf, aluminum-framed windows they could find. He then expounds on his theory that the divisions in the window glass are important on gray days when the sky needs to be reduced somehow rather than amplified. I like the idea but suspect that it is something he cooked up after the house was built, a poetic way of dealing with the prosaic.

The term "dream house" has never meant anything to me—just a crass expression used by game show hosts. And now, suddenly, I understand it. I am walking through my perfect house ignoring the signs—Melissa's big-screen TV, her firefighter's chin-up bar—that reveal that it is not my house. But eventually, the piercing parrot screams drive me out of the house, my house, and I watch Mark, who walks round and round taking photos of every detail, recording how the house has changed in its ten years of existence.

Afterward, we drive back to Mr. and Mrs. Anderson's to inspect the mega shed the brothers built for their parents to live in when the real place was under construction. It really is just a giant, two-story, 1,800-square-foot version of the cauldron shed, with one wall primarily composed of windows. I like it pretty well but I left my heart on Fox Island.

Mark, Peter, and I go down the steps to the water and sit on a small dock where the main house's yard meets Puget Sound, and Mrs. Anderson brings us a tray of tea and cookies. We sit in the sun and talk until I have to go. Not that I want to go but I have a dinner date with old college friends in Olympia. Really, I would prefer to stay right here, in the little world the Anderson brothers have built. I drive away reluctantly, wondering if there is a way for Mark and Peter's parents to adopt me.

In the months that follow my visit with the Anderson brothers, I begin to see pictures of the Fox Island house everywhere. It has become one of the poster houses for the increasingly fashionable prefab movement. At one point, I notice that a San Francisco–based start-up making unlikely promises about its ability to deliver prefab houses lists the Andersons as consulting architects on its elaborate Web site. By the time I call Peter to find out more about the company, the relationship has been severed. "Their marketing was getting ahead of what they have to offer," is how he explains the problem. Since then, the Andersons have stayed on the sidelines of the pre-fab game.

"That low end of the market is crowded with people and designs that are not anything that I want to try to compete with," says Peter. "There are a lot of hucksters getting into the business, people who see the fad and are trying to set up distribution companies.

"We've been doing a lot of studying," he adds, "of where costs go in building construction. The things that are getting prefabricated are a very small slice of the pie in terms of time, money, and complexity. They're not really solving a lot of the bigger problems. The part that has yet to be solved is not just how you build the wall panels but getting things connected to the site and appropriate to the site."

What Peter Anderson tells me jibes with my own suspicions about the prefab movement. The hard stuff—like building foundations, bringing in utilities, and getting approvals such as building permits—is all more expensive and complicated than putting up walls. But so far the existing prefab companies are mostly concerned with the walls. The only people who have streamlined the other processes—the foundations, the plumbing systems, the legal and financial niceties—are the big, conventional home builders. The thing that the tract house builders have to offer is not good architecture or superior carpentry but a well-practiced proficiency at taking care of the hard stuff.

California

7

August 13, 2003   The central plaza in downtown Arcata, California

It is about as idyllic a spot as I have ever seen. The perfect square of green, its appealing stores on four sides. Beautiful neon cocktail bar signs. The Sidelines. The Alibi. Toby and Jack's. Tastefully hip home furnishings stores and the Big Blue Café. It's all, as they say, good. It is the perfect Northern California college town scene, snug in its alternative character. I can't decide whether I love this place or whether it gives me the willies.

In California I hit a point where my fantasy life runs smack into reality or the accumulated effects of way too many of other people's fantasies. Eureka, California, is my destination. I had, in 2002, while reflecting my options if I left my job in San Francisco, considered buying a house in Eureka. I'd never stopped there, just driven through, but the real estate brokers' Web sites were full of sweet little $80,000 Spanish-style adobe houses. Typically, I would walk out of some meeting fuming and take revenge on my modernist magazine by looking at pictures of cute pink houses. But by the time I arrive a year later, there isn't much left. I began to have what I realize is the California real estate experience: if you make calls about houses at the low end of the spectrum, chances are that no one will return your call.

The Tramway gas station (1965) by architect Albert Frey,
Palm Springs, California

Chances are that the adorable house in the tiny picture in the real estate brochure is long gone from the market.

Admittedly, I'd first started thinking about the Eureka/Arcata area because *Outside* magazine had named it one of the best places to live in America, a miraculous spot where the cost of living is not too terribly high and you can cruise the redwood forests on your mountain bike without ever reaching the end of the trail. I had a feeling that all those little adobe houses went to *Outside* readers more decisive than I.

Still, it feels like a good moment to arrive in Eureka. The downtown is at a midway point in its transition from moribund lumber town to countercul-ture nexus: not too desperate, not too cute. I leave the heavily trafficked motel strip of 101 and stumble on a strange Victorian hotel called the Eagle House on the fringes of downtown. The building is a curious maze of stair-ways and empty ballrooms—very Agatha Christie—and my room offers a view of a municipal parking lot and the harbor beyond.

But all my calls to local realtors are in vain, so I drive up to Arcata, home of College of the Redwoods, and eat breakfast in a café.

The café waiter is a super-articulate kid, lingering here in a postgraduate holding pattern because, my god, how could he ever leave? Another guy warns his col-leagues in Big Blue that he is about to open and drink a Pepsi: "Tell me how I'm killing myself," he says. A woman explains that a toddler is her godchild because it was born just before her birthday. "It was a gift from god . . . or the goddess."

Sigh.

When I drove the back roads from Eureka to Arcata, I fantasized for a solid eight miles about picking up a piece of land, building a house, and growing—I don't know—artichokes or geraniums. In the café, I told myself that the reason I wasn't going to actually pursue this fantasy and check in with some of Arcata's real estate offices was that the town was pricier than

Eureka, and there was no real point. But the real reason was that the main square is beautiful in precisely the same way that portions of San Francisco are beautiful: the palm trees, the flowering shrubs, the greenest lawn, the bluest sky.

Maybe this is the result of reading too many Joan Didion essays, but there is something about that particular brand of Northern Californian beauty that I distrust. I always sense that beneath the greenery lurks trouble. Of course, geologically speaking, this is true, but my unease in Northern California has more to do with my personal seismology. This was the case long before I moved to San Francisco. It's not exactly a love-hate thing. It's more like I am completely seduced by the place but I can never quite get my balance there. So I drove on.

Let's just skip San Francisco. I stay a few days at my favorite budget lodgings, the "very quiet" Motel Capri. I check in with my friends and former colleagues. Then I leave. In San Francisco, where the median home price is $509,000 (and steadily rising), I can have no agenda.

Likewise, I decide to bypass LA because it will just be another place to socialize. I am pretty sure that there are no $100,000 houses to be had there, either. So instead of taking I-5, a fast but miserable drive, I follow 99, an older highway that runs parallel to 5 but somewhat to the east. I'm heading for the one spot in Southern California that might be in my price range, but I'm also angling eastward, beginning the long drive back toward Brooklyn. I pass through unforgiving desert towns like Bakersfield and Tehachapi and spend a night in Mojave.

August 17, 2003   Mojave, California

I am still in the real estate zone influenced by LA. Tehachapi, where I wanted to stay last night, is clearly a retreat for escaping urbanites—not totally colonized like Ojai, but known enough to be priced accordingly. Mojave is mostly a motel and fast-food strip, a place for trucks to pass through. The housing blocks behind the main strip seem sad, weary, baked by the sun, and ignored. This is just a flat spot. Until very recently, this is where they took new jets for testing, but it seems like the "test bed" is moving elsewhere.

I have breakfast somewhere south of Barstow, at the Slash X Ranch café. This turns out to be a crazy road-warrior hangout, where people go to race their motorcycles, their trucks, their all-terrain vehicles. The bar is lined with men and women dressed from head to toe in protective gear like armor. The ceiling is covered with caps, and the walls lined with photos of cars and trucks modified for desert racing. Everyone is polite and answers my questions about how fast they can go in as few words as possible. The answer is always roughly the same: "Yeah, really fast."

Pinned to the wall next to my table is a poem by "Scary Sheri" called "Desert Racing," which begins with the line: "It's the way the exhaust smells when you start your bike in the morning." I find it extraordinary that Californians can layer elaborate fantasies on even the least promising landscapes. I tell myself that this is a trick I need to learn.

My only hope in California is the desert area immediately north of Palm Springs, where semi-abandoned compounds with an acre or two of scrub and solid, low-lying concrete block houses routinely sell for $60,000 to $80,000. At least they did back in 2002.

I drive down Highway 62, and on the last stretch before my destination, Desert Hot Springs, I stop at a real estate office. It is Sunday afternoon, and the place is packed. Family groups keep streaming in the door. It is all I can do to get a brochure with listings and a business card from one of the salespeople. I feel as though I have stumbled onto a new Sunday afternoon family activity. It is like all-you-can-eat day at IHOP. This is not a good sign.

I check in at Miracle Manor, a 1940s desert modernist enclave owned and restored by LA-based architect Michael Rotondi and graphic designer April Greiman. For years, they had been coming to this motel, sited on a hilltop with a commanding view of surrounding valleys and situated directly above the hot springs that give the city its name. When the original owner died, they bought it, remodeled, and reopened in 1997.

I've spent a lot of time here, including a week in November of 2001, where the quiet and the hot mineral water were instrumental in bringing back my equanimity in the bleak months following 9/11. I love swimming in the hot spring–fed pool at night, doing the back float under the starry desert sky. And I've always admired the architecture of the place. The little buildings that house the motel rooms and the office form a slightly asymmetrical courtyard with a pool at the far end. In terms of materials—mostly cement block—the motel isn't that different from the crummy little desert rat shacks that I've always seen in the real estate ads, but there is something about the way the buildings are positioned—so subtly off square—that suggests to me that it was built by a contractor who'd worked on some of the houses designed by famous architects like Richard Neutra and Albert Frey in neighboring Palm Springs. Miracle Manor has very good bones. Of course, Rotondi and Greiman are both masters who stripped the place down, furnished the rooms with simple custom-built furniture, and gave it a perfect minimalist aesthetic. But it seems possible to me to take almost any concrete block desert compound and turn naïve, accidental minimalism into knowing, sophisticated minimalism.

Sadly, I am not the first person to have this idea. Or even the second. Sometime after I began thinking about buying a cheap house in the desert and long before I attempted to act on it, an artist named Andrea Zittel, known for creating modular living units that seem like the work of an especially doctrinaire interior designer, came along and bought one of the homesteader's cabins and outfitted it with her signature built-in cabinetry. Her goal was to make her 25-acre slice of the desert an art world destination. To that end, she's initiated an occasional art exhibit called "High Desert Test Sites," which consists of outdoor art installations by Zittel and her friends in the greater Joshua Tree area. And while I have nothing against art, I am not unaware of the effect the presence of artists has on real estate prices.

Honestly, though, I admire what Zittel has done and I don't hold her responsible for the real estate feeding frenzy I encounter. It is just the overflow from Los Angeles moving farther and farther east, deeper and deeper into the desert.

I had hoped to rendezvous with Rotondi at Miracle Manor and take a look at a few examples of the desert vernacular with him, to talk about their potential as habitable modern homes. But he got stuck in LA with a family crisis, so we wound up talking at a later date. One rainy afternoon in LA, we sit around an empty classroom at the Southern California Institute of Architecture, better known as SCI-Arc. The school's long rail freight building on the outskirts of downtown LA is full of students' models, clumps of polygons that look more like mysterious life-forms than buildings. SCI-Arc is perhaps the most intellectual and experimental of America's architecture schools, and Rotondi, one of its founders, is the perfect philosopher/architect.

By the time we meet the real estate bubble has swallowed Desert Hot Springs whole, and Rotondi isn't any happier about it than I am. He's particularly aggrieved that the old, uncomplicated, pragmatic approach to coping with the desert's temperature extremes has been abandoned, and the new homes going up are the same ones that conventional homebuilders would erect just about anywhere.

"The people that were building those [old] houses were people who lived there, and they understood the desert well enough and they had limited materials and other resources," explains Rotondi, whose years in Desert Hot Springs have made him a scholar of indigenous style. "The opportunities were out there. That is the place where, if you're looking to design something with natural ventilation and not to have air conditioning all the time, to really have something that works, yes, it would be concrete block. Well, it may be like what Albert Frey did—block and steel and glass."

Rotondi is referring to one of the notable Palm Springs architects. Albert Frey, born in Switzerland, designed some 200 houses in and around Palm Springs, as well as other buildings, including the iconic Tramway Gas Station, a modest structure dominated by a huge, angled awning that looks as if it's about to blast off into space. Abandoned in the 1990s, it's recently been used as an art gallery and is now the city's visitors' center. Frey also designed one of the most poignant buildings I've ever seen, the 1958 North Shore Yacht Club on the Salton Sea. It's a once cheerful, nautical, moderne building that was likewise abandoned when the shoreline of the huge lake receded, beaching the yachts. The building is now boarded up and surrounded by the corpses of fish that were left behind by the shrinking lake.

While Frey houses are well beyond my reach, the little anonymous concrete block homesteads shouldn't be. There are plenty of them in the real estate listings, houses of under 1,000 square feet on five acres of desert, all of them sold "AS IS." I have a feeling that "as is" doesn't include niceties like indoor plumbing, but that's a minor point, given that the prices for these marginal places rarely top the $50,000 mark. But my phone calls to real estate agents produce one of two results. Either my messages are not returned or I'm told that the house I'm interested in has been sold and they don't have anything else in that range at the moment. It feels much the way it did when I tried to buy a car at a Redwood City Volkswagen dealership in the middle of the dot-com boom. I am just too small-time for anyone to bother with.

Part of the appeal of those tiny casitas is that they represent a lost attitude toward homebuilding. Desert Hot Springs, which filed for bankruptcy in 2001, is now experiencing a housing resurgence. "It's basically small developers from other areas, and now there are these very large developers moving in. The desert from Highway 62 into town has been filled up with like three thousand houses," Rotondi tells me. (Later, I read the Desert Hot Springs "state of the city" report for 2005. It predicts 10,000 new homes.)

And these are not the kind of places I'm searching for, but normal subdivision houses. "I've talked to a handful of people out in the desert, developers, trying to convince them that there is a whole market that is untapped," Rotondi continues. "They said, 'What is this market?' And I said, 'Modern architecture.' In Palm Springs now, they're doing facsimile modern architecture. The buildings are boxy and white, with sort of quasi-pedigree pieces to them."

Across the street from Miracle Manor is Cabot's Old Indian Pueblo, now a museum, an outpost constructed by an early settler named Cabot Yerxa. The Pueblo is yet another reminder that the realization of elaborate fantasies in unlikely spots is pretty much the raison d'être of Desert Hot Springs, the surrounding communities, and, for that matter, the entire American West. Yerxa, after all, is the one who, upon finding the hot underground mineral springs, named the area Miracle Hill.

According to the "Legend of Cabot Yerxa":

In 1939 Cabot began the construction of a dream. It was his intention to build a monument to the Indian people he so admired. Without modern equipment he began the construction of what he came to call Cabot's Old Indian Pueblo. With only a pick and a shovel he carved the first room out of the hillside. It was little more than a cave to protect him as he continued with the rambling structure, sans blueprints.

Every portion of the overwhelming building incorporated the Indians' philosophy of life. Since the Indians believe that symmetry retains evil spirits, nothing is symmetrical in the Pueblo. Doorways and floors slant, walls are slightly uneven, and the windows form a puzzle of multi-shaped glass. The walls, measuring nine to ten feet in some places were designed to ensure warmth in winter and maintain cool temperatures during the summer months.

Somehow, I'd managed to never visit Cabot's museum, which is now owned by the city of Desert Hot Springs, but Rotondi had once taken me and a few other Miracle Manor guests on a walk up the dirt road behind the Pueblo to the ruins of a crazy house that Cabot had also built. It was a completely inexplicable assemblage of rooms that looked as if it might have been built by very industrious ants. There were no right angles, and the doors and windows were in completely irrational places. It was built out of whatever Cabot had on hand: adobe, wood, stucco, telephone poles. It made no sense but it was beautiful, like a house as a work of sculpture, the absolute antithesis of Andrea Zittel's hyper-organized desert abode just up the highway.

"I thought it was one of the best houses in this country," Rotondi tells me. "It was like outsider art." He pauses a moment and then tells me, "It burned down."

"It's not there anymore?" I'm shocked.

"I don't know whether it was burned, or maybe it was accidentally set on fire by somebody who built a campfire. It's like . . . nobody cared. And it was painful, because for me it was like somebody had been shot in the building and nobody cared."

Somehow, the demise of Cabot's crazy house and the unstoppable influx of normal subdivisions signal the end of my desert fantasy. In California I am simply undone by the pace at which collective fantasy becomes reality.

Subdivision Fever, Part I

8

August 22, 2003   Longmont, Colorado

After a completely glorious drive with the top down through Monument Valley, I was forced to stop in Moab, Utah, for the night, because I was in excruciating ovarian cyst pain that no amount of Advil would quell. Moab would be a great place to be if I felt like hiking and doing outdoor activities, but all I wanted to do was take a Vicodin and get into bed. I read the Book of Mormon for a while and crashed out.

All through California and Arizona I brood over what Mark Anderson said to me. Even as I drive through Monument Valley at 70 mph, my convertible top down, snapping digital photos of the crazy rock formations by bracing my little camera on the edge of the windshield, imagining Krazy Kat and Ignatz Mouse scampering around the surreal landscape, I can't shake the words of the elder Anderson brother: The least expensive house is the most conventional one.

Maybe I'm just wrong. Maybe I'm misguided. Maybe what I want simply isn't possible, not when real estate values have soared even in towns that just a year earlier were on the wrong side of the tracks or the wrong side of I-10.

And, much as I have tried to deny it, I know for a fact that Mark Ander-

The Rubik's Cube house by Prospect town designer Mark Sofield,
Longmont, Colorado

son is right. The easy way to buy cheap is to buy conventional. The simplest thing I could do is abandon my pretensions, park the car, and go directly to the cheap house specialists, the major homebuilders who bang together tens of thousands of houses a year and fill the American landscape with subdivisions named Terra Vista and Clover Glen.

Often, houses in these developments, especially when you get into Texas and the parts of the West where land costs are still low, sell for less than $100,000. Sometimes quite a bit less, like $60,000 or $70,000.

But of course these are never the houses I'm looking for. Part of the problem is that they are usually located on parcels of land far from urban centers and close to suburban malls. They are the progenitors of sprawl and are, for that reason, personally and politically repugnant to me. It's not just a matter of taste; it's a matter of ethics.

The fact is, I have been to the cheap house specialists. I know what they can and can't do. I know what they will and won't do. Back before I set out on my quest for the perfect house, I made a foray into the world of the imperfect house, trying very hard to understand the business of commercial homebuilding. To that end, I visited the Los Angeles headquarters of KB Home, one of America's largest homebuilders, turning out some 27,000 houses a year, as well as that company's architecture office in Pomona, east of LA off I-10.

I was there because I wanted to grasp the mechanics of the subdivision. I wanted to probe the thinking behind this staple of the American landscape. I wanted to burrow in deep enough to see the art in what they do, to understand why their houses look and feel the way they do. And to find out if they could build a house for someone like me.

At KB Home's headquarters on Wilshire Boulevard my expectations were both confounded and reinforced. On the one hand, this was a very sophisticated company. I was astonished as I sat in the waiting room with its pointedly domestic furnishings—incandescent floor lamps, warm brown sofas, vases filled with tulips—and flipped through the 2001 annual report. The cover featured a photo of a blue sky with wispy clouds. In large white type in its center was the word "EVERYWHERE." I turned the page and there was the same blue sky, now with the phrase "ALL THE TIME." On the adjacent page was the copy: "As the premier U.S. homebuilder serving first-time and first-move-up buyers, KB Home forges meaningful connections with consumers. We're in their sights and on their minds wherever they go, whenever they think of home."

As I looked through the report I marveled at the bold, high-impact graphic design and the intentionally blurry, fine-art-quality photography. KB Home's 2001 annual report was as contemporary, as knowing, as anything I'd ever seen. At the same time, the houses the company was selling during the period of my visit, that they are still selling, are those same nearly Spanish or moderately Tudor or ostensibly Craftsman houses that are the staples of subdivision life.

On my visit I met with Jeffrey T. Mezger, the company's chief operating officer, and Bruce Karatz, its chief executive officer. They were as articulate and passionate about what they do as any of the innovative architects or developers I've met. And both of them told me with great enthusiasm about how they design their houses based on data gleaned from some two million surveys they've conducted, asking recent homebuyers in KB's markets—although not buyers of KB's houses—what matters to them. In Mezger's words, they aim to discover "what gets into the psyche of that neighborhood."

For instance, in one survey book, a thick binder representing a twelve-to-fifteen-month period in Houston, participants were asked to agree or disagree with the statement "I would not buy a home that does not look impressive from the street." Forty-four percent of buyers in the $70,000 range agreed, as did 58 percent of those who purchased their homes for $150,000.

According to Karatz, the survey is one of a series of tools that KB uses to infuse a speculative business with stability and logic. He says it's the difference between the entrepreneurial model customarily followed by homebuilders and a strategic approach more typical of manufacturing. "We drill it into people's heads that we want decisions based on facts, not emotion."

At the same time that KB is asking homebuyers whether they would, for instance, prefer a house with more rooms or one with fewer but larger rooms, whether they would prefer a fireplace or 200 more square feet, whether they would pay extra for a basement, and then tabulating their responses, crunching them like the numbers in a political poll, they are also offering the homebuyer the kind of options menu that car dealers offer. The buyer goes to one of KB Home's "Design Studios" and chooses better than standard kitchen appliances, fancier than average bathroom faucets, pricier flooring, more stylish blinds.

"Everybody dreams of having a kitchen in the color they want," said Karatz. "Everybody dreams of being able to select faucets. We make that dream come true. And you don't have to write a check."

Indeed, all the accessories, all the upgrades are folded into the buyer's mortgage so that the interest that the buyer pays for all manner of household goods, from micro blinds to Berber rugs, becomes tax deductible. It's a brilliant strategy for adding $5,000 to $10,000 to the selling price of the home and deepening the company's revenue stream. A KB customer can get anything he or she wants, as long as it is an accessory, a detail. What the KB customer can't change is the architecture.

Nowhere were the contradictions between the company's overall sophistication and the retrograde qualities of its product more apparent than at the architecture and data center in Pomona. In the office of Ken Gancarczyk, KB's senior vice president of builder services, I meet with Ken, Eric Kough, vice president of architecture, and Todd Baker, the market research director. On a wall next to the conference table where we all sit, a series of renderings of houses is pinned to the wall: Craftsman, French Country, another Craftsman, Spanish, Farmhouse. "That's the streetscape," Ken pointed out. He then directed my attention to the wall behind his desk, which is completely filled with black survey binders.

"We ask questions that will assist us in delivering a product by keeping everyone's biases out," Ken declared, another statement of the now familiar company line. But what I really want to know, what I keep asking Ken, is, how do you actually design a house based on surveys? How do you go from opinion polls to bricks and mortar? If Ken were a hotshot—one of the young graduates of the Columbia University architecture program circa 1998—he would take the statistics generated by the survey and feed them directly into a computer drafting system that would spit out biomorphic blobs with the correct number of square feet apportioned to kitchens, bathrooms, and master suites, based on responses to the survey. KB's numbers combined with some radical thinking could generate remarkable results. But my dreams about what housing in America could be are usually stopped cold by the reality.

In the end, Ken never did answer my questions about the relationship between survey statistics and design to my satisfaction, but it seemed to be simply a matter of deciding which features were popular enough to make them standard and which should just be offered as options. "We come up with a preliminary design," he told me, "and we know that 25 percent want a fireplace and 75 percent don't. So fireplaces are an option."

Based on survey information, there's been a shift from having a formal living room to having an expanded kitchen called the "great room." And there's a free-form upstairs room called the "loft" that can be used as an informal family room or as a home office, a sort of basement rec room for houses without basements.

KB's homes are, as tract houses go, remarkably customizable. "We try to cover our bases and give people a choice," Ken argued. What you cannot change, however, is what the houses are. And the broader issues of architectural style are not addressed by the survey.

"If I asked if they prefer Craftsman to Mediterranean, they wouldn't answer," Ken told me. "They wouldn't know." As for the possibility of KB embracing modern design, Ken says: "Contemporary? I probably would never do anything with flat roofs. I can tell you that right now. No matter what they do, they're going to leak. . . ."

He speculates that Las Vegas or Houston might be cities where KB could, if the surveys dictated, try "contemporary." But the other problem is that there's something inherently difficult about building and marketing a low-end contemporary home. "To do a contemporary at $100,000 would be pushing the envelope," said Ken. "That clean look costs."

And I know that's true. The clean look costs—if not money, then time. You have to think about it to do it right. That's the cosmic joke about modernism. The Bauhaus architects believed, among other things, that by creating an architecture that celebrated technology, they were eliminating the need for handcraftsmanship, and thus liberating craftsmen from a life of tedious labor. The truth is that modern architecture, to be done right, requires just as much craftsmanship as more traditional forms. And in the world of low-cost, high-production homebuilding, some builders have been known to mask poor craftsmanship. If two surfaces don't come together in a straight, tight seam, decorative molding can cover that up. Trim can spruce up an ungainly facade. And homebuyers don't often look deeper than the stylistic touches like the Spanish roof tiles or the Tudor half-timbered veneer, at least not until they move in and start coping with a laundry list of structural deficiencies. A cursory Internet search will dredge up endless stories of homebuyers suing the big homebuilders over crumbling foundations and killer mold. With a modern house, the beauty is in the form itself, so you've got to get it right. And the other thing is that for much of KB Home's market the elusive quality known as "curb appeal" is all about having a house that exudes affluence. An unornamented box, to first-time homebuyers, looks exactly like the brand of affordable housing they're trying to escape.

So, honestly, KB can sell me a $70,000 house on the outskirts of San Antonio, but it won't be one that I want. I could get any number of options, including "Gas appliance fireplace with media niche in family room," but they wouldn't make me happy. I dream the wrong dreams.

Before I left the Pomona architecture offices, Eric Kough took me on a tour. He showed me stucco samples in twelve shades of toast and "theme boards," where designers tried to come up with new iterations of Spanish style. And, at some point, we walked past a printer that was spitting out construction drawings for a house in a development called Rancho Gabriela. I stopped for a moment and stared at the drawings. They were popping out of the printer like widgets off an assembly line. "They just keep coming," Eric observed. "They never stop."

And that's the thing. Companies like KB and Lennar and Centex and Hovnanian, they just keep on building, oblivious, it seems, to cultural changes. But it stands to reason that at some point homebuilders will have to get hip. Someone, somewhere will have to reinvent the subdivision.

And occasionally someone does. But those instances of reinvention are so rare, so special, that even if they start out with the modernist ideal of good housing for everyone, they quickly succumb to the laws of supply and demand.

For example, just south of Denver, in Englewood, Colorado, there is a 124-home postwar subdivision that is a perfect blend of European modernism and casual American style. Arapahoe Acres, as the development is called, is a time capsule of a moment when America's homebuilders were actually thinking progressively.

Its builder, Edward B. Hawkins, was a Denver native who in 1949 hired an expat Czech architect, Eugene Sternberg, then a professor at the University of Denver, to design the street plan and the houses. The result is a tightly arranged community of small homes—many of Sternberg's houses were only 850 square feet—that take their cue from the Bauhaus or Frank Lloyd Wright.

In the summer of 2002, not long after my visit to the KB Home architecture offices, I made a pilgrimage to Evergreen, another Denver suburb, to a retirement complex where Sternberg, eighty-seven, and his wife still live. Barbara Sternberg served us rhubarb pie while her husband, articulate and cantankerous, talked about his vision and how his vision had been compromised.

"The school of architecture in Prague had the philosophy of simplicity, down-to-earth honesty," he told me. After graduation, Sternberg moved to England and rode out the war there. He came to America to teach in 1947.

When he was hired by Hawkins, his intention had been to build small houses priced at $10,000, so that schoolteachers could afford to buy them. The perfect $10,000 house.

"At that time the builder agreed with me that he would sell it for ten thousand dollars because it cost him eight thousand dollars to build," Sternberg continued. "We had an open house one day. We had about nine homes built as a demonstration. About 40,000 people came to look. And they sold all of them right away, the same day." Because there was so much demand, some buyers offered as much as $13,800 for the houses.

"Then my talented, gifted builder said, 'Gene, I'm sorry. I know that you and I have an agreement, but how can I refuse this amount of money?' I said, 'You have to refuse it. Sell it for what you agreed on.'"

"Did the builder take the additional money?" I asked Sternberg, knowing what the answer would be.

"Money is God!" he replied.

That dispute precipitated the end of the first phase of Arapahoe Acres' development.

"He wanted to build bigger buildings for more money. But, whatever I say to you, he was an excellent builder. He was one of those builders who demanded quality details, had good taste. But that money spoiled him. And people wanted bigger buildings, could afford bigger buildings, and he went on, and the further he went, the bigger they became. I moved away from it, because that wasn't me."

Today Arapahoe Acres looks much as it originally did, with Sternberg's small houses, as efficiently planned as cabin cruisers, and Hawkins's larger, more assertive homes, still modest by today's standards, perfectly preserved. Ardent neighborhood historians have re-created the original street signage and house numbers. The place is a bit like a midcentury historic Williamsburg, with many of the houses furnished in authentic period style. The most dedicated guardians of Arapahoe Acres' heritage stop short at wearing 1950s clothing, but the place is so frozen in time that reenactments of the Eisenhower years seem like a distinct possibility. And today the going price for one of Gene Sternberg's modest little houses is easily $300,000. There is no one with Sternberg's sensibilities or talents building homes for today's schoolteachers.

The day I met with Sternberg, I invited Mark Sofield and Kiki Wallace to come with me. Mark and Kiki are, respectively, the town designer and developer of Prospect, another unconventional Colorado subdivision, located in Longmont, not far from Boulder, one I initially visited during the summer of 2001. It was Kiki Wallace who first gave me hope for the future of the American subdivision, because he built the only development where I thought—for a time—that there might be a house for me.

Kiki is one of those people who, if he didn't exist, I'd have to invent. Back at *Dwell* magazine, I had a couple of my editors assembling a package that was essentially a critique of New Urbanism. We were making fun of the retro architecture these communities typically use as their best sales tool and asking why the so-called neo-traditional neighborhoods couldn't incorporate modernism. Kiki got a call from someone on my staff who'd seen photos of the traditional houses in Prospect, and he was smart enough to know that he didn't want his development written about in that context. So he started calling my editors one by one, explaining that while Prospect had started out building cute little historicist houses, they were moving on to bolder things. Eventually he reached me. While the average New Urbanist has the low-key demeanor of Mr. Rogers, this voice on the other end of the line sounded as if it belonged to someone who urgently wanted to sell me a used car. I thought, *Who is this guy?*

Over the course of a year I had occasional conversations with Kiki and Mark and one or two of the Boulder-area architects who were executing modern houses for Prospect. I finally visited because I believed that Prospect might yield a modernist house or two suitable for publication. Instead, I found dozens, and I remember my first visit to Prospect as vividly as I recall my first viewing of a German Expressionist film. Mark; his wife, Kelly Feeney; Kiki; and I wandered through a subdivision streetscape that was unlike anything I'd ever seen, walking in and out of houses mostly still under construction. I remember searching for a metaphor that would somehow describe this surreal little development. I thought about The Village in the British TV show *The Prisoner.* I thought of scenes from the Ray Bradbury book *Dandelion Wine.*

Mark and Kiki instantly became my heroes because they had so adroitly scrambled the New Urbanist recipe, which calls for wedding a dense street plan to traditional architectural styles to make little developments all over America that seem to come from some Frank Capra version of small-town life. Instead, the Longmont developer and architect began to build houses that were rakishly modern, not in the midcentury European tradition but as part of an unestablished movement. They were building houses as unusual as the custom homes wealthy clients might commission but they were building them on spec, dozens and dozens of them, and mixing them with more traditional types of homes.

Mark designed many of Prospect's most idiosyncratic modern houses. Most remarkable, perhaps, is one that was nicknamed the Rubik's Cube (all Prospect houses have been anointed with unofficial names by the development's residents) because it consists of two volumes seemingly twisted in different directions. The house sits on a corner; the larger volume, a dark green shedlike structure, faces one street while the smaller volume, a paler green, one-story box, has seemingly been inserted right into the middle of the house and is angled toward the other street. On one of my early visits to their development, the house's builder was unhappy because this extremely unorthodox house had not found a buyer. Mark was convinced that changing the color scheme a bit, trading in the chartreuse of the smaller volume for something a bit more sedate, would help. I tagged along with Mark and Kelly—she was toting her Benjamin Moore paint chip kit—and watched them debate a new color scheme. They almost decided to paint the smaller volume gold. "I'm afraid people are going to say this is avocado and harvest gold," Kelly complained. They finally decided on a shade of pale green called "Puffball." Eventually, the house did sell.

Another Sofield-designed house, a long low single story with a double height tower at one end, was known around the subdivision as the Death Star or the Stealth House because the homeowner, a young tech executive, had decided, despite Kelly's call for mint, to paint it black. This house was one of my favorites because I loved the way Mark borrowed inspiration from the modest, low-slung homes typical of the isolated mountain communities outside Boulder without resorting to faux traditionalism or whimsy.

Prospect, however, where houses initially sold for prices in the mid-$300,000s, was swept up by the buoyant tech economy of nearby Boulder, and soon houses were going for upwards of half a million dollars. The economy had changed the tenor of the development.

Gene Sternberg came from Europe and brought the socialistic tradition of the original modernists with him. He wanted to design homes that were within the means of schoolteachers and college professors. Kiki Wallace came from Texas with the idea that he wanted to build big.

Somewhere along the way Kiki became an enlightened developer. "New development," he told me, "doesn't have to look bad. It doesn't. It's just that we accept it. Nobody's really made a choice, I don't think." So the aesthetics of suburbia became Wallace's main issue, but by the time I met him, he was troubled by the increasingly upscale profile of Prospect. He wanted to find a way through increased density or prefab construction to build more affordable homes.

I returned to Prospect in the fall of 2001 and began a dialogue with Kiki. On and off, over the course of months, we'd discuss the possibility of Prospect becoming a proving ground for some sort of prefab architecture. For a time in 2002 he was trying to get a variance from the city of Longmont that would have permitted the increased density necessary to building a low-cost component. But then, distracted by a series of personal problems and unwilling to devote the energy to the political battle he'd have to fight to get the variance, he dropped the ball.

By the time I return to Prospect on my road trip in the summer of 2003, I am beat. I'd driven by way of Flagstaff. I had spent a night in Moab. And somehow everyplace I wanted to stay in Boulder was booked, and so I wind up staying in Prospect itself, in Mark and Kelly's guest room. At first I considered staying in Prospect's new bed and breakfast, a garage apartment transformed into a themed environment inspired by the live-action version of *How the Grinch Stole Christmas.* But I am happier in the Sofield-Feeney residence, a traditional bungalow-style house that had been moved to Prospect from an old convent. It occurs to me that on my long quest to find a home, I've been staying in motels and the occasional hotel, but I haven't spent the night in an actual house in almost two months.

Only two years after my last visit to Prospect, some houses there are now selling for over $700,000. And Kiki's dreams of low-cost modular housing have been, for the moment, set aside. Over the course of two days of conversations with the developer, the town designer, and a couple of the builders, I tried to understand how and why the one subdivision in America in which I could actually imagine living had come to be priced so far beyond my means. Forget, for a moment, the $100,000 house. I couldn't even find the $300,000 house—still available elsewhere in Longmont—in Prospect anymore.

In a way, it appears that the free-floating, adventurous quality of the place contributes to the soaring prices of its homes. While the KB Home subdivision is all about building to a formula, a methodology that keeps everything, including the selling prices and the aesthetics, tightly reined in, Prospect is about defying the formula. Mark and Kiki have found a way of institutionalizing defiance; Kiki sells plots of land to independent builders who then construct and sell the houses. The builders who succeed in Prospect are the ones who are themselves characters. They can work within the architectural guidelines imposed by Mark and the overall atmosphere of eccentricity imposed by Kiki because they are a little bit wacko themselves.

Don Lucas is the most prolific builder in Prospect, and I spend a couple of hours roaming around with him one August afternoon. With his boyish enthusiasm for his houses and his shorts and baseball cap, Lucas, who had built twenty-five units in Prospect, is like an overgrown kid. By local standards, he is a mogul. Mark marvels at his ability to get the banks to back whatever he decides to build.

Lucas takes me to see the new townhouses he recently completed. The units have three bedrooms, high ceilings, and big balconies overlooking a street that no one has bothered to name because it's actually the development's central park. "I had $250,000 envisioned," he says, explaining how he attempts to set a sale price and build accordingly. "The six units are sitting on $300,000 worth of land," he continues. He claims he went to San Francisco architect Dan Solomon and gave him a price range. (In truth, Mark Sofield initially brought Solomon in before Lucas picked up the lots.) Solomon designed spaces that have loftlike drama. "It's real minimal stuff," as Lucas puts it. "To come out looking clean is harder than with fancy moldings and shit."

Solomon tried to stay within budget by specifying low-end bathroom fixtures. "He had the cheesiest, cheapest, ugly stuff," Lucas complained. The builder upgraded the bathroom fixtures, dropped the Kohler in favor of Dornbracht, and went crazy on the materials, installing floor-to-ceiling marble. "I think this is so much more elegant, to take this all the way to the top, the travertine tile," Lucas declares, as he stands in the total marble environment of a spectacularly high-ceilinged bathroom. He adds, "I never use those cheesy plastic shower pans." His preference for building the shower floor from scratch out of concrete, rubber, and tile adds $750 to each unit. "I'm my own worst enemy," notes Lucas. The selling price for these townhouses winds up being well over $400,000.

The other thing is that Prospect's eclectic architectural style takes time to execute. "Some of these houses are harder to do," Lucas explains. "The stuff that happens in the field in Prospect never happens in the real world." He points out a house that has a barrel-vaulted roof cut at an angle. And another house that has two sections of shed-style roof slanted at two dramatically different angles. "Mark has his computer do it. I have an engineered set of drawings. I order the glue-lams," he says, referring to prefabricated beams and trusses that can be custom-made to size. "It comes out right. It just takes a lot of time."

For comparison, Lucas drives me across the border of Prospect into the next subdivision, the conventionally luxurious Rainbow Ridge. He wants to show me a million-dollar house he recently built. I ask him which one it is, and he says it's the one with the beige stone facade. I sit in his truck staring at a long line of houses with beige stone facades trying to decide which one he means.

We pull up at a house with a sloping clay tile roof and lots of detail. Inside, the 5,000-square-foot house is like an appliance warehouse, with Viking stoves and Sub Zero refrigerators. There are three ovens, two wet bars, a wine refrigerator, gas fireplaces, steam baths, Jacuzzis, and two laundry rooms (one is in the master suite). It occurs to me that the conventional high-priced home is not expensive because it offers distinctive spaces—it's not about architecture per se—but rather because it gives the homebuyer lots and lots of merchandise. As Lucas leads me from room to room, pointing out the features, he sounds a bit like Monty Hall describing what's behind each curtain. And I realize, once again, how out of step I am with mainstream American culture. I am not exactly an ascetic but I can't imagine wanting more than one oven or washing machine. And, even well into my forties, I don't fully understand the purpose of a wet bar.

As I ponder the culture of materialism, Lucas rattles on about the structure of the house. The various pitched roofs, each facing a different direction, were actually pretty simple to assemble, he tells me. "It's all trusses. I brought it out and I put it together like it's ABC. This house took six months. That white house in Prospect has taken me a year and three months, and I'm not even done."

Well, now I know what a million dollars will buy. It occurs to me that if I multiply my budget by ten, perfection might be harder, not easier, to achieve.

We head back to the other side of the divide between the standard-issue beige subdivision and Prospect, where the houses are typically painted deep, couture shades of red or blue or, occasionally, black—colors chosen by Kelly, an interior designer with the most sophisticated set of paint chips in Colorado. Mark and Kiki are at a loss to control the trend toward ever larger and more expensive houses in the community that they spend most of their waking hours creating and guiding.

We sit around at Prospect Land Company's architecture office, directly upstairs from Mark and Kelly's garage. There, Mark works with one or two young assistants. Alternative rock is the usual soundtrack. Ray, the pit bull, canvasses the room for attention. We sit near the wall of architecture books, in chairs arranged around a little coffee table. Compared to the architecture offices of KB Home, there is a healthier balance here between facts and emotion.

Kiki, who spends his days driving around Prospect's 80 acres in one of his secondhand Mercedes and rarely wears anything more formal than a pair of khaki shorts and moccasins, never owns up to having a business plan. He recalls that back in 1996, when the property was annexed to Longmont as an official subdivision, he had to come up with a set of projections. At the time, he estimated home prices would be $125,000–$175,000. "I thought I was stretching."

"How did you guess?" Mark asks Kiki. Funny, I think, the questions the town designer has never gotten around to asking the developer. They see each other practically every day.

And Kiki replies, "I sat down like I did with the street names."

The street names in Prospect are part of the antiformula: Tenacity Drive, Incorrigible Circle, Ionosphere Avenue. They came out of a brainstorming session that Kiki had with Andres Duany, the leading New Urbanist planner, when he was doing the layout for the development.

When I ask about the fact that the home prices in Prospect keep going up, despite the fact that the technology industry in Boulder has yet to recover from the bust, Kiki blames it on the growing prices for lots. This would seem to be something he controls but, with customary Texan insouciance, he shifts the blame to the builders who buy lots from him. "Land has gone up because of the time factor involved. The builders build so slowly that the carrying costs go up."

While Kiki owns the land outright—he bought out a family-owned tree farm—he had to borrow money to put in the streets, utilities, and other infrastructure. At the outset prices were double what he'd expected, $78,000 lots producing $385,000 houses; now the lots themselves typically cost over $100,000.

"Part of it gets out of control when the builder tries to lower the per-square-foot price by building a bigger house," Kiki acknowledges.

"The builders are competitive with each other," Mark observes. "Whoever's house sold for the most is top dog. $729,000 is the record."

Another experienced Prospect builder, Tony Beck, says the lot prices have gone from $50,000 to $125,000 and "the prices of the houses reflect that." He blames the increase in the lot prices on the rising land values around Boulder.

Kiki described the vicious cycle in the simplest possible terms: "I push up lot prices. They get mad. They pick up house prices, I get mad."

The cycle seems impossible to break. Mark and Kiki tried to build four houses themselves with the idea that they would sell for under $400,000. They couldn't get financing to do what they planned, so they sold the lots and the plans to Don Lucas, who wound up asking $480,000.

Ultimately we get tired of talking and Kiki, Mark, and I wind up doing the same thing we did on my first visit to Prospect, walking the dusty streets where the newest houses are under construction, wandering in and out of the nearly completed units. It feels a lot like one of the best forbidden activities of my childhood, sneaking into half-built houses in the neighborhood. Except we don't have to sneak. And, naturally, I start thinking about my first visit, the first time we ambled up Tenacity Drive together. The summer of 2001 was a more innocent time. It was a lot like childhood.

Two years later the world has changed, but Mark and Kiki are still pretty much the same. They still take pleasure in making fun of all the aesthetic decisions made by the builders: the increasingly garish plumbing fixtures, the ugly overhead lights. Here and there Mark notes some minor violation of his architectural standards and reminds himself to call the builder on it.

And while I love hanging out with these guys in the unconventional neighborhood they've bravely fashioned, I wind up feeling sad that Prospect is falling victim to the same plague of gigantism that afflicts the rest of the country. I worry Mark is so preoccupied with the small, specific problems—a fence that doesn't conform to Prospect's building codes, a troubling window treatment—that he doesn't have the energy or ability to tackle the big ones. Mark argues that he can't, that it wouldn't even be legal for him and Kiki to try. "You can't intervene directly," he points out. "It would be . . . whatever the opposite of anti-trust is."

A 5,000-square-foot house, whether it's Mediterranean style or radical and modern, is still an enormous house. I drive away from Prospect worried that it will lose its quirky charm as the houses grow bigger and more expensive. And when I call Mark to discuss that possibility, I discover that he's concerned as well. "Prospect is a victim of its own success," he concurs, "and the demographic is so narrow now that it's not living up to its promise. We're always encouraging smaller, less expensive units and, as we're fleshing out the downtown part, there are a lot more condos and small units, which," he notes, "are less expensive to buy but they're more expensive per square foot."

He tells about me the latest attempt to keep things interesting: they're going to buy a zero-energy house designed by students at the University of Colorado in Boulder that won a U.S. Department of Energy Solar Decathlon.

"We're going to buy it and put it on a lot here. It's like a 600-square-foot, one-bedroom house. It makes your money back by selling power to the grid—and it will actually be the cheapest house in Prospect. But we don't even know if we're going to be able to sell it. Kiki thinks he'll be renting it out for a while. But, if it does sell, it will sell for what we got it for."

Mark points out that the cost of the lot is now $150,000 and he figures the zero-energy house will go for between $300,000 and $350,000, which, he admits, "is a lot for a 600-square-foot house."

Earthship by architect Mike Reynolds, Greater World Earthship Community, Taos, New Mexico

Subdivision Fever, Part II

August 25, 2003   Morning in my rented Earthship outside Taos

I find it refreshing to be here. I liked walking around this morning in the sweet, high desert air. But I suspect this enlightened subdivision has many of the same problems that plague more conventional subdivisions. I don't honestly know if this place is liberating or stifling.

Taos is farther away from Longmont than I thought. Or maybe I took the long way around. In either case, I'm in a hurry because Hillary, the woman who has the keys to my Earthship, is only going to be in the Solar Survival office until six.

At six, I'm still on the slow road, State Highway 64, that noodles from I-25 through mountain meadows, past resort and retirement developments that have the look of late-night TV commercials selling a slice of paradise, before it reaches the seamless adobe environment of Taos. Fortunately I find a spot with cell phone connectivity and call Hillary. She agrees to leave my key and my Earthship operating instructions taped to the office door.

The Earthship subdivision lies some 12 miles west of Taos, across the Rio Grande bridge, where lightly populated desert terrain rolls on and on. When I finally arrive I peel a handmade envelope—actually a recycled "What's an Earthship?" poster—off the door of the building with a sign out front advertising Earthship tours. Inside the envelope is something that, in the fading evening light, looks like a treasure map with pink dots representing existing and proposed dwellings. The streets have names like Humane Lane and Happy Trail. Well, what do I expect from a place called "the Greater World Earthship Community"? No stranger, I guess, than Kiki's street names.

"Make a right out of drive onto Hwy. Take a right onto the third dirt road, Earthship Way. Follow that until it splits. Go right. Make your first left. Follow that road to the last ship on the right. The key is above the door. Enjoy."

There is also a typed letter with the following instructions:

"Once inside, located in the first closet doors is the inverter. You will need to turn this on for any AC appliances, like the stereo and TV. Please turn it off when going out, to bed, or when not in use. To turn it on push the red on/off button twice until the line is under on. . . . The Water board and the Gray Water board are also located in the cabinets near the inverter. These pumps will run after showering or using sink water or flushing the toilet. You do not need to do anything to these pumps. Have a great time!"

Inverter? Water board? Pumps? Have a great time?

I drive up the dark dirt road until I arrive at what appears to be a big mound of topsoil, but it is, in fact, my Earthship. I'm relieved when I walk around this giant anthill and discover that the other side, where the door is located, is made mostly of glass. The key is right where it's supposed to be.

A year earlier, just after the movers had come and emptied my San Francisco apartment, I spent a few days in a borrowed house in the Marin County hippie enclave of Bolinas, just off Highway 1. Bolinas is most famous for having removed the highway sign that would have allowed tourists to find the place. That and the fact that the whole town rose up in rebellion when it was rumored that Martha Stewart planned to buy a home there. My friend Alex had given me directions to the little house he'd been renting from an artisan couple. The key was supposed to be under an urn by the front door. When I arrived at the beautiful little half-moon-shaped adobe cottage that was, like an Earthship, all glass on the south side, I found the front door open a crack and the radio on, tuned to a classic rock station. I walked in and called out a hello. A man, perhaps sixty years old, with long gray hair, emerged from the bathroom, naked. We stared at each other for an instant, then he scurried back into the bathroom and reappeared with a towel wrapped around his waist.

As it turned out, he was the landlord. He and his wife, a sculptor, lived next door. But they had recently split up, so he was camping out somewhere nearby. Alex, who wasn't around much, let him use the bathtub. It seemed like a plausible story to me, and it didn't occur to me to be afraid. All I thought, as I waited for him to finish up in the bathroom and be on his way, was that he looked pretty good for a man his age.

As I approach the front door of this dark, strange, isolated house, I brace myself for the unexpected. But the only real surprise is that my "packaged" Earthship is a lot nicer than I believed it would be. Its design is cleaner, less hippy-dippy than I'd predicted, given what I knew about the culture of Solar Survival, an organization dedicated to renegade architect Mike Reynolds's vision of sustainable living.

I feel as though I've wandered into an article in *Sunset* magazine. The south wall of the house is all glass for passive solar heating and to provide sunlight to the indoor planters that filter the gray water, the waste water from the sinks and shower. The gray water is pumped back indoors and used to flush the toilet.

I explore the house, padding around on the cool brick floor. It's a nice feature in summer, but I'm not sure I'd like the brick underfoot as much in winter. The view from my windows is of an earthen berm. At first I assume that it's another anthill, the back of my neighbor's house, but later it becomes obvious that it's actually the wall of a gravel pit. The Earthship that I've rented for the night is in the least desirable part of the 633-acre

Greater World Subdivision, the section that is called the Leumuria Gravel Pit Project. Down here in the rehabilitated gravel pit, lots are small, a half acre. Elsewhere in the development, houses are built on three-acre spreads.

The north wall is an unwindowed earth and tire bunker. It insulates the house against heat in the summer and cold in the winter. This business of building dense, medieval-style walls out of discarded tires packed with dirt is the heart and soul of this whole operation. While the Earthships collect rainwater, recycle wastewater, and run on solar power from rooftop photovoltaic cells, the tires are their true raison d'être.

While most rooms where I've spent the night on this trip come with bibles—or the book of Mormon—my Earthship is furnished with the seminal text of the local religion, *Earthship, Volume I* by Mike Reynolds. I lie in my comfy, southwestern-style bed and fall asleep reading "How to Pound a Tire":

> *Tire walls are made by laying tires in staggered courses like brick or concrete block. Each tire is filled with compacted earth, so that it becomes a rammed earth brick encased in steel belted rubber. As you will find, a pounded tire weighs over 300 pounds. So all tires are pounded in place and only minor movements can be made. . . .*
>
> *Tire pounding should be done in teams of two people, a shoveler and a pounder. Depending on your strength and endurance, a team should be able to pound a tire in five to fifteen minutes.*

I wake up, fix coffee, and listen to the low-frequency rumble of the big DC refrigerator. I sit at the kitchen table and read the guest book, which includes many affirmations like this one: "Staying in an Earthship is everything I thought it would be, warm and cozy and makes you feel connected to the Earth." There are also a fair number of complaints about the smell generated by the gray water pump whenever you flush the toilet, something I've also noticed.

I start exploring my Earthship, examining carefully all the control panels necessary to run this house. I open the cabinet next to the bathroom and note the gray water pump and the filter that cleans the collected rainwater for drinking. There are lots of PVC pipes, and hoses, and widgets. It feels a bit like looking under the hood of a car.

And then I investigate closely the "power conversion center," the device I'd had to turn on the night before. It's a series of metal boxes and arrays of buttons and indicators that resembles a standard circuit breaker box but it's larger and more complex. One thing baffles me. The indicator lights say the battery level is low. I can't figure out why, as I haven't watched TV, and the only electricity I've knowingly used was my bedside light the night before. And today is a sunny day. The battery, based on what I know about solar power, should be practically overflowing. I file this question away for later.

My neighborhood, I discover when I take a walk, is a network of dirt and gravel roads spread across gently sloping desert acreage, the intersections marked by wooden posts dug into the ground, topped by yellow reflectors. I make my way out of the Leumuria Gravel Pit and up Earthship Way through the sparse high desert terrain and past houses that look a lot alike, the way houses in a subdivision often do. Except here, the commonalities are the windowed south wall, the thick dirt north wall, and occasionally rounded sections decorated with the ends of bottles—discarded bottles and cans, like tires, are often used as bricks—or primitive mosaics. The Earthships, taken collectively, are a true alternative to Tuscan- and Mediterranean-style subdivision houses. Arguably, they are all about function, but there is also an aesthetic: Taos meets Teletubbies.

I spend part of my afternoon watching a crew of two, Ted Elsasser and Braden Trauth, at work building an Earthship for a client. It's a $162,000 midsized house, about 1,300 square feet. Ted, a permanent member of the Earthship building team, is a stringy, sun-wizened, good-looking guy with a malleable, Jerry Lewis kind of face, and Braden, an intern from the University of Cincinnati, has long blond hair, a straggly beard, and an amiable demeanor, all of which remind me of the hippie boys I knew in college. As I look on, they move dirt. It's actually gorgeous dirt. Adobe, as it turns out, is made from very dark, fine earth that looks like French roast coffee beans ground for an espresso pot. The dark dirt is mixed with sand, sawdust, and water to form adobe.

As he shovels and Braden stirs, Ted tells me about his life as an Earthship builder and his work on his own house, located in the part of the subdivision known as "the subculture," where Reynolds sold land to a dozen of his employees at a very low cost.

He's been building his house in his spare time: "I'd work nine to five on other people's homes. Then I'd come home and pound a few tires. My goal was five to seven tires a night."

He prefers doing the work on it himself, slowly, to hiring a crew to get the job finished. "My body gets tired of digging, but my pocketbook gets tired of paying for the backhoe." He sees his house as his personal laboratory, a place to test the relative merits of vertical and sloped glass for passive solar. More by accident than design, the house wound up being a split-level. "I didn't have a builder's level," Ted explains. "So I thought, 'Fuck it, let the contours speak.'

"I'm building mine for $45 a square foot, doing my own labor," Ted continues. "I've been working on it since 1994, and have been living in it since the day I started. I just camped out." In that time he's also constructed eighteen client houses, start to finish. Trained as an architect, Ted sometimes moonlights designing Earthships. "I got snowshoes for one set of drawings, candelabras for another."

As I sit in the strong sun watching Ted and Braden labor, I think about how simple the Earthships are, on the one hand, and how complicated they are, on the other.

"Another thing that's beautiful," Ted says, as if reading my thoughts, "is the building process. It requires little to no building experience. We've designed out complicated roofing systems. It's tire wall to wood roof with concrete bonding." The typical Earthship, according to Ted, requires 11 or 12 "courses" of tires, maybe 13 if there's going to be something fancy like a loft. Compared to a conventional house, the labor required is very low-skill. Pounding tires requires strength and a modicum of technique but it doesn't demand precision; no right angles are required.

At the same time, Earthships are outfitted with very sophisticated energy-generating and water collection and recycling systems. In effect, they are double or triple plumbed and they contain all the utilities that a normal house would draw from an outside source. At the end of the process there are licensed electricians and plumbers who install the solar power system that Mike Reynolds designed and the Power Organization Module, the thing that looked to me like the world's most complex fuse box.

Ted invites me to come see his house that evening, and I accept, noting the fact that his girlfriend moved out long ago and the shed he originally built as her pottery studio now houses his motorcycle. He gives me another idiosyncratic set of Greater World directions: "Take Earthship Way. Bear left toward Margaret's house. Take a right at Private Keep Out. Take a left and look for the white truck."

What I learn during my afternoon spent visiting with various residents of the Earthship subdivision is that Ted's method—what I think of as the Vermont 1970s method, living in a house that you build gradually, day by day, year by year—is fairly typical. Kirsten Jacobsen, the education director—again, I feel like I'm dealing with someone I knew at Evergreen, an archetypal hippie circa 1975, with wavy blond hair and cutoff shorts—came to Taos when she was in college to write a paper about Earthships and never left. "I did construction for four years, was a total little grunt construction worker. But I never made it past a certain level." After two or three years in the Earthship culture, she wanted to start building her own house. She made a sweat-equity deal with Reynolds for the land and began building.

"Personally, I don't know anyone who has built their Earthship in less than five years," Kirsten says, as we chat in the Solar Survival headquarters. "Slowly, out of pocket, you create a structure that will take care of you. I started by building a tire wall, a dome that will be my bedroom."

She lists the materials that she used, besides tires and dirt:

Rebar

Birdcages

Ferro-cement

"I have a camp stove and one solar panel," she adds. "My situation is still pretty modest." She calculates that her house will wind up costing "way, way less than $100,000." Although one of the tenets of Earthship culture is avoiding debt, Kirsten is considering taking out a loan for $30,000 and getting the crew to build her a kitchen and a bathroom.

Once again I begin to feel as if I have traveled back in time some thirty or forty years, until Kirsten begins telling me about the culture shift that's taken place at Greater World. It involved Reynolds's ongoing legal troubles with Taos County. The community started out in 1994 as a loosely knit "land users association" with all the homeowners jointly owning the acreage. But in 1996 the county said, in Kirsten's words, "Forget it. You're an illegal subdivision."

The cost of fighting the county over variances and the improvements that had to be made in the roads—like creating cul-de-sacs big enough to accommodate fire engines—raised the land cost and forced a collective to become a group of small stakeholders. "Now it's a subdivision and people own their lots." Lots that once sold for a maximum of $15,000 now cost from $20,000 to $80,000. As a result, there's been a shift toward wealthier homeowners, people who can afford to hire a crew to erect a house in the space of a few months. And there are a growing number of retirees moving in. "Their relationship to the land is different," Kirsten observes. "There are more private property signs."

On the northeast corner of the property, where Ted lives, it's still the old school. "It's the main owner-builder area," Kirsten explains. "It's called The Subculture. There are eleven homesites on ten acres. It's people who worked for Mike. He gave them a good deal."

While Mike Reynolds comes up in every conversation one has at the Earthship subdivision, he doesn't seem to be an authoritarian presence. The feeling is less that of a cult and more that of a funky small town. "It's nice," Kirsten observed, "that there isn't a strong top-down utopian vision from Mike."

Eventually Kirsten leads me out the back door of the Earthship office and along a narrow path skirting a string of strange man-made formations that look as though they were unearthed in an archaeological dig: a grayish dome built in part with beer cans, the aluminum ends shining in the desert light; a curved wall of tires enclosing a few weedy-looking sunflowers; a pile of empty bottles, a rusty barbecue. At the end of the path is a low earthen building containing a chaotic maze of offices. Reynolds's office is all the way at the back, as if he had burrowed, over the years, into a corner.

With long gray hair and a pair of red-framed glasses perched atop his head, he looks as if he has escaped from an episode of *Star Trek*. Reynolds is wearing a tightly fitted shirt of some synthetic material, with a zipper open from neck to mid-chest. I was expecting Mr. Kurtz from *The Heart of Darkness,* but instead I'm confronted with a slightly dissolute Captain Kirk. Reynolds is an architect from another planet, sitting behind a big desk piled with books and papers in a cramped office, also piled with books and papers. On one wall there's a whiteboard listing things to do: "Culverts. Stop signs. Street signs. Cul-de-sacs."

"That's fifty hours right there," Reynolds snaps when he notices me reading the board. He informs me that he spent the early afternoon repairing the photovoltaics on my Earthship. The reason my Earthship's battery wasn't fully charged is that the solar collectors had been zapped by lightning. It happens, he acknowledges. But then, regular electrical utilities can get knocked out by lightning just as easily. (In fact, this conversation takes place only a few weeks after a blackout knocked out power to the entire northeastern corner of the country.) I don't know quite what I expected from Reynolds, but what I get is a sales pitch, a more focused one than I've been given from anyone since, perhaps, Josh Shelton back in Kansas City.

The house I'd spent the night in, Reynolds explains, is what they call a "packaged Earthship." It's his attempt at doing what more conventional homebuilders do, simplifying and standardizing. "Off the rack," Reynolds states, "is cheaper."

"After being involved in this for twenty-five years, we sort of thought we knew what we were doing. That design is our answer. We're putting everything we know into it."

Reynolds is trying to convince me that the packaged Earthship is my Perfect $100,000 House. He argues that a mortgage payment on a typical $100,000 home would run to about $900 a month, but most houses would also require something like $300 in monthly utility payments. The Earthship is entirely self-sufficient.

Eventually, Reynolds sets aside his sales pitch to tell me the history of the Earthship, which, he says, "was simply a response to the news." He recalls watching Walter Cronkite in the early 1970s talking about clear-cutting practices in the timber industry, and Charles Kuralt talking about the problems with beer and soda cans all over the landscape. "That was before recycling was a word."

So he began gathering cans and using them as a building material, but the idea never took off, because "there's no can-layers union." What he means is that the building trades, set in their ways, are a major force in maintaining the status quo.

Reynolds kept on watching TV. News reports about the energy crisis made him start thinking about the importance of thermal mass. And stories about mountains of worn-out tires made him start figuring out a way to reuse them.

"I looked at tires over three or four years. Finally I developed a way of beating earth into them. So, there I am using another by-product of our society. It just kept on going."

By the early 1990s Reynolds's reputation was spreading. I remember hearing his name from a couple of guys I met while walking in the woods in Vermont. They were building a little shack and told me, their voices full of reverence, about the man who was building houses out of tires in New Mexico.

Over time, news stories about Santa Fe and Albuquerque's depleting their aquifer motivated Reynolds to think about water, how to catch rainwater and how to recycle gray water to flush the toilet. "Toilet flushing uses 48 percent of the water supply," he points out.

The Earthship, Reynolds insists, was less a vision or coherent scheme than simply an accumulation of responses to the state of the world. "There was no plan to this. We're making absolutely sustainable housing, but we didn't plan to do it."

Of course, lack of planning is what got Reynolds in trouble with Taos County officials. The original idea was that the community was supposed to have "common ownership, like Pueblo Indians."

Reynolds, who'd been building his peculiar houses in and around Taos since the 1970s, had actually established two earlier Earthship communities, one called Star, which consisted of 20 houses on 650 acres, and a smaller one called Reach. Both of those developments, though, were tucked away on back roads. Reynolds thought they were too inaccessible, so when he found acreage with more than a mile of frontage right on State Highway

64, he decided it was the perfect site for a new, more ambitious community. But the newfound accessibility exposed the development to increased scrutiny. According to Reynolds, the banks bought into the community ownership concept, and all was well until someone noticed that they were at odds with New Mexico subdivision law. And since what they were building was a little outrageous to begin with, the local officials were more inclined to go after technicalities.

"We were pushing a lot of envelopes. We were containing sewage in the living room, for God's sake." Reynolds had gotten variances, but mostly they were granted verbally by county officials who retired or died. "I turn around, and I'm in trouble on every level."

Being a subdivision in New Mexico, as in most localities, means putting in utilities, and utilities were the one thing that the Earthship subdivision didn't need. (Although phone lines would be a nice addition—most people have rooftop antennas that provide cell phone reception.) Ultimately, Reynolds was so "uptight and pissed off" about New Mexico subdivision law that he got a bill introduced in the state legislature that would have loosened some of the restrictions. The bill was opposed, however, by environmentalists who were afraid that developers less enlightened than Reynolds would benefit from fewer safeguards.

"New Mexico is that state that designated acres to testing the nuclear bomb. They should be able to dedicate acres to test sustainability," Reynolds grumbles. "The thing is that we lost, so we can't do it as cheaply as we used to. You could get a membership for $600, and now a lot costs $30,000. It's no wonder that there's no sustainable housing going on, because it's too damned hard to do."

So now the Greater World is, on paper at least, a standard subdivision, with cul-de-sacs and model houses. That's essentially what the "packaged Earthship" is—Reynolds's equivalent of the homes a company like KB builds in subdivisions called Crestview and Sundance. "You have to make this like regular housing," Reynolds declared. "Generic. Permittable."

He says he can build me a one-bedroom Earthship for $100,000 or a two-bedroom for $130,000. It sounds like a pretty good deal. Of course, that doesn't include the land, which will add another $25,000 to $100,000.

His latest plan, he continues, is to make the rental Earthships like the one I spent the night in a little slicker. "The one we're building right now will have a flat-screen TV and an Internet office," he brags. "All the goodies people want they can have off the grid."

Currently there are about 35 homes in the community; Reynolds figures that someday there will be 130, but it's hard to say when. "I don't want to grow more than four or five homes a year. I don't want to turn into a totally stressed-out businessperson."

It might be too late for that. I notice as I make my way out of his office that his door has a sign that says "Bang Head Here."

As I wend my way through the maze that is the Earthship world head-quarters, I realize something: I have just been presented with my first honest-to-god offer on a house. Every other possibility on the trip has been qualified, conditional, an elusive maybe. I could do this. At this moment I have enough money in the bank to buy a small, packaged Earthship . . . were it not for the land costs. And if I want to buy a used one, one of the smaller ones, the 600-square-foot nests, I notice in the Taos real estate listings that they are on offer for $85,000. It's tantalizing, but practical considerations give me pause. The biggest thing stopping me is the fact that the Greater World subdivision is still a subdivision. For all its alternative intentions, for all its sustainability, Greater World is a dozen miles from Taos. To buy gro-ceries or do just about anything, you're forced to drive.

Admittedly, it's a decent blend of subdivision and commune. The setting is rural, in that there's no real community infrastructure and no commercial core. But it's suburban in that there's not all that much privacy, either. While the newer Earthship owners, the people who can pay higher land prices and have their homes completed before they move in, are reputed to keep to themselves, the members of the subculture form a pretty well defined little tribe. One woman I visit, Margaret, a skinny twenty-eight-year-old with long dark hair, who left college in Staten Island with her boyfriend and came to Taos to volunteer building Earthships, lives in a half-built house. There's now a working kitchen, but she points to some Rubbermaid bins sitting on the floor: "That was the kitchen from the first year." And to some slabs of wood leaning against a wall: "These are the kitchen cabinet doors, and they've been in process for three years now." This work-in-progress feeling pretty much typifies the culture of the place.

My Vermont cousin, Verandah Porche, who lived for years in a house under construction, e-mailed me a song she wrote about that way of life:

> Once I had a house ten miles out of town.
> Couldn't tell if we were building it or taking it down.
> Didn't know what we were doing but we figured we'd try.

It could have been written about Greater World.

"It's more of a neighborhood than a community," Margaret tells me. "The only thing people share is Earthships. Among the owner-builders there's a certain camaraderie. We all know what it's like, 'Oh, a light bulb!' But that culture in this neighborhood is starting to die out."

Before I leave Greater World behind I visit Ted, to see what he's been working on for the past decade. His place is less like Vermont hippie architecture and more like that crazy man's labor of love near Miracle Manor in Desert Hot Springs, the house up the road from Cabot's Old Indian Pueblo.

Nothing is symmetrical at Ted's, either. It's a series of spaces that look as though they were carved out of the earth—more like a cave than a methodically assembled structure of adobe and tires. The curving interior walls are built out of the bottles Ted accumulated before he stopped drinking—lots of jug wine, lots of Tanqueray—and multiple levels, including a sleeping loft, a roundish living room, and the requisite indoor jungle. But nothing is as well defined as a room, and from inside it's hard to tell where the house ends, because the place is so much a work in progress that there are few definite edges. It is like one of those objects you learn about in topology, a bottle with no inside or outside, or an infinite sphere.

And, although he's been working on the place since 1994, Ted still doesn't have a toilet. Earlier in the day, watching Ted work on the Earthship, I developed a small crush on him, but there's something about his house that dampens my enthusiasm. Maybe it's the wall built of gin bottles or the daisy pattern formed from wine bottles. I find myself thinking, *What kind of person would work ten years on a house and not bother to install a toilet?* The idea of waking up in this house destroys any quiet fantasies I have.

Just before I leave Taos, I stop on the Rio Grande bridge, a steel structure that spans the river's narrow gorge at a dizzying height. I do the lonely tourist thing, something I'd been doing all the way across the country: I take a picture of myself—head, shoulders, the river far below—with my digital camera. There are two problems with doing this. One is that some guy—it's always a guy—offers to take my picture for me, but these photographic good Samaritans are invariably incapable of framing a shot and tend to cut me off at the knees. So I started refusing their kind offers. The other problem is that I am bad at smiling in photos to begin with, but find it impossible to do anything but look grim when I'm taking my own photo.

Anyway, I'm standing in the middle of this epic bridge, concentrating on the problem of framing my shot, avoiding the gaze of well-meaning tourists, when an advance crew for a wide-load truck roars up in pickup trucks and on motorcycles and closes the bridge to traffic. The workmen shoo me away and along comes a truck carrying a house. It isn't one of those manufactured home halves you often see on the highway, with their bathrooms and kitchens exposed like the guts of a dissected frog. No, this is a whole house, a neat rectangle with a perfect sloping roof, which extends beyond the edges of the two-lane highway. I watch from the west side of the bridge as the house, so wide it nearly brushes the railings, moves slowly through space on the back of the truck like a fat man moving down the aisle in economy class.

Later it occurs to me that I should have followed it, found out where it came from and where it was going. But at the time, it appeared like a vision, like what I'd see if I'd been doing peyote. Or maybe it was a palate cleanser, something to relieve the heaviness of the Earthships. Those houses are so freighted with dirt-filled tires and purpose, while this one, this stupid assembly line special, can practically fly.

Anyway, the house is traveling east, and I am heading west, backtracking. I need to drive back into Colorado to check out a place called Crestone. Mark and Kiki had told me a little about it. All they'd really said was that it was a *Glengarry Glen Ross* subdivision that had gone belly-up and was being reclaimed by New Age types who were building cool houses there.

Crestone is, essentially, in the middle of nowhere, about 60 miles north of the New Mexico border, and 15 miles east of a minor highway. The road to Crestone leads there and then just stops. An 1880s gold rush town, Crestone is built into the side of the Sangre de Cristo Mountains, an exceptionally beautiful but very rugged spot. By the early years of the twentieth century, the gold boom was over, and the town's population dropped from its peak of 2,000 to about 100. Then, in the early 1970s, the Arizona Colorado Land and Cattle Company, the town's landlord, formed the Baca Grande Corporation and subdivided a 14,000-acre parcel into 3,000 lots. They put in roads and utilities and sold the parcels, mostly sight unseen, and mostly to members of the military looking for a dream retirement home. The developers failed to hold up their end of the bargain. By the end of the

1970s AZL, as the land company was known, was owned by Saudi arms dealer Adnan Khashoggi, most of the original investors had sold out, and this mountain subdivision became known as a source of cheap acreage, attracting people who wanted to build alternative and unconventional housing. AZL was bought out by Maurice Strong, the businessman and philanthropist who rose to prominence as the force behind the Rio Earth Summit. His wife, Hanne, began a spiritual mission, giving away tracts of Baca Grande land to groups representing as many of the world's religions as she could. Crestone is now home to a wide variety of ashrams, zendos, and churches.

But all of this history is unknown to me on the day I visit. What I find is a sleepy mountain town with a sandwich shop, a liquor store, and a handsome, well-dressed, somewhat agitated man on the town's only pay phone explaining to someone that he wasn't allowed to take phone calls at his spiritual retreat, that whatever business needed to be discussed would have to be discussed right then.

After an agent from Northern Valley Realty gives me a list of Baca Grande lots for sale, mostly half-acre lots with utilities for $6,000 to $10,000, I drive around to try and get a feel for the place. I start in the section of the development known as Chalets I, built in the Sangre de Cristo foothills, its roads winding through chaparral and wildflowers. At irregular intervals, houses have been built on half-acre lots. Some are vintage 1970s A-frames. Some are eclectic Western contemporary. Some are clunky straw bale. Some are simple sheds with solar panels on their sloping roofs. The cumulative effect is strange, because while the bones of a subdivision layout are so clear, what's been built is more free-form. Crestone is full of people trying to live a "sustainable" lifestyle on a piece of land that was master-planned for unsustainability.

One thing stops me dead in my tracks: the sign with Smokey the Bear holding the words "Moderate Fire Danger" in his right paw. Not so unusual, except for the fact that this Smokey is seated in a cross-legged yoga position, his paws facing upward, resting on his knees. Contained in his upturned left paw are mystical-looking flames. "Kundalini Fire Management," it says along the bottom of the sign. "Baca Grande VFD."

Again, I am having the same attraction and avoidance I experienced at the Earthship subdivision. Here I could easily buy a rehabbed A-frame with a splendid mountain view or a cluster of buildings described as "Hobbit domes among the trees" for somewhere in the mid-$100,000s, but I'm not sure I could live in a place as New Age as this one. I mean, it's one thing to do yoga in New York City, where it feels like preventive medicine, a way of maintaining sanity in the madness, and quite another to own property in a place where yoga is all anyone does. My concern is that spirituality, when it dominates a place so thoroughly, is every bit as oppressive as soulless materialism.

I'm fascinated by Crestone but I don't stay more than a few hours because I'm eager to get to Marfa, Texas. It takes me a day longer than it should, in part because at a few critical junctures I neglect to look at my road atlas. I don't hit El Paso, which is still 150 miles or so from Marfa, until evening the next day. Then I opt for a state highway when I would have been better off sticking with the interstate. I decide that I'll spend the night on Montana Road, aka Highway 62-100, which on the map, at least, appears to be a promising motel stretch on the east side of town. But it turns out to be a toxic combination of businesses serving the nearby air-port, prisons, and auto wrecking yards. So I keep driving, confident that this highway, once it gets out into the desert, will yield a beautiful 1950s motel. And, were this still the 1950s, it might have. But, once I get past a weird immigration checkpoint, where an INS agent speaks to me long enough to determine that I'm not Mexican, all I find on this highway are ruins—abandoned gas stations, abandoned motels. Clearly, I-10, running parallel about 50 miles south, had sucked away whatever life this highway once possessed.

I drive through the most glorious sunset, with the last light of day behind me bathing the road ahead in an otherworldly gold. My car is a long, skinny shadow racing ahead of me. I am both exhilarated by the sheer beauty of the moment and scared that I will be on this desolate road after dark. More than anything, I want to pee. But I'm afraid to pull over, afraid that some desert fiend will materialize out of the emptiness or that squatting on the ground I'll be bitten by a tarantula. It's strange, but in nearly two months that I've been traveling all over the country by myself, this is the first time I'm afraid. It's the kind of fear I used to have when I was a kid, alone in the house while my parents were at work. It is based on reason—clearly, this is not an ideal place to be alone—but it's also totally crazy.

My turnoff is about 100 miles east of El Paso. It's well marked, and I find it in the dark with no trouble. Then I set out on a 50-mile run down narrow Route 54 to Van Horn. I know that there will be a motel in Van Horn, because it's right on the interstate. I remember the town from a cross-country drive I'd made twenty years earlier as the "city of motels." But this last stretch of highway is, if anything, spookier than the previous one. The road crosses an unending series of desert washes, low places that can turn into a stream in wet weather. Each time the road dips, the water gets deeper. I am aware that somewhere ahead of me, to the south, lies a huge storm. But instead of seeing streaks of lightning, I see blankets of flashing white light, which remind me of the northern lights. On the radio, all I can pick up are AM stations with strange talk radio conversations about business opportunities, people singing hymns, and Mexican music. Behind me is a lone pair of headlights that somehow spooks me even more. And by now I desperately have to pee.

As an indication of how shaken I am, the motel I choose in Van Horn is a Days Inn, the most corporate, the most predictable possible lodging, and one I'd normally never set foot in. The only place to get anything to eat is the Subway franchise at the gas station, where I wait in a long line with local teens and large families. I take my sandwich to my tidy white room, along with a tallboy can of bad beer, and am grateful for my simple meal, appreciative of my flush toilet, and glad to be alive.

In the morning I finally exhibit some common sense and call ahead for a hotel reservation in Marfa. It's Labor Day weekend, time for the Marfa Mystery Lights festival, and I assume the town will be full. Which it is. But I luck out and get the last available room in the Holland House Hotel in Alpine, some 20 miles down the road from Marfa. By Texas standards, that's right next door. The room is the "penthouse" and it is mine because there was just a cancellation. The woman who books my room tells me over and over that I am the luckiest person alive. "You should go right out and buy yourself a lottery ticket," she insists, and I assure her that I will.

I know about Marfa, as I've been hearing about it for years. It's the little town that minimalist artist Donald Judd practically took over in the 1970s. After buying up an old army base outside of town and a number of warehouse and office buildings downtown, he set up the Chinati Foundation, which basically exists to propagate minimalism. As a result, Marfa is the most aesthetically perfect small town I've ever seen. I drive in and gawp. It looks as if Martha Stewart came in and chose the tasteful colors for every building on the solid little main drag. Everything is creamy and subtle. There's a big courthouse that was featured in the movie *Giant*—the fact that James Dean and Elizabeth Taylor spent time here is the town's other claim to fame—and the Hotel Paisano has been renovated and made wonderfully hip. I stop to take care of a little business. I need Internet access and, finding that the computers in the local designer bookstore are down, I visit the library, where I can surf the Internet for free. The whole experience makes me happier than I've been for days. I love civic infrastructure. How could I exist in a place without a public library and a courthouse?

I drive to Alpine to check in to my penthouse, a room carved from the hotel's old elevator housing, and quickly drive back to Marfa in time for the afternoon half of the Chinati Foundation tour. It's led by a tall, thin man dressed head to toe in Western wear. He turns out to be a German actor spending his summer as an intern in Texas. And he seems to have bought into the culture with a vengeance. The German cowboy leads three of us through the sprawling complex, building by building. There are the U-shaped barracks where the interiors have been turned into a series of light sculptures by Dan Flavin. There is a building that has been transformed into an abandoned Soviet schoolhouse by Ilya and Emilia Kabakov. And there are the giant armory buildings that Donald Judd used to display his polished steel cubes. What interests me most was the fact that Judd, whose artwork tends toward the rectilinear, had chosen to add curved metal Quonset-hut-style roofs to the brick and concrete box buildings. Somehow, he prefers his art to be square but his buildings to be rounded. As a fan of rounded roofs in general and Quonset huts in particular, I approve. Chinati is, of course, very cool and very impressive. But I have a hard time conjuring up the reverence that the occasion merits. The German cowboy, unlocking each building for us, speaks softly about what Judd intended each space to be, how he felt about each artist he invited. It is too much like a shrine and too little like a living place.

My friends go to Marfa in October for the Chinati open house, a big art party that attracts black-clad minimalists from all over the world. But this weekend is a very different event, a celebration of the Marfa Mystery Lights, mysterious illuminated blips that you can see from the road between Marfa and Alpine. There's even a Marfa Mystery Lights viewing post. This festival is the townie equivalent of Chinati's open house, something more egalitarian, unpretentious, and fun.

I am very happy that evening at the Marfa Mystery Lights parade, which is odd and lovely. Toward the beginning, after the local amublance drivers show off all their bells and whistles—literally—and drive through the center of town behaving like lowriders, the owner of the Hotel Paisano, a woman roughly my age, sails by on her skateboard waving at the crowd. She has glowing stars pinned to her clothing and is followed by a band of children dressed up as the Marfa lights, with costumes consisting of life preservers and Bubble Wrap. She just looks so cool and so peaceful as she zips by, like an Olympic skater doing a victory lap. The strangest part of the parade is the Border Patrol teens going by on a float labeled "America's Future Front-line." They wear uniforms that make them look like Hitler youth, or so the German cowboy says when I run into him at the street dance. He buys me a beer and puts his own longneck bottle into one of those foam insulators that are common in the Southwest. I point out how well he's assimilated, and he thanks me.

I listen to the country western band play and watch one man in particular, a lanky Willie Nelson type, dancing with his vaguely Native American–looking wife. He is so confident and graceful, with a beautiful high-stepping style. I recognize him as the man I saw earlier in the evening, the one who'd driven into town in a limo-length car with Western murals on the side, longhorns on top, and a roof rack made of horseshoes. I am smitten. I think of him as the local Baryshnikov.

The German cowboy introduces me to a guy named Nick. He and his wife, both painters, have just moved to Marfa from Brooklyn. He tells me about how he bakes his own bread because he now has the time, and because you can't find good bread around here. And somehow this breaks the spell. Too many Nicks, I think, and Marfa would be very boring. The trick is to be Donald Judd, the first guy on the scene, and not Nick, the last guy in the door. Where does that leave me?

It's like Crestone. What fun is it to be a yogi in a town where there's nothing but yogis? What fun is it to be an artist in a town where everyone's an artist? I love Marfa, but it's not what I'm looking for. I'm not after an elitist enclave. I'm after a heightened state of normal.

On Sunday of Labor Day weekend, driving from Marfa to Austin, I have my only accident of the trip. (Okay, I did back into a light pole in a Denny's parking lot somewhere in the middle of the country, but I didn't do any damage.) On an empty two-lane highway heading north out of a town called Marathon, I encounter these huge birds in the middle of the road, eating carrion. Turkey vultures, I figure. As my car approaches, the fat birds wait until the last moment to fly out of the way—turkey vultures playing chicken. One of them, hanging out on the right shoulder, sees me coming and takes flight a little too late. He flies directly in front of my car, and the impact causes a tremendous thunk. I assume that I've lost a headlight. When I pull over to inspect the damage, expecting to find something that looks like the worst imaginable Thanksgiving on my bumper, the only trace of the bird is a bunch of feathers stuck so tightly into the grille, that I can't pull them out.

Interior, the Cedar Avenue house, by KRDB, Austin, Texas

Populist Modernism
in Austin

August 31, 2003   Austin, Texas

I check into the Austin Motel, a semi-rehabbed Tex-Deco retreat for scene makers on South Congress Avenue, a strip of slacker heaven that frames a perfect view of the Texas capitol's dome, and marvel at the wonder of it all. It's Sunday night of Labor Day weekend, and I imagine that I'll participate in Austin's peculiar Labor Day celebration: free yoga classes all over town. But I can't. Either the greasy burger I ate back in Marathon or the splendid Mexican dinner I ate at Guero's, just a block up the street, has done something unfortunate to my digestive system. Or maybe it's divine retribution for the death of the turkey vulture. You know, karma. In any case, yoga is not possible.

Architecture, however, is. Sort of. When I rendezvous with Chris Krager, who, together with his business partner Chris Robertson, runs a company called Krager Robertson Design Build (KRDB), I feel almost too drained. I figure I'll just go through the motions, coast through the day as he talks about houses. I pop a couple of Imodium on my way out the door and hope for the best.

We meet at an outdoor coffee bar next door to my motel. It is clearly the local daytime hotspot. A stew of Austin life is here: tattooed bottle blonds and their dogs; abundantly pierced, shave-headed men and their cell phones. Austin is one of those cities, like Seattle, like San Francisco, that has the reputation of being a hub of the counterculture. It routinely turns up at the top of pop economist Richard Florida's charts of cities that the so-called Creative Class calls home. It has that combination of a high-tech economy and anything-goes culture; Florida cites the custom of drinking at "Hippie Hour" instead of "Happy Hour." I think of it primarily as the setting for Richard Linklater's meandering film *Slacker*. It's a city where twenty-somethings can live a peaceful, undirected, undriven existence. It's not an image that makes me expect a lot. On the other hand, I also think of Austin as the birthplace of the health food supermarket chain Whole Foods.

Even though I've never met Chris Krager before, I recognize him instantly. He's a slight, dark-haired, well-groomed young man in work boots, gray pants, a yellow shirt with buttons, and a pen in his pocket. His look suggests engineer more than architect. Or maybe Chris Krager, thirty-five years old, just looks like what he is, a designer/builder. In any case, Chris's appearance, the purposeful way he talks about his work, the quality of KRDB's design . . . all those things make me suspect that Whole Foods, which grew from a single store in Austin into a $6 billion company by expertly marketing and aestheticizing the tastes of the counterculture, might be the more relevant point of reference. But, because I'm feeling so run down, it takes me a few hours to appreciate that fact.

Shortly after we climb into Chris's well-used Saab, he explains that he got together with Chris Robertson in grad schoool, at the University of Texas, Austin. "Both of us had an interest in affordability and sustainability. We thought that there's no reason why design services shouldn't be accessible to people like myself."

The goal of KRDB from the outset, he tells me, was to produce "affordable modern housing." Chris Krager, more than anyone I've met thus far, has religion. He isn't just a member of my peculiar church, worshipping at the altar of cheap but good. He's an apostle. I should be crazy with excitement. But, having met my share of visionaries thus far on my trip, I am moving slowly.

Anyway, I'm happy to be in the passenger seat as we drive the leafy back streets of Austin. Chris starts telling me about a new kind of concrete block that reduces the "thermal bridge" between interior and exterior. In other words, it insulates much better than conventional concrete blocks.

"Our practice," Krager says, "we consider it a laboratory. We're looking for products that balance performance and economy."

And this, of course, is precisely what I want to hear. It's like Krager is waving the banner of the Holy Grail at me the way a football fan waves one of those jumbo foam fingers. It is right in front of me, but I'm not quite paying attention. I have, on this particular morning, no capacity for abstraction and don't begin to perk up until we arrive at a house that's nearly complete. It's a long, narrow box with a black slate tile wall facing the street. The front wall is punctuated by a couple of skinny, translucent windows, one horizontal and one vertical. The real front of the house, the entrance, is on the side. Framing the entry is a wall covered with cypress siding, a warm, light-colored wood, and more irregularly shaped windows. At a break in the wall is a deck, a kind of minimalist front porch, that serves as the main entryway and divides a single-story front volume from a rear volume that dips down into the landscape to create a double-height kitchen and living area. From the outside, it's a slightly awkward house. The process of puzzling out how to merge the desires of the clients—art collectors—with a narrow, somewhat rugged lot still shows. It's a rawness that many new houses have before the surrounding property has been landscaped. What strikes me, looking at the exterior of this building, is how carefully it's been detailed: the positioning of the windows, the strips of metal sealing the corners, the palette of materials. There is nothing about it that suggests economy. Yet KRDB built it for $125,000. It's a 1,400-square-foot house, and Krager figures that it cost $85 to $95 a square foot, "turnkey, including our fees."

The low price even includes the time and effort that it took to cope with an unpleasant surprise: "When we started to excavate," Krager recalls, "we found huge chunks of concrete." And it also factors in some sweat equity, as the owners are doing some of the interior finishes themselves. But the KRDB approach to low-cost housing doesn't depend on free labor. One of the primary ways KRDB saves money is by working with contractors who are sympathetic to their aims. For example, the unorthodox windows would be hugely expensive if they were being outsourced, but one of KRDB's regular team built the steel boxes for the translucent windows on-site. And the architects know when to cut corners. For instance, the house has black melamine kitchen cabinets from Home Depot that look perfectly fine without the telltale store-bought doors.

Actually, this house isn't typical for KRDB, in that it was commissioned by a client. Usually, the firm prefers to build on spec. As Krager points out, "It's hard doing commissioned projects with this kind of budget. Clients say up front that they have certain expectations, but then the expectations change."

He adds something that I think is the essence of what sets this firm's houses apart: "This kind of work forces us to focus on the essentials of architecture, the quality of space, how space is experienced. There's a lot you can do with Sheetrock and studs." While the brothers Anderson in Seattle were all about using materials—even low-tech materials—in high-tech ways, KRDB seems more about thinking through the space and doing extraordinary things with ordinary materials.

It's the quality of the space, Krager says, not the quantity of the space. This is what modernism used to be about. I think about the midcentury houses that I most admire, whether it's Gene Sternberg's little Arapahoe

Acres homes or the simple 1,100-square-foot houses that populist architect Gregory Ain built in Los Angeles in the late 1940s. They always had features like sliding walls or accordion walls that allow two rooms to become one or vice versa. And they always came equipped with clever built-in cabinetry or tables, things that were about maximizing the efficiency of the house and also maximizing the architect's role in determining how the homeowners operated in the space. There is, of course, an inherent contradiction: flexibility as dictated by an architect is not true flexibility. But that's more of a philosophical discussion. The point is that these houses were all about function, while today's modernism is chiefly about style. It may be minimalist in design but it is maximalist in budget and attitude.

That is not the case with KRDB's houses. The firm is deeply engaged in creating a business model that allows them to design and build and also to develop. By doing all three, they can make money at the low end of the market. "It's a nontraditional model of practice," says Krager. "We try to be more entrepreneurial, to go out and make work ourselves."

The best examples of this way of working are a pair of simple, lovely butterfly-roofed houses the firm did on Cedar Avenue, in a part of East Austin that is traditionally black and had been the scene of what Krager terms a "mini-riot." KRDB picked up the two lots for $15,000 apiece and built houses with the assistance of Austin's housing department that sold for $105,000 and $125,000, including the land costs. Krager figured that the city agency, by waiving fees and expediting the approval process, saved the firm between $10,000 and $15,000, a savings they passed along to the buyers.

We pull up to the Cedar Avenue houses, and Chris gripes about the wooden fence that one of the homeowners built, obscuring the view of the house from the street. Now I am finally fully alert. All the little hairs on my body are tingling. I am experiencing something that feels a lot like desire.

More than the house we had just visited, this one conforms to my notion of perfection. The walls are made of 12-inch-thick insulated concrete block and HardiPlank, a commonly used siding material made from fiber-reinforced cement. The floors are polished concrete. The roof is metal. All of these are the standard materials of low-cost housing, but the distinction here is the way these components are put together. This house, KRDB's cheapest, is as beautifully laid out and articulated as houses that cost five or ten times as much.

The open kitchen is separated from the living room area by a large blue built-in table that matches the countertops. The kitchen cabinets and drawers aren't fancy, but there are a lot of them. The roof has a gentle slope. At the low end of the slope, hidden in a gap between the drop ceiling and the exterior wall, is a row of recessed lights running the length of the house. On the opposite wall, beneath the high end of the roof, are clerestory windows that also run the length of the house. The long hallway that functions as a kind of spine—it leads to the two bedrooms and the bathroom—has a floor-to-ceiling operable window at either end. The bathroom is tiled in red, KRDB's favorite accent color.

The house is a study in the science of space and light. The same space without the careful placement of windows and lights would be much diminished. It all appears so simple that it looks as though anyone should be able to do it—modernism at its best—but the elemental quality conceals a tremendous amount of craft.

At times like this I think about the Bauhaus. I wonder if Gropius knew, if Mies knew, how hard it would be to execute the brand of simplicity they advocated. I stand in this house in East Austin thinking that this is exactly the place to which modernism was meant to lead, that houses like this should be the rule, not the exception. I think about the Bauhaus and its founders because it keeps me from thinking how jealous I am of Chia and Javier, the young couple who own the house. I focus on the Bauhaus because it keeps me from crying.

Chia, the homeowner, goes by only one name. She is a local entrepreneur, in the business of making and selling fake fur hats with animal ears in both children's and adult sizes. She's got a head of free-form frizzy hair and is dressed, on the day I visit, in alternachic—a flowered skirt with a belly-revealing top—and has tattoos on her ankles. A couple of dogs laze on the cool concrete floors. The furniture is pure thrift shop; wobbly wooden chairs are pulled up to KRDB's crisp blue table as if they belong there. Funky ceramic teapots and candles are on display everywhere. Chia refers to her home as "The House of Taurus." Clearly she doesn't realize that all of twentieth-century architectural history leads to her door.

She tells me that she and Javier (his last name is Arredondo, but he's also known as DJ Big Face) simply drove by when the house was under construction, saw the rendering on the sign, and applied to the city's department of housing to buy it. She tells me all this blissfully unaware that I would kill to own such a house, that my counterclockwise drive around the country has led me to this very spot.

While this covetousness I have feels like something that the Ten Commandments specifically forbids, I'm clearly not the only one who has been stricken with it. The house next door—slightly larger, a bit more complex, furnished more stylishly by the couple who owns it—was published in a national magazine. Afterward, KRDB got 200 e-mails from all over the country from people who wanted to buy just such a house. And there was nothing the firm could do. KRDB is set up only to build locally and can build only one or two houses at a time. This is when Krager and Robertson got the prefab bug.

Like other architects I've met in my travels, they are now cultivating relationships with manufactured homebuilders. "We're developing some designs, using the limitations of their module, that we can deliver."

Krager admits that manufactured housing "has a stigma to overcome." He explains, "It's like the bus stigma," meaning it's downscale and has the smell of desperation about it. But he thinks that stigma could be overcome, and when he actually visited a Texas manufacturer, he was "surprised at the quality. You can have quality control throughout the process."

I leave my perfect house behind with some reluctance. If I were staying in town another day, maybe I would have found an excuse to come back, to hang out, to make friends with the owners or their dogs, or buy a furry hat, or something. But I don't really know what to do. It's like seeing the man of my dreams on the down escalator when I'm on the up escalator. And he has some other babe on his arm.

So we get lunch. We stop at a Mexican health-food restaurant, where the woman behind the counter asks if Chris and I are brothers. I hope that it's a language problem, that she can tell I'm a woman but thinks English works like Spanish: *hermano, hermana.* But maybe I've been on the road too long. Maybe I do look like Chris's brother.

Then Chris takes me out to see the site of what might someday be KRDB's most ambitious project, five acres in a rural, outlying Austin neighborhood where the firm hopes to build twenty-four units, a mixture of prefab and stick-built. The idea would be to test out a number of building systems in one development.

The land is owned by a retired firefighter named William Mosley, for whom the firm has already done work. We sit in Mosley's driveway for a moment, staring at the house they built for him. It's two distinct volumes, a single-story red brick box attached to a two-story HardiPlank-covered box painted fire engine red.

"I wanted something that would jump out at you, " Chris says. "Mission accomplished."

This one, about 1,400 square feet, cost $137,000. "We were very fortunate to have begun this endeavor when we did," says Chris. The building market in Austin had just crashed—the half-built Intel headquarters downtown was an icon of the dot-com bust—and subcontractors were calling for work.

Well, maybe it was good timing. Or maybe it was magic. I don't know how they did this house for $137,000. It's one of the nicest houses I've ever seen at any price.

Mosley, a handsome, solid black man in, perhaps, his fifties, dressed in overalls and a short-sleeved shirt, greets us and shows us around. He hasn't moved in yet. He's waiting until his retirement after twenty-five years in the fire department is official, when he's going to start his new life as a real estate developer. The house is divided into two discrete pieces: the single-story brick building, which contains the kitchen and living room, and the two-story red HardiPlank building, which holds a downstairs study and an upstairs bedroom with a spectacular bathtub cantilevered over the floor below. The two volumes are connected by a narrow breezeway. The idea is that the kitchen and living area can be rented out for special events.

And as quickly as I fell in love with the smaller Cedar Avenue house, I fall for this one, too, because it is remarkably warm, richly detailed, and has so much personality. The living room has concrete floors dyed a deep mahogany, a brick wall surrounding a fireplace, and built-in shelves. The adjoining kitchen, demarcated by a step up, is nicely and simply laid out and has a skylight and one of those long vertical windows that KRDB loves to do. The whole space is so beautifully conceived and framed.

I ask Mosley about his role in the design process, and he tells me that, in all his years as a firefighter, he's been in and out of a lot of houses. He'd learned something about what he did and didn't want.

My conversation with Mosley reminds me of a running theme we had back in the early days of *Dwell,* when we loved to feature modern houses built for civil servants. It started with the very first issue, which included a house in Phoenix that a married couple, both firefighters, were building for themselves. They chose a modern design in part because they wanted their own home to be as efficiently made as the firehouse where they worked. They wanted floors you could just hose down. Subsequent issues featured houses for a retired narcotics officer and the Andersons' Fox Island house, built for another firefighter. In a way it was an accident, highlighting the homes of so many uniformed public servants, but in another way it was the perfect expression of my conviction that good design isn't just for the elite. And Mosley has the potential to be the ultimate icon of this revival of modernism's populist streak because, during his years of fighting fires, he'd also been buying up land. Bit by bit he amassed five acres that KRDB wants to develop.

Inevitably, what happens to firms that build great low-cost housing is that they attract the attention of wealthier clients. "Clients with obvious resources and savvy," Chris notes, "want us to build for $125 a square foot in a neighborhood on the west side." In other words, wealthy clients are very interested in building low-cost houses in the better parts of town.

"We've started doing more expensive houses, " Chris acknowledges. "But we don't want to wake up and find out that's all we're doing."

KRDB's business seems to be heading in two different directions. They are dedicated to inexpensive housing but they are eager to team up with a manufacturer to cut costs and to allow them to build more houses with less design time. "We're moving toward modular," Chris says. "It decreases building costs 20 to 30 percent."

Like other architects I've met around the country, he's had discussions with a manufacturer who's willing to customize and to send houses out without cladding so the exteriors could still be, for instance, fire engine red. Inevitably, they will be turning out a better class of manufactured housing, but I can't imagine that they will still be able to get the kind of detailing that makes their houses unique. I begin to think that the triple-wide manufactured house I saw crossing the bridge in Taos was a harbinger, a warning that I won't be able to escape the modular fad.

Later, Chris e-mails me a proposal for the "Jackie Robinson Modular Housing," as the project on Mosley's property is called. (Jackie Robinson is the name of the adjacent street.) The PDF file opens with a 1957 quotation from midcentury LA architect Craig Ellwood: "Eventually all homes, except those for the very wealthy, will be bought in prefabricated form." And the optimistic declaration: "No longer just a promise." And there's a lovely rendering of a house squeezed into an alley. It has the dimensions of a manufactured home combined with the thoughtful window treatments and cladding of a KRDB house. It's two stories tall with the main living space on the second story and a carport on the ground floor. In the rendering, there is a red motorcycle with rider in the carport, and I assume that's meant to be the homeowner. As with everything else I've seen from KRDB, I have just one thought: *That's my house.* It makes me think that KRDB might be able to cut costs further by teaming up with a manufacturer and not compromise the quality of their designs. But I'd have to see an actual house to be sure.

The proposal goes into a little more detail about the three methods of home construction that KRDB would try out in the development. One system would use SIPs panels (structural insulated panels, each made of a polystyrene core sheathed in oriented strand board or metal) that would be assembled in a factory. Another system would use more traditional stick-built manufactured houses configured to KRDB's specifications. The third system would use a steel frame and prefabricated panels assembled on-site. The homes would be affordable to the people who make 60 percent of Austin's median income, and a 1,400-square-foot house would sell for $112,000. The various different kinds of houses would be accessible from a public alleyway that looped around the site, so that parking and automobile access would be from the alley to the rear of the houses. The fronts of the houses would all face on a common green.

I love the spirit of the proposal but I'm still not convinced that the alliance between a conventional house manufacturer and an unconventional design/build firm will yield a house I want. I'm not convinced, but if the project goes forward, I will be first in line to see the results.

At the end of my day in Austin, we pick up Chris's girlfriend, Amy Grappell, and get margaritas at a bar downtown. We sit outside, surrounded by the corporate part of the city, and Amy tells me about her film project, a documentary about the Ukraine, where she happened to be at the moment the Soviet Union fell apart. As we sit and relax halfway between the capitol dome at one end of Congress and the hipster enclave at the other end, I imagine that I could stay right here. Later, when we drive across the river separating the Austin of business and politics from the Austin of alternative culture, I consider asking Chris to pull over so I can watch the swarms of bats fly out from under the bridge at sunset. But I pass, figuring that I will return to Austin someday. After all, my house might be nearby—and the bats will still be flying.

The Shot-Trot

September 3, 2003   Empire Coffee, Houston, Texas

The fact that I just got an oil change—about 600 miles overdue—gives me a sense of satisfaction. New wiper blades, too. I love Jiffy Lube.

Brett Zamore and I are having dinner in a Houston seafood restaurant done up to look like an old stainless steel diner. I'm showing him pictures of KRDB's Austin houses in the tiny monitor of my digital camera. I keep talking about William Mosley's kitchen and living room.

Brett says, "You really like that one, don't you?"

And suddenly I feel as though I've been cheating on him. The way this story is supposed to work is that I'm fated to like Brett's house best. His house, his way of thinking about houses, his essential pragmatism, have been on my mind this whole trip.

Brett Zamore. I had visited him earlier in the year, before my road trip began, on the February weekend when the space shuttle fell out of the sky. Young, with an open face, a broad smile, and curly reddish hair, he looks more like a baseball player than an architect. I can more easily picture him in a catcher's mask, squatting behind home plate chanting, "Swing, batter, batter" than sitting at a conference table wearing a black suit and speaking gravely in the secret dialect of architects about programs and conditions.

The Shot-Trot house by architect Brett Zamore, Houston, Texas

Brett comes across as a kid, dressed in sneakers, faded jeans, and a lived-in sweatshirt, but he's a kid with things on his mind.

Back in February, Brett had a secret. He confessed it to me as we sat on the patio of a coffee bar in Houston as a mild winter afternoon was disappearing into evening. The family with the screeching toddler was packing up to go home. The white parrot that had been perching on one of the wrought iron chairs, conversing with a mynah bird up in a tree, had moved on. The girls with the brightly colored hair and the multiple piercings had decamped for some more exciting place to spend their Saturday night. And, at the end of a long conversation about how to understand what the house he'd designed for his first real client would cost to build, Brett admitted that he has been moonlighting, working for a local developer on cookie-cutter houses.

This may not sound like much of a secret, but consider it in the context of the fact that Brett was a thirty-two-year-old graduate of Rice University's prestigious architecture school, did his undergraduate work at Yale, and was employed by Carlos Jimenez, one of the city's best-known architects. He was now dabbling with the dark side not just because he could use the extra cash but also because he wanted to know the things developers know.

"I think you have to be smart," Brett explained. "I think you have to think like a developer, something architects don't do."

It was precisely Brett's take on "smart" that first brought me to Houston. The young architect was building a long, narrow house for David Kaplan, an unmarried newspaper reporter, someone a little bit like me. David needed a home designed to accommodate the life of a single person, rather than that of a family. Brett's design for him was a hybrid of two elemental Southern housing types, the shotgun—a narrow gable-roofed house with rooms laid end to end—and the dogtrot—a house characterized by a covered central breezeway—but it was also sleek and modern, a hybrid that borrowed from the past without nostalgia and that seemed effortlessly farsighted. I looked at the rendering of this house and I could imagine a life inside its walls that was sane, comfortable, and thoughtful. I could imagine a future that was good.

And this time machine of a house was also very inexpensive. The budget, including the quarter-acre site in a still largely undiscovered neighborhood on Houston's less glamorous east side, was $150,000, a figure tantalizingly close to my $100,000 goal.

If I were being true to my injunction against uninspiring landscapes, I would skip Houston, all low-lying and swampy, a sinkhole about to happen, and head for Texas's hill country. The drama of Houston's landscape, when there is any, is entirely man-made.

If I were being true to my nature as an urbanist, the kind who likes being able to walk everywhere, who feels burdened rather than liberated by a daily routine that requires driving, I would stay far away from this city. To the casual observer, it is nothing but malls, parking lots, and freeways.

But Houston is a funny place. Although it is the fourth largest city in the United States (after New York, Los Angeles, and Chicago), a city built on the proceeds of the oil industry, and a magnet for an immigrant population as large and diverse as any in America, it has the unstudied, unplanned qualities of a much smaller town. Like other sprawl-intensive cities—Los Angeles, Phoenix—it is full of pockets, areas where extraordinary beauty is possible, where experimentation is, if not encouraged, then tolerated. It is a city invented by oil wildcatters and even though it has grown more economically diverse, it has not gotten appreciably tamer. Houston, alone among sizable American cities, has no zoning laws. The anything-goes mentality that allowed Enron to spiral ever upward, propelled only by hype and deceit, seems very much like an outgrowth of the local variety of laissez faire. So does the set of circumstances that permits an entire neighborhood to adopt corrugated metal siding as its architectural symbol or encourages an artist to completely cover his home with beer cans and surround his porch with strings of aluminum pull tabs that clink and clatter in the wind like industrial wind chimes. There is room in Houston—physical space, psychological space—for anything to happen. Good things. Bad things. The horrifying and the wonderful. And to me this swirl of possibility is what makes this city great.

"Never had I seen a city so immense or one so alien to my sensibilities," observed architect Carlos Jimenez in an essay he wrote on the occasion of the millennium. "In Houston, one is immediately overtaken by the horizon's imperturbable presence, concealing and revealing an urban destiny of waste and potential." Jimenez went on to probe Houston's status "as a city caught between short-term greed and the occasional long-term vision."

One of Jimenez's examples of long-term vision is the Menil Collection, also the key site in my Houston, the version of the city that I keep in my head. This museum, housed in a long, low, white building designed by the architect Renzo Piano, sits in the middle of a verdant neighborhood of well-maintained bungalows. Instead of dominating its surroundings like any other great institution would, the Menil hunkers down amongst its neighbors and acts as an aesthetic center of gravity, exerting an otherworldly glow that bathes its particular spot in the museum district in a benevolent light.

As it turns out, the otherworldly harmony I see and feel in the blocks around the museum is not a hallucination. John and Dominique de Menil actually bought up much of the neighborhood as part of their plan to endow and grow the University of St. Thomas. Ultimately, their vision of an open-minded, ecumenical, liberal Catholic university was thwarted by the school's administration, and they wound up using much of the real estate they'd accumulated for the school to build a museum to house their collection of some 10,000 artworks. In the 1970s and '80s, when Dominique de Menil was planning the museum, she decided that the surrounding bungalows should be preserved. Indeed, the lovely little houses were restored and, in some cases, relocated, painted a uniform shade of gray, and rented out to a deserving cadre of artists and intellectuals. De Menil also required her architect, Renzo Piano, to design a museum building that respected the scale of the neighborhood, in order to demonstrate how modern architecture could fit into an ordinary Houston landscape. In other words, the neighborhood looks like the peaceable kingdom because it more or less is.

The Menil Collection includes modern art, surrealist art, and rooms filled with ancient and primitive art that has clearly been chosen and displayed for its beauty rather than for its historical significance. I have never been so taken with Russian icons or African fetish objects before. One night at a Menil opening, a bit drunk on white wine, I stood in front of an African figure and looked into its unexpectedly blue eyes and had another one of those satisfying moments that made me want to stay.

Certainly it was a sense of possibility that drew Brett Zamore to Houston. He had a choice of attending architecture school at Harvard or at Rice. Rice sweetened the deal by offering him a full scholarship, but there was also something about the place, something that promised an escape from the rigidity of New England culture. Then he fell in love with the city. After only eight years here the thirty-two-year-old sounded like an old-timer, grumbling about how much of old Houston has been bulldozed into oblivion.

To understand Brett's sensibilities, you'd have to go with him to the Alabama Ice House, where they serve long-neck beers wrapped in napkins and, on Friday nights, free barbecued hot dogs. "This is the real Houston," he exclaimed.

Or you could visit the 1920s shotgun house that Zamore rebuilt as his thesis project.

On Buck Road, in Houston's Fifth Ward, one of a string of ragtag neighborhoods nestled between downtown's skyscrapers and the freeway loop, Brett's shotgun had sat abandoned for years before he discovered it. "There are empty shotgun houses all over the city," he said, explaining, "I fell in love with the simplicity."

Brett regards Houston's derelict row houses as both an inventory that can be restored and as a resource that enlightened developers can draw on for inspiration. He was not the first to be seduced by this traditional form of housing that some historians believe has its roots in Africa.

The shotgun house has been associated with African Americans since its first appearance on this continent. Scholars have traced the history of the shotgun backward from black neighborhoods across the Deep South to New Orleans, where, in theory, the original shotguns were built by free blacks who had in the early nineteenth century fled a bloody slave revolt in Haiti. Progenitors of the typical shotgun form—a gabled roof facing the street and a progression of narrow rooms laid end-to-end—still stand in Port-au-Prince. Going further back, the Yoruba people of West Africa constructed two-room buildings, longer than they were wide.

In other words, the architecture has a heritage—in this case, one that fascinates cultural historians but puts off contemporary homebuyers, whatever their race. Consider that most developers design homes that, whether they sell for $100,000 or $1 million, project a vision of affluence and well-being. This quality is what real estate agents call "curb appeal": people want houses that remind them of Buckingham Palace or the Alhambra. The shotgun, by contrast, is a symbol of slavery and segregation. It was the kind of house that both African Americans and poor whites owned when they had few options. As a friend who grew up in Texas remarked on seeing one of Brett's computer renderings, "That's a white trash house."

In 1993 a group of Houston artists began to transform a cluster of twenty-two abandoned shotguns in another inner-city neighborhood, the Third Ward, into a series of spaces for art installations, preserving the homes as a sort of architectural petting zoo. Today these houses have all been whitewashed and assembled around a central yard. The overall effect is that of a Caribbean resort, something more organized and sweeter than the immediate surroundings. Some of the houses are galleries open to the public, and some are devoted to an educational residency program for single mothers. These shotguns have sponsors. "Shell Oil Company Foundation," reads a painted sign hanging over the porch of one such house. "Alpha Kappa Alpha," says another.

Project Row Houses is, for Houston, a rare success story in preservation. This well-maintained fragment of neighborhood is a bit like the area around the Menil, a conscious effort to honor the city's vernacular architecture. It is a wonderful little enclave, but it treats shotgun houses as museum pieces, relics.

What intrigued me about Brett's approach was that he viewed the shotgun as a starting point, an architectural form that has a future as well as a past. He was less interested in preservation as such and more interested in identifying the practical elements of shotgun design, elements that could still be useful today.

Several years ago, through a Rice connection, Brett found an abandoned shotgun house on property that was owned by the Fifth Ward Community Redevelopment Corporation (FWCRC), an organization that has succeeded in refreshing the area's housing stock, building affordable homes for the largely black population of the neighborhood.

When Brett first got his hands on the shotgun he named "House 00," he once told me, "I had no clue what I was going to do with it." He thought he might, like the artists before him, create some sort of installation. As he began to study his house and the history of shotguns, he developed an appreciation for the typology's understated virtues.

"Why is it such a beautiful, successful house?" Brett asked himself. "It doesn't ignore the street. It doesn't ignore the landscape as developer houses do." He came to recognize that having a door at each end promotes ventilation. He realized that setting a house on blocks, instead of on concrete pads like most contemporary Houston homes, allows air to circulate below, keeping the shotgun cooler.

Brett declared that he developed "a simple love for the house." But really, it was more like the grad student and the battered old house had become physically involved, as if they were having an affair.

For two years the shotgun where Buck Road dribbles to an end by an elementary school was Brett's life. He put new beams under the house to support a sagging floor. He pulled out all the doors and windows and reinstalled them. He removed most of the interior walls, and left them out, creating a more spacious interior. Those he didn't remove he preserved under a heavy coat of clear varnish like archaeological treasures. He tore out the ceiling but left the joists in place so you could see how the house had once been divided.

"I installed this roof," said Brett, pointing to the sheets of corrugated metal atop the house. "I think I lost 10 pounds doing it. It was a nightmare but it's going to last forever."

Brett got local businesses to donate or discount supplies such as insulation and light fixtures. IKEA sold him the kitchen cabinets at 40 percent off. He also received grant money and $16,500 from the FWCRC. All told, the house cost $70,000 to renew. The only trouble was that Brett was an architect without a client. He didn't know for whom he was working. He was pretty sure he wasn't going to live in it himself, that someone from the community should take possession of it. But because of the shotgun's troubled heritage, its association with poverty and the bad old days, most local people regarded the house with disdain.

Nonetheless, Brett endeavored to make the sturdiest structure and most flexible layout that he could for some unknown future occupant. Whenever he caught himself thinking too hard about how exactly this someone would live in the space, he'd stop himself. "I was becoming too much of an architect," he observed. "I was programming it."

Eventually, Brett's shotgun was sold for $30,000 to Bert L. Long Jr., a leading Houston artist who grew up in the Fifth Ward. ("It used to be called the 'Bloody Fifth,'" he recalled.) "Now I'm back home, right around the corner from my mother," said Long, just before he moved in. At the time, he was excited about the ways that his art "can help to heal and grow the community. . . . It's a very conscious thought. Bringing back, instead of taking from, you understand."

Brett also designed a simple studio building for Long, which the FWCRC built next door. Long saw this pairing of the shotgun house and the art studio as a new prototype for the neighborhood. "We'll do fifteen or twenty row houses with studios attached. It's our way of using art to affect the community," Long asserted. "We need a core, a cultural core."

For a while, it seemed as if Long's dreams for the unassuming little house dwarfed even Brett's. The architect, however, found a way to move his dream forward.

One Friday night Brett, his girlfriend, Rene; his new client, David Kaplan; and I went to Ninfa's, a Mexican joint near downtown that spawned a chain of shopping mall restaurants. Everyone told me that this bustling, low-ceilinged maze of rooms—Ninfa used to live right upstairs—was far superior to its chain progeny. Rene pointed out Ninfa's portrait on the wall, her maternal visage sanctifying the scene. I didn't have the heart to mention that I had eaten at a shopping mall Ninfa's the night before and had seen exactly the same portrait. Over fajitas and sugary margaritas we talked about the house that Brett was designing for David.

David Kaplan is a thin, studious-looking man in his early fifties. He is from Houston but seems nothing like a Texan, lacking that extrovert bluster that I imagine is the birthright of everyone in the state. Instead, he is quiet, tentative, carefully choosing his moments. He works as a reporter for the

Houston Chronicle where, he told me, his beat is "small business." I began to think of him as the hero of a Raymond Carver story.

David knows Brett and the original shotgun project well, because he used to work at Rice as a publicist in the university's communications office. "I was his promoter in a way," David explained. "I pitched stories to the media. I had more success with Brett's house than anything else I worked on."

It took me a while to fully appreciate the relevance of David Kaplan to my own search for a home. Eventually it dawned on me that the thing we have in common is that we are both single individuals looking to mold a space to our own needs. Out in the larger world of homebuying and building, the assumption is that couples and families buy homes. Major real estate purchases are typically part of a larger package of commitments, going hand in hand with marriage or, at least, a long-term serious relationship. But it's a big decision to buy a house for yourself, because it suggests that there's no sense in waiting for Mr. or Ms. Right to come along before making this life-changing investment. David has never owned a house; he's always rented. "I'm fifty-three," he said. "There was sort of a now-or-never aspect to it. Time's running out." He paused and added, "I guess it's a different kind of biological clock."

When his best friend bought a bungalow in Eastwood, a pretty but economically marginal neighborhood east of downtown and the north-south freeway that divides good neighborhoods from bad, David decided to go see if there was anything in the area that interested him. "I picked out two houses," David said. "One weekend I took Brett to look at them."

Brett recalled that David brought him to look at a couple of bungalows, both selling for a bit more than $100,000. "My fear," he said, "was that David would have to put in another $100,000 on renovation and repairs." Still, Brett was taken with the neighborhood: "The houses had a beauty to them. I saw a lot of opportunity, maybe the opportunity I saw in Houston when I moved here."

"Then," David continued, "we saw the empty lot and thought, why not start from scratch?"

The empty lot was a full quarter acre and sold for about $22,000. It was narrow but deep, the length of two typical lots. "As soon as I saw the narrow lot and the depth of it, it made sense," said Brett. David bought the land almost two years ago, and he and Brett have been hammering out details of the design and trying to get the financing in place ever since.

Although the house was designed for occupancy by one individual, David figured that it had enough room for two and maybe even some kids, if he ever did get married. But mostly the space was about him. Originally, there was only one bedroom in the plans. In order to get financing, Brett had to redraw them so that the study appeared to be a second bedroom. The bank's assumption was that a one-bedroom house would have insufficient resale value.

David pointed out that if he had a family, he'd be far less likely to build in a marginal neighborhood. He'd be in the sort of safe, prosperous area where most of his childhood friends landed. But then, most of the kids he grew up with make more money than he does.

"I'm a reporter," David pointed out, "not a lawyer. That's a huge factor."

Like the archetypal shotgun, David's house was long and narrow, 16 × 80. The model made it look more like a Greyhound bus than a building. It had the typical front gable facing the street, though Brett gave his gable an exaggerated angle and cleaner silhouette so it looked more assertively modern and less traditional. The house had a front porch, a back porch, and a central breezeway that could be sealed up with glass doors or left open to the air, with a pair of sliding louvers to provide privacy and security.

There was nothing nostalgic about the house. Rather, it took what it needed from the past but was styled with an eye toward the future. The house was a wonderful balancing act: the past and the present, openness and security, a low budget and the client's hunger for luxe details.

The design of any house is a dance; sometimes the architect leads, sometimes the client leads, and sometimes the process is a perfectly balanced pas de deux. In this case Brett seemed like the obvious leader, because the outward appearance of the house was dictated by his fascination with vernacular forms.

Although David claimed that he was "intimidated" by the process of designing and building a custom home, he was not so cowed that he didn't voice his ideas about what he wanted. For one thing, he craved a fireplace, "even if it was a tiny fireplace," which was not a standard Houstonian feature. And he wanted a yard. When he saw the breezeway that Brett put smack in the middle of the house, an architectural detail stolen from another vernacular southern style, the dogtrot, David embraced it. He knew that this would be the place where he would sit and read his newspaper every day.

Initially, David was hoping for "a clean, simple feel to the house. I want it to have different influences, maybe Asian, even though it's a shotgun house."

"Brett's stronger willed than I am," David noted. But David stuck to his guns on a number of issues. He turned out to have strong feelings about the exterior. Brett originally proposed corrugated metal siding, something industrial as a nod to the mixed nature of the area, but David rejected the idea, explaining, "I thought it would be too shocking to the neighborhood."

They settled on HardiPlank. "It's the perfect material for Houston," Brett explained. "It looks like wood but it's concrete. You don't get termites. It doesn't rot."

Brett thought that industrial chic, medium density fiberboard (MDF) flooring would be a good, low-cost idea, but David wanted wood floors, which they wound up getting cheap, salvaging them from old houses that were being demolished.

The funny thing about this particular dance was that Brett, the Connecticut Yankee, designed a house that reflected his infatuation with Southern vernacular styles. David, who was born and raised in Houston, kept looking for ways to give the house more of a Japanese flavor. He wanted to add long, trisected windows to the exterior walls of the two bathrooms because they would have a sort of shoji screen quality, but Brett argued for less window on that side of the house, which would bear the brunt of the summer sun.

After dinner at Ninfa's, we drove over to see the lot—to the extent that we could see anything in the dark. Brett called my attention to the coffee factory that prompted him to name David's house The Maxwell House. The drive around the neighborhood was a blur: tiny houses, shadows, funky old bars, and restaurants built from cinder block and neon. All I remember from the excursion was David talking about his friend who had bought the house in Eastwood, "the pioneer," David called him. His house had just been robbed, at night when the family was at home asleep. Not much was stolen, except for their sense of well-being. David and Brett will have to have another conversation about how much glass to use and how to make the sliding louvers even more secure.

Meanwhile, back at the old shotgun that Brett dubbed House 00, Bert Long's dreams were moving forward, as well. More than two years after our first meeting in 2000, I returned to Buck Road for lunch with the architect and the artist.

It was the day of the *Columbia* disaster. Since my run, I'd had some coffee, showered, and spent much of the morning planted in front of the TV. Brett picked me up at my hotel on Houston's fashionable west side, and we drove east, journeying to the far side of the freeway, past the bail bond shops and barbecue joints to the spot where Buck Road ends in a schoolyard fence. And there was the double shotgun that was Brett's thesis project, painted a rich shade of red, surrounded by greenery.

Bert and his girlfriend, Joan, had planted flowers and papayas in the front yard, a cornucopia of vegetables in the back, and tomatoes along the side fence. Strewn everywhere were blankets left over from Bert's efforts to save his salad greens from a recent cold snap. The papaya tree out front was still all bundled up. However, by the time I arrived it was a balmy 70-degree day and the winter ryegrass that surrounded the little red house was the lushest thing I'd seen in months. It looked to me as if Bert was living in Eden.

Bert gave me a tour of the garden, uncorked a bottle of red wine, and talked nonstop about his art as he served up barbecued brisket, fresh-picked Chinese cabbage, and roasted potatoes.

Seeing House 00 so full of life made me happy. Some people don't see the connection between the formal attributes of architecture and the quality of life within the walls but, rightly or wrongly, I do. Seeing Brett's thesis project transformed into a real home gave me renewed confidence in his instincts and skills.

After lunch, on the car radio, the men from NASA were having a press conference, speaking mournfully about the day's events, about losing contact with the space shuttle, about the unwelcome knowledge that radio silence brings. The men talked. We drove.

First we went looking for a house in Bert's neighborhood. The local redevelopment group had, a couple of years back, sponsored an architectural competition. Sixteen well-known architects designed houses that could be built for $103,000 and sold to community residents with subsidies under a federal voucher program. Seven were chosen for construction and one, supposedly, had been built. But Brett and I couldn't find it.

The voucher house idea was wonderful. It was a way of demonstrating that low-income housing and innovative architecture were not mutually exclusive categories, an idea very dear to my heart. Sadly, the organizers of the competition had moved away from Houston. Left to its own devices, the development group that was supposed to construct the winning plans just wanted to build what it had always built, plain old colonials and salt-boxes, with vinyl siding and faux historic lanterns by the front door.

Brett and I drove on. We did slow loops around downtown Houston, checking out the mighty black glass cylinders that Enron built as their head-quarters, and admiring sleek oil company towers from less bombastic eras.

We drove at a crawl through neighborhoods like the Sixth Ward, where all the little cottages have been bought up and lovingly restored, where prices are high. I pointed to a house with an example of indigenous Texan art on the roof, and Brett responded, "A house like that, with the bull on top, is probably worth $350,000."

And we visited the "Tin House" district, which started a few years ago when an artist clad his home in corrugated metal. Then other people fol-lowed suit, building more houses with rippled metal exteriors. Finally devel-opers joined in and built apartments and town houses that mimicked the look of the artist houses. The district is a perfect example of how life with-out zoning plays out. In another city, the original innovation would have been prohibited, the use of industrial materials forbidden, if not by law then by some form of homeowners' covenant. In Houston the innovation was allowed to happen—which is good—but then, once the faux industrial look had caught on, there was no device in place to slow the transformation of a modest, single-family neighborhood into a high-density landscape of town houses and apartments.

The thing that all the metal houses have in common—the little quirky ones and the big, ungainly developer ones—is that they are metal only on the outside. Brett and I sat and stared at one that was under construction, and I realized that I was looking at a conventional wood-frame building going up. The metal building phenomenon in this corner of Houston, then, is not so different from the adobe phenomenon in Taos: a structural material—metal here, or clay in New Mexico—is turned into an aesthetic, a style. Here in Houston an assertively modern material is used in exactly the way that fake half-timber and wattle are used in some homebuilders' subdivisions as a decorative appliqué. Right then and there, I decided that I wouldn't want a house with metal skin, that HardiPlank, in its dishonest way, is a more honest material.

Driving around, it wasn't as if Brett and I were looking for anything in particular. He was trying to show me some of the local styles that inspire him, and I was just soaking up the feeling of the place. I didn't think my perfect house existed on any of those streets, on any of those blocks, but what I got from that kind of aimless slow-motion tour was the same thing I get from going for a run in a city. It's a way for me to develop an intimacy with a place, an intimacy that's necessary, I think, before I can make any kind of commitment.

Ultimately, we wound up sitting outside at a coffee bar not far from Rice University, and Brett and I started deconstructing the Shot-Trot house. Brett talked about plywood, specifically the standard 4×8 sheets that he used as the basis for the design. Brett was talking plywood, and I was thinking Le Corbusier.

Back in the 1940s Le Corbusier had developed a system of proportions, his answer to the golden section used by the ancient Greeks. Corbu believed there needed to be an intelligent system based on the proportions of the human—by which he meant male—body, to introduce both standardization and flexibility into mass-produced building components and even into urban planning. "The 'Modulor' is a measuring tool based on the human body and on mathematics," wrote Corbu. "A man-with-arm-upraised provides, at the determining points of his occupation of space—foot, solar plexus, head, tips of fingers of the upraised arm—three intervals which give rise to a series of golden sections, called the Fibonacci series." Using his proportional system, Corbu could calculate everything from the proper size of doors and windows to the optimum scale for a neighborhood. It was his own system of measurement, intended, he said, to bring a degree of perceptual and psychological comfort to spaces that would, as the modern age moved on, be increasingly standardized and smaller. He was correct in assuming that mass production and standardization would, to a great extent, determine the size, shape, and appearance of many buildings. His system, however, was never universally adopted, and building industries, from country to country, came up with their own arbitrary standards.

Brett embraced the 4×8 plywood board for reasons of economy. If he based a design on readily available, precut materials, it would be less work for the builders and less expensive for the client. "I tried to be religious to the standards I laid out for myself from the beginning," said Brett. But there was something in his use of these materials that also suggested the beginnings of an aesthetic philosophy. The 4×8 is the pragmatist's golden section. It is Brett Zamore's Modulor. The 4×8 board determines the Shot-Trot's 16 × 80 dimensions.

In Houston, noted Brett, the tract houses that developers build can cost as little as $75 a square foot. The more modest homes his employer, architect Jimenez, designs go for more like $110 to $130 a square foot. Brett was aiming for a point in between. "I worked out a base plan. It's 1,200 square feet. I asked David, 'How much can you spend?' If it was me building it, I could do it for $90 a square foot. With a builder I figured $100 a square foot."

Actually, the house, if you count the 400-square-foot loft and mechanical area upstairs, is 1,600 square feet. With a $130,000 construction budget, that's $81 a square foot. If you don't count the upstairs, then the budget is more like $108.

Naturally, the client determines the budget. But what if Brett were to build the house for me, with my $100,000 limit?

"I don't think the character of this house would have to change at all to bring it down $25,000," Brett claimed.

"Well, let's see," I replied.

And so we began a process of subtraction. If we value engineered the

Shot-Trot, the first thing Brett would rethink is the roof. He had specified a standing seam, galvanized aluminum roof—the sophisticated version of the tin roof that was once a sign of poverty. Today, this kind of roofing, made from long strips of metal joined by double folds that stand upright like the wales on corduroy pants, costs perhaps twice as much as the conventional asphalt-shingled roof. While David, for the most part, demanded the expensive finishes, it was the architect who lobbied hard for the metal roof. "I put my foot down," said Brett. "I said, 'David, I'm not thinking about short-term. I'm thinking long-term.'"

Well then, I may be guilty of short-term thinking, but, hey, I save $10,000.

"Okay," I continued, "how do we get rid of another $20,000 without ruining your beautiful design?"

"Drop the ceiling in the living room," Brett responded. "Get rid of the vaulted space."

Having a double-height space requires that something called a ridge beam run the length of the house, front to back, to provide structural support that in a more conventional design is provided by crossbeams at ceiling height. With a vaulted space, there's no place to hide those crossbeams. Lose the vault and we shave $10,000 or $12,000 off the price.

So we're down to a $110,000 house.

Simplify the back of the house so that there's less glass, and the price drops another $3,000. Substitute standardized sliding glass doors from Home Depot for the custom glass doors that enclose the dogtrot breezeway, and we lose another $2,000. Use less expensive windows throughout the house for a savings of $4,500. Make the floor from MDF, a cheap material that is currently in fashion—its Presto Log texture has a certain industrial je ne sais quoi—and we drop $3,000.

So we've shaved another $12,500 from the cost, and we're at the $97,500 house.

And we can keep going. Substitute less fancy kitchen appliances and save $4,000. Skimp a little on the lighting fixtures, and another $1,000 disappears from the cost. Substituting wood handrail on the front porch for the metal rails in the plans would shave off another $2,500. Now we're down to $90,000, and I can afford to bring back the vaulted ceiling. Or maybe the metal roof.

I wonder, though, at what point do all these changes and cuts degrade a wonderfully wrought, high-quality, low-cost home into a tract house? Where is the boundary? When have we cut too much?

I don't know that there's a clear demarcation. It seems to me that it's essential to use very meticulous contractors, because nothing looks worse than a modern design built badly; there is no ornament to cover up the mistakes. But I think the real trick to saving money without compromising quality is to understand how to balance: you splurge on some things (bathroom tiles, kitchen appliances) and cut back on others (the flooring, the use of standard glass doors instead of custom). You try to figure out what's important and what's not, and edit accordingly. There are no rules. You just have to know.

Me, I figure that in a smallish house, a double-height main room is essential. Openness gives the illusion of space. Le Corbusier knew it. Brett Zamore knows it. And I know it.

Brett's ideas about how to trim the budget on David Kaplan's house kept coming: get rid of the fireplace, ditch the outdoor shower, get the kitchen cabinets from IKEA instead of custom building them.

As Brett told me, "You have to be smart. You have to think like a developer." Actually, it seemed to me that we were talking about the Shot-Trot as if it were a car with a list of options. Do you really need the leather interior? How about the state-of-the-art sound system?

But it's also the way that the most sophisticated large homebuilders now operate. Today you don't buy a completed home. You pick out your lot and then you go to the so-called design center and start selecting options: Spiffy micro blinds or less expensive shades? The fancy bathroom tile or some sort of laminate? Media niche or no media niche? All these options are tacked on to the base price of the house and folded into the mortgage, where even the most extravagant additions seem minor compared to the overall cost of the home. Besides, you get thirty years to pay for all that cool stuff. Brett was right. Developers are smart. Too bad the houses they build are so ugly.

On the other hand, architects don't generally work with their clients this way, not routinely or methodically, not at the beginning of the design process. Usually, at some point during the construction period the client realizes that the house is going to cost way more than it was supposed to and, in a panic, eliminates or puts on hold certain features or even entire wings.

"I could copyright this house. It could be marketable," said Brett, who then spun out an elaborate fantasy that involved selling not a house, or even plans per se, but a set of instructions, sort of like the architectural equivalent of a Sol LeWitt painting. Go to such and such an aisle at Lowe's or Home Depot and pick up the following items. . . .

As we left the coffee bar and headed back toward the Galleria area, a maze of shopping malls and highway interchanges into which my hotel had been deftly shoehorned, Brett kept talking. He told me about going, at the invitation of the homebuilder for wshom he secretly worked, to the grand opening of a subdivision and just listening to the way this man and his employees sell.

"I'd love to start a little development company based on this," said Brett, meaning that he wanted to put his design together with the developer's tricks he's studying in his spare time and figure out a way to market the result. "I want to question how development is done," he declared.

"Yeah, me, too," I said. "Me, too." I got out of Brett's car convinced that he's on to something.

Now, six months later, in the first week of September, Brett is in trouble. He takes me to visit David Kaplan's property, this time in daylight. It's a big patch of deep grass surrounded by tall shade trees on a street lined with sweet little bungalows. It is a part of Houston that could be every bit as nice as the manicured blocks around the Menil, but gentrification hasn't been here.

And the sad thing is that it's clear from Brett's troubles with the city that what the local government is looking for here is not infill development that will preserve the character of the neighborhood but big-ticket development that will come in and change everything.

"There's old infrastructure," Brett explains. "There's a one-inch-wide water main feeding all the houses on the street."

Even though the previous building on David's site was a duplex and the new house will be less taxing on the water system, the city is demanding that David provide a new 8-inch water main from his house all the way to the main line at the next intersection. "Essentially, they want David to pay for the infrastructure," Brett complains. I make sympathetic noises and notice that Brett has aged a couple of years since I last saw him. He figures that it would cost an additional $10,000 to $15,000, an amount that David's tight budget wouldn't allow.

It seems inexplicable that the city would obstruct the construction of a single house that way, crazy that they'd expect a newspaper reporter and a young architect to pay to replace the city's inadequate water main. Of course, if a large developer came in with a plan to redevelop a whole block or a whole neighborhood, they would think nothing of replacing the water pipes.

Brett, if anything, is resourceful. He got in touch with the city council, and when that didn't work, he contacted the head of the plumbers' union. Back when Brett was working on his original shotgun house he'd gotten support and free labor from them, and now he was using that connection to work his way through the city's bureaucracy. The head of the plumbers' union offered to contact the head of water and sewage and the plumbing inspector.

"That's the water meter right there," Brett points out, as we stand in front of the empty patch of green, so peaceful in the fading light. Among other things, the city is claiming that the previous house on the property had no water hookup, so the new house isn't entitled to one. But that's clearly crazy, and the water meter in the ground out front is proof.

"This is what happened with the voucher houses," Brett explains. He's referring to the seven architect-designed houses that were supposed to be built under the auspices of the FWCRC. Those houses never got built. "It's gonna happen, but it's been hard . . . the time that's been wasted."

As we drive out of Houston's east side on our way to dinner, Brett points out that a new "loft" building is under construction on the fringes of the neighborhood. "See, here," he says as we drive past. Gentrification is coming. As we trace the perimeter of downtown Houston, I notice that Enron Field is now called Minute Maid Park.

Maybe it's because I've just been in Austin, where the city went out of its way to encourage and assist KRDB, that I can't understand why the city of Houston isn't bending over backward to do whatever is necessary to make this house happen. It seems to me that this is exactly the sort of development they should be encouraging, development that treats existing neighborhoods with respect. In the presentation booklet Brett made about the house, he demonstrates over and over again how it relates to its neighbors and how the house could serve as a prototype for a larger-scale development.

"The option of building another shot-trot on the adjoining lot or within the neighborhood furthers the idea of a rhythmic recurrence of a basic, simple, geometric form," Brett wrote. "Borrowing forms from existing local vernacular architecture, the shot-trot creolizes them in order to emerge as a hybrid system . . ." He goes on to describe how the basic Shot-Trot could be customized to the needs of each homeowner. "The shot-trot type could be an important and powerful cultural diagram reconnecting the home back into the community."

It sounds very idealistic, but like Dominique de Menil, Brett is able to look at Houston with an outsider's perspective and see what's valuable there, to see what's worth building on instead of demolishing. Unlike the Menils, however, he is just a junior architect at a small firm. He's got no money to throw at the problem.

As we sit down to dinner at the seafood restaurant he tells me about the other obstacles he's encountered. "The past four months of this project, I've lost five years."

For example, he had to fire the structural engineer who had overengineered the place, specifying steel floor joists instead of wood. "I feel happier about the house now. I'm building it the way it should be built. The new guy made it a very modest structure."

Still, despite all the trouble, despite this completely unexpected roadblock from the city, Brett believes the project will go forward. And, in fact, a week or so later, I get e-mail from him. The subject line is "green light":

I have some great news. I finally got in touch with the deputy director of engineering for the city of Houston today. He responded quite positively. After all the waiting, all he wants is David to write a letter stating that he understands the implications of the 1" water line. He was sensitive to the project and its most definite impact . . . to the neighborhood.

"I'm very excited," he continued. "I'm pretty sure things will finally begin construction within the next few weeks."

Let Us Now Praise Famous Men

September 14, 2003   Greensboro, Alabama

At this moment I am the sole occupant of a sprawling antebellum bed-and-breakfast. I am perched on a king-size four-poster bed in a private suite. Scott Wing, who is supposed to be lecturing at Rural Studio tomorrow, hasn't arrived. The other occupant isn't coming. Just me, reclining in the lap of luxury.

I think of the South as the obsessive corner of America, where people are passionate in a way that northerners don't understand—the Civil War being a case in point. And also the South seems to speak a different language. For instance, I stop at a McDonald's somewhere in Louisiana (an act of sheer desperation—I somehow can't find anyplace else to eat) and order two regular hamburgers, the little ones without the secret sauce. The young woman behind the counter can't understand a word I say. And I can't understand a word she says. In theory, we are both speaking the same language, in a situation that really requires no nuance. The upshot is that I wind up with two double cheeseburgers.

I stop for the night at a Sleep Inn on the outskirts of Jackson, Mississippi. It's a newish motel, the kind that likes to pretend it's a hotel, built on

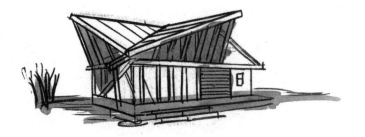

Two butterfly-style roofs by Rural Studio: the Harris house,
Mason's Bend, Alabama, and the Antioch Baptist Church,
Perry County, Alabama

the edge of a strip mall that also has a sushi bar where I have dinner, grateful for a meal that involves no melted cheese.

Back in my room I watch Channel 6, the real estate channel, which shows nothing but homes for sale, all still images like the kind of ads they show in movie theaters before the lights go down.

"214 Memory Oaks $239,000 . . . storage isn't a problem in this house. . . . 143 Beaver Bend $239,000 . . ."

They all look the same, these houses, big spreads with pointy roofs. Each house seems to have half a dozen peaks, like a bowl of meringue. In the morning, before I check out, they show the $100,000 houses. They look just like the $200,000 houses but they're smaller, with fewer peaks, and tend to be in newer subdivisions, farther from the desirable parts of Jackson, I guess.

Eventually, I pack up my car and drive a largely featureless road to Starkville, where I spend much of the day steeped in Dan Camp's obsession, a part of town he built and owns, a place Camp named "The Cotton District."

This neatly contained, dense neighborhood in the middle of Starkville, a smallish college town (population 22,000), is Dan Camp's private fiefdom. A trim man of about sixty, with a slightly scraggly white beard and a khaki baseball cap that he wears the way another man might wear a crown, Camp rules by driving around in his golf cart, keeping an eye on the dozens of crazy little houses he built, all with some sort of historicist charm, whether Italianate details or New Orleans style. Almost all of them are student rentals with prices ranging from $375 a month to $750 a month. "If you're in Starkville, that's kind of pricey," says Camp.

Mark and Kiki from Prospect have been telling me about Dan Camp for years. He's the one guy who regularly shows up at important New Urbanist meetings whom they actually like. The New Urbanists tend to be a sober, sanctimonious bunch who don't stray too far from the neat town plans and clean, historically inspired architecture specified by the movement's found-ing mother and father, Elizabeth Plater-Zyberk and Andres Duany. But Camp, like Kiki, is a renegade.*

I meet him at his office in one of his miniature villas just off Starkville's main street. Students file in and leave their rent checks in a basket on the front desk or give them to his assistant. In back, Dan, in khaki shorts and a polo shirt, sits behind a big desk.

"I'm a classicist," he announces right off the bat. And he makes it clear that he's not the theoretical sort. "These guys on the Internet, all worked up with intellectual fervor. . . . Some of us actually go out and design things and build things."

I ask him if his background is in architecture.

"Of course not," he growls. "I wouldn't be doing this if I came out of an architectural background."

Camp made money in the stock market in the 1960s. He'd toured places like Alexandria, Virginia, and New Orleans, Charleston, and Savannah and noticed the way that successful Southern cities used classical architecture as the basis for their own tarted-up styles. When he settled in his hometown of Starkville, he decided to go into the real estate business in his own pecu-liar way, buying up dilapidated old houses and replacing them with little neoclassical gems. "One thing we Camps do, we believe in cash flow. We rent them."

We tour the neighborhood in his golf cart, and Camp keeps a running narrative going, pausing every so often to call out greetings or instructions to maintenance crews working on one property or another. The houses are like marzipan confections: a pink one with two porches, a wee Palladian villa, an antebellum mansion with eight apartments inside.

"In the middle 1970s, I started to hide the cars," notes Camp, riffing on

*Camp was elected mayor of Starkville in June 2005.

the New Urbanism rule that garages go in back. "I began to be sensitive. Now there's my first Charleston number. With a Charleston side yard. That's one of the original mill houses. There's my Mississippi dogtrot Italianate. I got into a pink mood."

He transformed a 1950s duplex into a Roman villa and, as we turn the corner, there's a miniature temple complete with a *Venus de Milo* up top and a Weber Grill on the porch. "No villa is complete without its temple," says Camp.

It makes no sense, all these tiny, cute houses, really only big enough for a student to live in. It follows no planner's playbook, but it's Camp's business and his life. I am a little jealous of the fact that this man has found his spot, that it is his whole universe. I also feel as though I've detoured into a Faulkner novel.

He has built a number of houses that he's sold outright and a couple he's built for favorite employees. They're nice little bungalows priced at under $100,000, but it's not clear who you'd have to be to get Camp to let you have one. Real estate doesn't seem as if it's ever a simple commercial transaction with him. And you'd have to be willing to live in his version of history.

After lunch with Camp at a restaurant in one of his buildings, a place with white tablecloths and big-city élan, I take off in pursuit of my next obsessive southerner: Elvis.

His birthplace is in nearby Tupelo. And the Presley house, a white, two-room shotgun, so unadorned, so pristine, and so rectilinear that—but for its modestly peaked roof—it looks like something Walter Gropius would have built for the workers of Dessau. Inside there's a hostess, a friendly, white-haired lady named Juanita Robison, who tells me all about Papa Presley building the house for $130. She points out the original doors and moldings, but explains that the Presleys had it wallpapered with newspaper instead of the pretty flowered paper that's there now. Sadly, the family couldn't keep up the payments on the place and had to move to public housing in Memphis. I tell Juanita about the purpose of my trip, and she says I should visit Graceland, because $100,000 is exactly what Elvis originally paid for the place. I tell her that I'll keep that in mind.

And then there's the obsessive Southerner I really care about, a man who played a big part in cultivating my obsession with low-cost housing. I guess I feel about architect Samuel "Sambo" Mockbee a bit the way other people feel about Elvis. Mockbee was an architect and a teacher and in June of 2000 he won a MacArthur, the prize for geniuses. He ran an architecture program called the Rural Studio at Auburn University, in Hale County, Alabama. Since 1992 his students have designed and built houses for poor Alabamians, per capita income $8,000. I met him once, at an awards event at the Cooper-Hewitt National Design Museum in New York. He was burly and shaggy and looked out of place in a sleek, black-suited New York design crowd but he was quick on the uptake. He took one look at me and instantly had my number. "My students," he told me, "are building a house out of old car windshields. And they're building one out of bales of cardboard. You come down to Alabama, we'll show you around and feed you some ribs."

Visiting him was on my list of things to do, but Alabama wasn't really on the way to anyplace I needed to go, neither a spoke nor a hub in my flight plan, so I never got there. In December of 2001, Mockbee died of leukemia. He'd been fighting it for a while but he hadn't told most people, not even his colleagues at Rural Studio, that he was ill. He just left for Christmas break and never came back.

Sambo, as his friends called him, wasn't like anyone else building for the poor. He wasn't like Habitat for Humanity or all the urban housing authorities across America that are methodically replacing bleak, uninspired high-rise projects with equally uninspired row houses.

Rather, he built houses that are the envy of design fanatics everywhere. There's one that his students designed for the Harris family. It's called the Butterfly House, because the roof tilts upward in two directions like a pair of wings. The angled roof collects rainwater that flows into a cistern and is used for washing the clothes and flushing the toilet. The materials are cheap, like tin, or salvaged, like 105-year-old lumber. The whole place is handicapped accessible, because Mrs. Harris is in a wheelchair. But on top of all that altruism, it is a gorgeous piece of architecture, as delicate in appearance as a Noguchi lamp. I could easily envision it sitting proudly on a choice piece of Long Island beachfront or tucked into some Marin County cove.

Sometime after our one face-to-face encounter, I called Mockbee to talk to him about an idea I had for a building competition. I was trying to figure out whether his methods, whatever they were, were transferable. Like everyone with whom he came in contact, I wanted a little of his magic.

He explained that he could build for next to nothing because, in the rural South, even people with no money, who live in leaky, unheated shacks, often own land on which to build. And, with student labor and scavenged materials, a small architectural wonder could be built on a $30,000 budget.

The next time I tried calling him, someone picked up the phone and hung it up without saying a word. Later I realized that at that moment he was dying.

At one point I conducted phone interviews with a group of Rural Studio students who had crafted a surprisingly elegant, freestanding dormitory room out of 1,000-pound bales of industrial waste cardboard. The most impressive thing about the project wasn't the beauty of the structure itself but the dedication of the students, kids from towns like Wetumpka, Alabama, and Marietta, Georgia. Clearly, Mockbee had inspired them. They had caught the spirit of the place, not just the desire to do good but a pride in craft that made the good deed even better. It was such kids, rather than the computer jockeys that many architectural programs churn out, who seemed as if they might have the skills to actually change how people live.

Still, most of what I knew about Rural Studio I knew from looking at pictures, mostly gorgeous photos by an architectural photographer, the kind that transform buildings into perfectly lit, pristine works of sculpture. Now, finally, I was going to visit this legendary place.

Which is how I find myself at the Muckle House Annex, the overflow building of a bed and breakfast, in Greensboro, Alabama, the only town near Rural Studio's home in Newbern to have a McDonald's and a proper strip mall.

I arrive after dark, following instructions e-mailed to me by the proprietress. She is busy at Muckle House itself, tending to the guests who are in town for a major football game up the road in Birmingham on Sunday. I go out in search of food and come back with a McDonald's Cobb salad and a six-pack of beer. When Andrew Freer, formerly Mockbee's second in command and now the codirector of Rural Studio, and Scott Wing, a visiting instructor from Penn, show up, I offer them beers and tell them how amazing it is that absolutely the only wine for sale at the local convenience store is Boone's Farm.

"Welcome to my world," says Freer with a sigh.

Freer is a tall, skinny English architect whose curly hair appears to have gone gray rather recently. Or maybe that's my imagination. His very presence in the middle of Alabama seems like a strange accident. Picture him as Arthur Dent, the bathrobe-wearing Englishman who accidentally travels from planet to planet in *The Hitchhiker's Guide to the Galaxy*. He seems that out of place. Freer, who took over the day-to-day operations of Rural Studio when Mockbee died, has yet to replace himself. He has no assistant. He drives the backroads of Hale County from student project to student project, multitasking as he hunches over his pickup truck's dashboard, opening mail and fielding phone calls when there's actually a cell phone signal. He seems, at every moment, to be exhausted.

On Friday morning I have breakfast with Wing, Freer, and John Forley, an architect from Birmingham who pitches in at Rural Studio. Mostly they talk about how to run the charrette they are having that afternoon intended to get the students interested in renovating an ugly duckling high school home ec/shop building in outlying Thomaston. A firehouse for downtown Newbern was the sexiest of the year's major projects, the one everyone wants to work on; the high school building project needs to be sold. The idea this year, Freer explains, is that instead of everyone going off immediately to work on their own project, the whole group of thirty students has to spend a few weeks discussing all of them.

After quick stops at the various Rural Studio properties in Newbern—like Morissette, a big old house that contains offices and girl's "dorms" (the "pods" where the male students live are out back) and the Red Barn, where studio work is done—we drive on to Thomaston. There we sit around in an old classroom for hours discussing simple logistical problems: how to cover the windows of the big old high school room so Scott could show his slides; where the students should work on their part of the charrette.

Andrew and John send Scott and me off to buy lunch. We are told to go to a gas station where "buffet pizza" is sold. The word "buffet" means that one price will buy you all the toppings. The pizza crust is preformed and probably frozen and the pizza is baked in a big assembly-line-style toaster. While the pizza cooks, Scott and I watch the locals come in to buy stuff and hang out at the tables. The gas station/convenience store/buffet pizza joint is the only place in town. Freer can go on at length about the sociological significance of the gas station/convenience store in rural southern life.

The four of us eat our gas station pizza and, eventually, the students trickle in and gather on the vast front lawn of the defunct high school. (The old gym is a kudzu-choked ruin.) More than an hour after the charrette was supposed to start, we are divided into groups of three, with each group assigned a single facade of the ugly little building—slated to become the headquarters of the Alabama Rural Heritage Foundation—to rethink. Andrew and John decided to use me as the "wild card" student and place me in a group.

I work with a cocky fifth-year student, Matthew, and an artistically talented, shy second-year student, Mary-Michael. While it isn't my intention to dominate the design process, it is hard not to. I have ideas I'm willing to discuss, and the students are either uninspired or, more likely, are feeling too intimidated to bring their ideas to the table. So the design we came up with—turning a blank brick wall into a billboard and putting in a pavilion that echoes the shape of the old gym—are mostly my concepts. My position becomes even more awkward because I am expected to be both a kid—participating in the design process—and an adult—commenting on the other team's work. It is tough to play both roles because, by the end of the day, I also want my team to win.

In any case, over the course of the afternoon I become increasingly interested in the future of this undistinguished building, which will eventually house a gift shop and a commercial kitchen turning out limitless quanities of pepper jelly, exactly the effect the day's activities are supposed to have on the students. I am having Yestermorrow flashbacks. We finish after sunset, with the mosquitoes biting and everyone beyond the point of exhaustion, leaving me with the crazy, overextended feeling of a Yestermorrow day. In theory, this is a good thing. These kids are getting their money's worth. On the other hand, I am beginning to feel the way Freer looks, totally drained.

Finally, much too late, much too hungry, Andrew, John, Scott, an architect named Dick, and I go to a joint in a town called Faunsdale for crawfish étouffée, catfish (Greensboro is Alabama's catfish capital), and Cajun sausage, and I am grateful to be eating in a real restaurant. On the way back to Greensboro after dinner, Andrew and John decide that they have to show Scott and me one more thing. A softball field that several of last year's students—"leftovers"—are struggling to complete now has night lighting donated by a local company. We drive down some pitch-black back road—in truth, back roads are the only kind they have around here—park, and walk into an open field. Then Andrew turns on the lights, which gives the whole place an otherworldly glow. The perimeter of the park is defined by a wall of cardboard bales. The bleachers will eventually be enclosed in catfish netting on a frame of metal hoops. The hoops are there, but the netting hasn't been installed. It is a crazy, beautiful place. I haven't seen a single house all day, but I now possess a bone-deep understanding of Rural Studio's culture and aesthetic.

The next day Andrew and John take Scott and me on a grand tour of Rural Studio projects all over Hale County. Our first stop is Morissette, where I get a chance to go back and take a good look at the pods. In real life, these ramshackle little buildings are occupied by college boys, which means they get all the wear and tear of dorm rooms even though they're built with more fragile materials. So when I finally see the cardboard bale pod that I'd once written about, it is no longer the pristine, monkish little shelter I've admired in architectural photos. Instead, there is dirty laundry everywhere, a dart board leaning against a window, an empty Boone's Farm bottle on the floor. Dangling from the steel cables that anchor the roof—one of those perfect architectural details I'd noticed in the photos—are hangers holding clean clothes. Stolen traffic signs have been added to the décor. And, in the context of this dorm room squalor, the bales of industrial cardboard with their messy, flocked edges have begun to look less like an amazing new building material and more like the recycled paper products they actually are. This is not to say that I am disillusioned—quite the opposite. It's always instructive to see one's favorite architectural icons in use, as they are meant to be.

We drive around Hale County in two cars. Sometimes I ride with Andrew and sometimes with John. This is the same Alabama county where James Agee set up shop with Walker Evans when they worked on the *Fortune* magazine assignment that eventually became the book *Let Us Now Praise Famous Men*. I think it was John who explains to me that Agee and Evans spent their time with the white tenant farmers of Hale County, who traditionally lived in the hills, while the black farmers lived in the flatlands. The places we're going are in the flatlands, as Rural Studio's clients are most often black.

In Mason's Bend, an end-of-the-road enclave where Rural Studio started out building just a bus shelter and went on to build three houses, a community center, and a chapel, we first stop at the famous Harris house. No one is home, so we can't go inside, but from outdoors it looks just a little worse for wear. While it may have alluded to a Noguchi lamp in the official photos, a pristine objet, in real life it is someone's home. A satellite dish is prominently mounted at the V of the butterfly roof, while an artificial Christmas tree is on display in the overhead storage area of the screened porch that comprises most of the house's square footage. Cars and trucks are parked everywhere on the property.

Another house looks like an elongated bungalow, its exterior walls made from carpet tiles stacked like brick. At one end of the house is a misshapen tower of the sort that Daniel Libeskind proposes to plop down on the World Trade Center site, if anyone would let him. It's crumpled and asymmetrical inside and out, with a bunker-type room below and a bedroom above. A big, soft man sits in the living room surrounded by lots of whirring fans, watching TV, and a little girl watches another TV in her own room.

We also visit the original "charity house," the Bryant house, a low, dark, straw bale number with three Quonset-shaped projections—bedrooms—out back, that houses an elderly couple and their three grandsons. The boys are playing Nintendo football on the living room floor, and the old man can barely walk well enough to make it into the kitchen to greet us.

Toward the end of the day we come to a trailer enclave in Greensboro where a leftover student named Lucy is finishing up a lovely, colorful screened porch that will double the floor space of a beat-up trailer occupied by a woman and her son. Lucy has moved all the woman's possessions—crumpled clothes, dirty old cans of food, broken small appliances—to the porch so that she can re-floor and paint the trailer's interior. I am struck by both the

beauty of the porch itself and the poverty suggested by the client's possessions. I find myself thinking, as I had back in Lawrence, Kansas, about
whether improving someone's home also improves their life. On one hand,
it seems clear that the best help you can offer someone who's struggling to
survive is a decent home. But Studio 804 in Kansas and Rural Studio are
both dedicated to giving impoverished clients a home that is more than just
decent. These programs try to create homes that are actually inspiring, as if
the quality of the design will lift the lives that are lived inside its walls. And,
as much as I'd like to believe that's the case, I leave Mason's Bend (and
Greensboro) thinking about the ways that the real lives lived in an architectural icon are very different from what the icon suggests. A great house is,
after all, just a starting point.

The Rural Studio projects that I wind up being most impressed with are
not the charity houses but the public buildings. I'm not sure whether it's
because these buildings—churches, recreational facilities, senior citizens'
clubs—simply strike a populist chord or because the fifth-year architecture
students who work on them are more skilled than the second-year students
who build the charity houses. Or maybe it's simply that the organizations
that maintain these facilities take better care of them than the homeowners
do of their houses.

The four of us stop off to visit three leftover students trying to finish a
project from the previous year, three architecturally ambitious restroom buildings for a new park. The construction schedule had been defeated by inces-
sant rain, and so the bedraggled kids are still here, months after they've
graduated, fighting the mosquitoes. The most ambitious of the trio of latrines
is a forty-foot-high tower, a toilet with a view. Other students had already
built a wooden boardwalk into the woods. When I follow the walkway it
leads to yet another Rural Studio project, a pavilion with an undulating
steel roof supported by thick wooden beams and benches made of the same
wood as the floor. The benches seem to just pop up out of the flooring. The

pavilion is a phenomenal piece of architecture, and looks like something one would stumble upon in a Swedish park, not in America, and most particularly not in Alabama.

The most stunning of all the public buildings is the Antioch chapel, which was built on the site of an old black Baptist chapel. The students incorporated, Andrew tells me, some 70 or 80 percent of the materials from the old church into the new building, including the pews. The new church is an asymmetrical bow tie with a butterfly roof, one upturned wing shorter than the other. The interior is mostly wood, with a glass wall facing the cemetery so that parishioners can have visual contact with the place where their dead are buried. The exterior is a very tasteful combination of seamed metal siding, wood, and concrete block. The Antioch Chapel is a surprisingly well wrought, elegant piece of design sitting in a tranquil clearing. Again, I feel as if I've been transported to Scandinavia and I start thinking about how, year by year, project by project, Rural Studio is transforming Hale County.

The church reminds me of my favorite passage from *Let Us Now Praise Famous Men:*

> It was a good enough church from the moment the curve opened and we saw it that I slowed a little and we kept our eyes on it. But as we came even with it the light so held it that it shocked us with its goodness straight through the body, so that at the same instant we said Jesus. I put on the brakes and backed the car slowly, watching the light on the building, until we were at the same apex, and we sat still for a couple of minutes at least before getting out, studying in arrest what had hit us so hard as we slowed past its perpendicular. It lost nothing at all in stasis, but even more powerfully strove in through the eyes its paralyzing classicism: stood from scoured clay, a light lift above us, no trees near, and few weeds; every grain, each nailhead, distinct; the subtle almost strangling strong asymmetries of that which has been hand wrought toward symmetry . . .

It shocked us with its goodness straight through the body. Yes. Exactly. That's what this church does. It is so beautifully intentioned and so well executed that it just radiates goodness. It exudes a magic that most buildings have only in photographs when they're staged and lit just so.

I've always had a notion about the power of small aesthetic gestures—architects call them "interventions"—that I acquired early in childhood from a story called "The Magic Geranium." The story concerns a woman who lives in a shabby house. One day, she gets a red geranium and puts it on the kitchen table. The beauty of the geranium forces her to notice the shabbiness of the table, which she then replaces. The new table reveals the shabbiness of the wallpaper. And so on. The beauty of one flower winds up transforming the woman's life. (Later the Magic Geranium was reincarnated as the Broken Windows theory, popular with New York mayor Rudy Giuliani and his police commissioner, Bill Bratton. The idea is that if you take care of the small things, like broken windows, a neighborhood will not deteriorate into a slum and, likewise, if you prosecute minor offenses, you create an environment less appealing to felons.)

I guess I'd always regarded the Rural Studio charity houses as Magic Geraniums, believing that they would, bit by bit, remake their surroundings, starting a chain reaction that would spread the kind of shocking goodness about which Agee wrote throughout Hale County and beyond. But I leave questioning the wisdom of the school's piecemeal approach. Maybe planting the occasional hothouse flower isn't the most effective thing they could do. Maybe they'd accomplish more if they designed and built half a dozen houses at a time. Or twenty. Or fifty. The houses would be less quirky and charming. They'd perhaps be less photogenic, but they would have the civic heft of the school's public buildings. I leave Rural Studio thinking that maybe one house at a time isn't enough.

STRETCHER

CONTROL JOINT

SCREEN

CORNER RETURN

SOFFIT

FLUTED

OFFSET FACE

SPLIT RIBBED

LINTEL

Assortment of blocks

Breeze Blocks

13

September 8, 2003   Decatur, Georgia

I am late for dinner in Decatur, Georgia, having taken back roads from Selma, where I stayed at the St. James Hotel, one of the few buildings the Union army neglected to burn down. My room had a view of the Alabama River and the Edmund Pettis Bridge, where state troopers and local policemen attacked civil rights protesters who were marching to Montgomery in 1965.

I am late, and I'm navigating the complicated maze of interstates that either hold the Atlanta metropolitan area together or tear it apart, depending on how you look at things, and William Carpenter, Fellow of the American Institute of Architects (FAIA), keeps calling my cell phone.

I'm joining him for dinner in downtown Decatur, along with his friend, a publicist named Liz Lapidus, whose father was the legendary Miami architect Morris Lapidus, and her artist husband, Tony Hernandez. Carpenter, whom I've never met, used to send me long letters about his work and his ideas. He has done a number of modest houses and additions for a clientele dominated by artists. His most famous client is Jimmy Carter's daughter, Amy. Carpenter has endless notions about place, about how Atlanta, a city with a bad reputation for soulless sprawl, is actually a city of intimate little neighborhoods.

Over time I got to feel as if Carpenter were somebody I actually knew well, so I decided to accept his offer of a place in Atlanta. Again, it has been weeks since I've stayed in an actual home—the four-poster splendor of the Muckle House Annex was as close as I'd come. (Actually, Andrew and John at Rural Studio had offered me use of what had been Sambo's pod, a cool little building on stilts. But it had no bathroom, which meant I'd have to navigate the outdoor stairs in the dark if I needed to pee. And I was warned that the the pods' outhouse was so rank that most of the guys who lived there just urinated in the field. As much as I thought it would be good journalism to sleep where Mockbee had slept, I politely declined.)

So Bill keeps calling to get my ETA, to find out if I like Thai food, to direct me to the restaurant, to find out what I want to order. We are in a hurry, I discover, because Liz needs to get home to watch *Sex and the City*. She thinks that the final episode is airing tonight and doesn't want to miss it. I can empathize.

I finally arrive in downtown Decatur, find a parking space and the restaurant, wishing desperately that I could shower and change my clothes before dinner. A nap would also be good.

Bill turns out to be a completely different person from what I had imagined him to be. His writing style and his phone voice suggested a classic, buttoned-down, bookish guy. I had envisioned Atticus Fitch from *To Kill a Mockingbird,* as played by Gregory Peck. Instead, he is a gangly, middle-aged hipster with whatever hair he still possesses neatly shaved away. Liz is stylish and charming, and her husband is understated and cool. I am trying very hard not to let my road weariness show. It is difficult to overstate the disappointment I feel when I discover that the Thai restaurant can't make me a vodka martini. I settle for white wine.

The conversation at dinner is a blur. I notice that Bill talks a lot in a soft monotone and drops many important architecture names—Sambo, Jennifer (for Jennifer Siegal, known for her book on modular housing)—and there is something about his tone or my fatigue that makes me want to pick a fight.

We make it to Liz's place in time for *Sex and the City.* The episode ends with Carrie kissing the character played by Mikhail Baryshnikov, an ending so ambiguous that we decided that it can't possibly be the season finale. And we spend a lot of time admiring Liz's beautiful home. It's a former hardware store converted into a rambling modern spread with an enclosed patio off the kitchen and Tony's paintings of children with wizened, sad faces like the boy from *The Tin Drum* everywhere.

When we finally arrive at Bill's I am beyond exhausted. We drive off a main street in the center of Decatur, down a driveway, and behind a row of buildings that face the street. Tucked away in a back parking lot is a squarish, cement block structure. My room for the night is on the third floor in a loft overlooking the main floor of the house. This is Bill's bedroom. He is spending the night in the little bedroom downstairs shared by his daughters, who shuttle between here and his ex-wife's place.

It isn't until morning that I realize that this funny concrete house, hidden away behind a row of institutional buildings, is the closest thing I've seen to the house I'd designed at Yestermorrow. It has the lofted bedroom and the concrete block walls. It has a garage below and a main floor that is primarily an office.

And I don't especially like it. The theory of it is fine. But there's something about the reality that is a little bit off.

Partly, it's the site. The house feels wedged in. I'm all in favor of density and I love infill development. I assume Bill got a good deal on the little piece of land, and here, deep in the middle of the block, the house is well insulated from traffic noise. But somehow the site makes it feel as if the house, with its view of the backsides of its not terribly distinguished neighbors, is nowhere in particular. I have an innate bias toward street views. I've always resisted buying or renting apartments with back or courtyard views, choosing visual excitement over tranquillity. I believe that you should be able to look out the window of an urban house or apartment and see the life of the city, and you can't exactly do that here.

Mostly, though, my problem is with its finishes and details. I stand in the loft bedroom overlooking the main downstairs space where Bill has a small dining table, a drafting table, and a computer area. I mentally take inventory, noting all the details, trying to understand my reaction to them. The concrete block walls here are too raw, too cold. They have none of the beauty of the polished concrete block walls on which I'd based my Yestermorrow design or even of the painted concrete block walls that KRDB favored back in Austin. There are no floor-to-ceiling bookshelves here to add color or warmth; nor is there any art. And the finish work is sloppy. Flecks of paint from the ceiling dot the adjacent walls, and mortar from the concrete blocks spills over onto the blocks themselves. It all looks hasty, as if at a certain point in the process Bill was just in a big hurry to get it all done.

My reaction to the house surprises me, because I have had a long romance with concrete blocks. Back at Yestermorrow, I briefly considered designing an interior wall for my house out of decorative screen blocks, the kind that are square with different patterns cut out of the concrete and are often used in situations where you want more of a fence than a wall, something that offers privacy and security but also admits light and air. I remembered driving around some of the older residential neighborhoods surrounding downtown Las Vegas and admiring the way builders had used screen blocks; each facade would have a slightly different block pattern. I thought it would be cool and kind of elegant to have a solid wall of little niches formed by screen blocks, until Kathy Meyer pointed out that the niches would inevitably trap dust and spider webs, and that I'd be forever vacuuming them.

Still, I spent a lot of time looking at the page from one of the builders' reference books at Yestermorrow that showed all the different varieties of "concrete masonry units." I was amazed that there was a concrete block designed for every purpose, special shapes for corners and columns, and blocks with a fluted pattern to create an undulating finish. I found myself thinking of concrete blocks, which became popular in the early 1900s as an inexpensive method of fireproofing, as very handsome, almost heroic objects. I began to regard concrete blocks the way someone with a more classical sensibility might regard the orders of columns.

At the time I wasn't even thinking about Frank Lloyd Wright, who built some of his most beautiful buildings—the Arizona Biltmore, the Ennis-Brown House—out of concrete blocks he designed himself and often had fabricated on site. Whenever I visited Wright buildings, I was invariably moved by their integrity.

And even other forms of unornamented masonry sometimes get to me in ways I find difficult to explain. For example, when I visited St. Mark's Church in suburban Stockholm, designed by architect Sigurd Lewerentz, the brick walls, so raw in appearance that they practically looked medieval, almost moved me to tears. Yet they were just bricks and mortar, intentionally laid to emphasize the handmade nature of the place. No bricks were cut to make them fit; rather, the width of the joints was altered to make measurements work out. In a way, the walls were sloppy looking, like Bill's walls.

Bill and I talk a lot about the technology and economics of concrete blocks. He used a type of block that is made in part from recycled blocks, nominally a green product. Bill says he initially considered using autoclaved aerated concrete (AAC) manufactured in America by a German company, CSR Hebel. AAC is interesting stuff, based on an old Swedish process. The concrete is exceptionally porous and, as a result, it has about a tenth the strength in compression as regular concrete block but a much higher insulation value. While this qualifies it as a green material, it's friable, meaning it has a tendency to dissolve, so exposed walls have to be covered with stucco or siding. And it's more expensive, about eight to ten times the cost of regular blocks.

Compounding the coldness of this house for me are the heavy metal fire doors separating the floors, not a design decision but something required by law. Then there are the huge industrial windows equipped with rolldown steel shutters. But more than all those individual details, is the fact that the house may be a reflection of Bill's life. He has impeccable taste, but his divorce may have left him without a certain vitality or joie de vivre. The place has a feckless bachelor quality to it.

"I was shooting for $100,000," he explains. Because of the tight infill location in the middle of downtown Decatur, the fire code was unusually strict. Hence the heavy metal doors and window shades. "I had to get a second loan." It wound up costing $140,000. Still, it's not bad.

The basic rectilinear shape of the building, to Bill's thinking, represents a sound economic decision, for as he says, "I think the boxiness is a way of streamlining the construction process." But it's also an aesthetic choice. "I like boxes," Bill declares. "They're interesting to live in."

He says of his 2,800-square-foot house—the measurement includes the loft, the garage, and the ground floor workshop—"I see this as a live/work prototype." He figures that "next time" he could build one for $90,000.

The house itself is the outgrowth of an earlier project, a $5,000 one-room studio he had built for himself in the backyard of the house where he had lived with his wife. It was a 12 × 12 × 12 box with a hammock out front. "You know, Thoreau and Walden Pond, that's what this was based on." The little office outbuilding, he explains, made a statement about "the balance between work and leisure." The hammock "is right here for returning phone calls."

But the live/work connection isn't Bill's main interest: he devotes more of his energy to the idea of design/build, stressing the importance of programs like Rural Studio, where young architecture students learn to build. "A lot of architects are known for not knowing how to build," he says. "I've been looking at how this act of building affects students while they are developing their design minds, at how the way they think about design changes. It makes them better designers. My thesis is that architectural education, this delivery method, is changing the way that architects think."

He now runs something called Urban Studio at Southern Polytechnic State University in nearby Marietta. "Sambo," he adds, "helped me start the Urban Studio." Carpenter's students have built small huts for the homeless in Atlanta and a variety of park and garden structures.

Bill and I spend the rest of the morning driving around Decatur, stopping at several additions he's built to local houses. Most of his built work is much softer in appearance than his own house. We visit a string of wood-sided, gentle modern additions with butterfly roofs and whimsical names like "rain catcher" and "light catcher."

And then we do my favorite thing: drive around Atlanta's little neighborhoods looking at the occasional new house under construction and at old houses. Bill points out the various hipster enclaves like Cabbage Town and Candler Park, and we cruise through the Martin Luther King district, past the great man's birthplace.

In the afternoon Bill heads off to Marietta to teach, and I go back to his house and spend some time carefully considering why I don't love this place. Is it the placement of the windows, which are somehow more like retail display windows than windows in a house? Or that the big expanses of glass just underscore how tightly boxed in the house is? Or is it the enormous ceiling height that feels wrong? Or maybe it's really just the concrete blocks themselves that continue to bother me. Whatever it is, my thoughts keep drifting back to that warm living room/kitchen that KRDB did for the firefighter in Austin.

It's funny. I've spent so much time insisting to people, "No, modern architecture isn't cold." But this house seems like a potent counterargument. It's a very subtle thing. When does a home that borrows its material or its architectural language from institutional or industrial buildings cross over and stop being a clever appropriation and itself start being industrial or institutional? When does architecture that flirts with a language we've all found alienating and unyielding go too far and actually become alienating and unyielding? How much skill does it take to avoid the kind of sterility that up until recently most people associated with modernism? Bill's place suggests to me that the boundary between success and failure is very, very thin. And maybe the problem is me.

As I near the end of this long trip, I'm discovering that road weariness accumulates. My stint at Rural Studio seems to have used up my meager reserves of physical and emotional energy. I've reached a point where no amount of sleep makes me feel rested, and fatigue makes me susceptible to doubt; it's like what cults do to brainwash would-be disciples, except I've done it to myself. Now, confronted with Carpenter's house of concrete, I'm beginning to second-guess myself on matters of taste. But, as tired as I am, I don't want the road trip to end because I haven't quite found what I'm looking for. I'm too tired to go on and too anxious to stop. As a result, I'm feeling more than a little peevish and I'm taking it out on the home of my generous host.

Some months later I get an e-mail announcing Bill's new Web site, www .lightroom.tv. He's formed an interdisciplinary design studio with a graphic designer and a Web designer whose office is the main floor of his house. The studio, as it turns out, is named Lightroom, and the home page—a big photomontage of the view from the loft where I slept—is intended to show what a wonderful space it is. But even at its most photogenic, with sunlight flooding in, new furniture, and Bill looking pensively out the window while his partners are at work, it still looks a little too cold.

The Pursuit of Happiness

14

September 11, 2003   The Clarion Hotel, Raleigh, North Carolina
I guess this may be normal, but I've had a sense of foreboding about this day for
days, an uncomfortable sense that there is something up ahead, around the
corner, that I can't see or imagine, a deer about to cross the highway.

Once again I'm backtracking, driving south when I should be continuing north. I am heading to Americus, Georgia, home of Habitat for Humanity. My stated goal is to visit the organization's Global Village and Discovery Center, billed as a museum village of substandard housing around the world.

I have a fascination with museum villages and someday will do a whole road trip devoted to exploring little faux towns erected specifically for didactic purposes. I still haven't forgiven myself for skipping Henry Ford's Greenfield Village back in Dearborn in favor of a dip in Lake Michigan. And I almost missed this one, too, having initially arrived so late on a Sunday, after a stop at the Jimmy Carter Center in Plains—how could I resist?—that I just have to retrace my steps.

I check into the handsome nineteenth-century Windsor Hotel in the middle of town. The words "I'm here to visit Habitat" are enough to shave thirty bucks off my room rate, no questions asked. I set out on a walk

The Haitian house, Habitat for Humanity Global Village and Discovery Center,
Americus, Georgia

around town before dinner and find the Global Village, locked up for the night, and also locate the Habitat headquarters in a small office building downtown. I formulate my plan for the following day. First thing in the morning, I call Habitat for Humanity and ask for whoever handles press. I leave a message saying that I very much want to tour the facilities and get a quick call back from Linda Mills, visitor services manager. My day is set: Global Village in the morning; Habitat with Linda in the afternoon.

Along the way on this trip, I have from time to time pointed out that architects I've visited built low-cost housing that improves upon the houses constructed by Habitat for Humanity. For example, back in Kansas, one of the Studio 804 houses stood right next door to a Habitat subdivision where all the homes were standard-issue tract houses with big garages front and center. While it seems churlish to criticize an organization that has built over 175,000 homes for low-income families all over the world, and while I respect their goals, it does bother me that they mostly feel compelled to sponsor such unlovely work. This has changed in at least one instance in recent years. A Seattle architecture firm, Olson Sundberg Kundig Allen, designed a very simple modern house, with the same butterfly roof that turns up on many of my favorite buildings, for a local Habitat group, which built eight of them in West Seattle. "All for an unbelievable $45 per square foot, less than what most Olson Sundberg Kundig Allen clients might spend on a square foot of marble countertop," reported the *Seattle Post-Intelligencer.*

Anyway, I walk into the Global Village Welcome Center with my prejudices intact and proceed to the first dot on the map, Poverty Housing. I immediately encounter an assemblage of shacks and shanties that resembles nothing so much as the pods out in back of Morissette at Rural Studio. In fact, the poverty housing this exhibition decries, with its use of whatever scrap material is near at hand, strongly echoes the Rural Studio aesthetic.

The Habitat version of poverty as education tool is well intentioned but a little strange. "Notice the hanging light bulb in this dwelling," says the sign affixed to one of the shanties. "There is no electricity, but the bulb symbolizes hope of a better life."

I quickly make my way through the poverty row and move on to examples of the types of houses Habitat builds in various countries around the world. "From Poverty to a Simple, Decent House," says the interpretive sign as I approach an example of a steel-reinforced concrete block house of the type the organization builds in Guatemala. It's crazy, but I love it. It is approximately the shape of a modest suburban ranch house but much smaller and it's made from concrete blocks fabricated by the homeowners themselves (just like Frank Lloyd Wright!). In other words, it's what architectural theorists would label a trope, a mixture of fashionable industrial materials and traditional domestic form. And it costs only $3,300 to build one. Forget Elvis's birthplace—this is my kind of house.

And then there's the little brick shed Habitat builds in Botswana, with its sloping corrugated tin roof, steel window frames, and doors painted a pretty shade of blue. It's the Primal Shed; its price tag, $3,500.

The Haitian house is better still and is, in fact, so pretty that I can't stop looking at it. It has a double barrel-vaulted roof, two curves of steel-reinforced concrete side by side, and looks like something the Italian architect Pier Luigi Nervi or Eero Saarinen would have built in the 1960s. The roof is supported by concrete block walls, and the windows are made of patterned breeze block. The front entrance has a little covered porch area, and the doors are made of wood. It's a perfect little Third World house with a design that could easily be modified for First World consumption. It is graceful in a way that Bill Carpenter's concrete block house isn't. The difference, I think, is that the curved roof softens the hard edges of the concrete block construction, and the breeze block is a nice decorative touch. Of course, in a weird way, it also echoes the house I designed for myself at Yestermorrow.

The Global Village was planned to include some twenty Habitat models from around the world, although a few are still under construction when I visit. The tour ends with a sign that says: "Poverty housing is a worldwide scourge, and the United States isn't exempt." It shows a picture of a beat-up mobile home and contrasts it with a tidy Habitat house, not the kind I've been seeing with a two-car garage out front, but a somewhat more modest design that Habitat builds here in Sumter County, Georgia, its home base.

As it turns out, the modest design is actually what the organization's founder, Millard Fuller, prefers. That's what I learn during the second half of my day, which I spend driving around with Linda Mills. She takes me to see a 130-house subdivision called Easter Morning, which was completed a few years earlier, where low-income homeowners also receive social services. Or, as Mills puts it, "a nurturing committee helps the homeowners." The homeowners are mostly black, because in Sumter County, that's where the poverty is. "The average black income is under $12,000. The average mortgage [at Easter Morning] is $200 a month." The houses sell for about $45,000. Of course, that price is based on donated labor and donated materials (like vinyl siding and Whirlpool appliances). Habitat provides the financing and no-interest mortgages, and Habitat is funded, in turn, by the fund-raising efforts of its network of largely church-based affiliates.

"It's a nice pyramid scheme instead of a bad pyramid scheme," is how Mills puts it.

Habitat grew out of a cottage-industry farm called Koinonia, organized in the 1940s by a man named Clarence Jordan, preaching pacifism and shared possessions. The idea, a radical one for Georgia at the time, was that black and white people would live together in a Christian commune. In the 1950s Koinonia established an interracial summer camp, which was closed down by the local health department presumably for political reasons, and a roadside produce stand, which was attacked by area residents and in 1957 destroyed by a bomb. Millard Fuller arrived at Koinonia in 1968 and began a homebuilding project that became Habitat for Humanity. After a stint in the early 1970s working with the Church of Christ in Zaire, he came back to the states with a vision of how to build affordable housing in this country.

While I am wary of Fuller's vision, driven as it is by his Christianity and the notion that he is doing God's work, I'm surprised to find much that I admire in what Habitat has done in its own backyard. The Habitat houses I see in the communities they've built around Americus adhere to Fuller's guidelines for "simple and decent houses."

When I read the actual Habitat guidelines that local organizations are supposed to follow, they make a lot of sense. The largest Habitat houses are supposed to be 1,150 square feet. Of course, four bedrooms are supposed to fit within that area, which is a lot more rooms than I would try to squeeze into a relatively small footprint, but still, I admire the spirit. The basic house is intended to have only one bathroom (although additional baths are permitted if the family so chooses). The stated goal is to have families "affect the design of their houses as much as possible." Houses should be designed to accommodate people with disabilities. And "homes should not have garages or carports." The Habitat houses in Lawrence that are dominated by their garages, like bad suburban houses everywhere, are not just contrary to the current thinking about what constitutes a well-designed, pedestrian-friendly neighborhood but are contrary to Habitat's own rules.

In other words, there's nothing in the Habitat design criteria that dictates the ugly houses that most often get built. And the purist houses I see around Americus are not so different from Brett Zamore's updated shotgun house . . . and Elvis's birthplace. If Habitat could somehow wean itself from the donated vinyl siding, something they are considering as they focus more on environmental concerns, they could sponsor housing that Millard Fuller and I would both like.

Leaving Americus with more sympathy and respect for Habitat, I head to Tybee Island, near Savannah, for a little beach time. I feel overwhelmed by my whole trip through the South and wish I could just sit at the beach for a while and process everything that I've learned in the past week. But I have only one night before I need to be in Raleigh, North Carolina, and wind up spending my evening on Tybee listening to a man with long blond hair, Frank the Beach Bum, tell me about the beauty of the ocean. He's a guest in the same downtown motel where I'm staying and, before I leave him to get dinner, he tells me his room number and invites me to visit. For a moment, I'm tempted.

I wake up in Raleigh on September 11, 2003. On NPR three of the last four people to get out of the Windows on the World alive are being interviewed. They had just finished their regular 7:30 breakfast, gotten into the elevator, and were descending as the first plane hit. The Clarion Hotel, where I've spent the night, is one of those round towers that Holiday Inn liked to build in the 1960s. At twenty stories, it's the tallest building in town. The continental breakfast that comes with my room is served in the top floor restaurant. I drink my coffee and eat my pastry at a table by the window feeling a bit uneasy.

Raleigh is home to Bryan Bell, who runs a nonprofit called Design Corps, which specializes in building housing for migrant laborers. I had met him earlier in the year at the opening of the triennial design exhibition at the Cooper-Hewitt. At the time he told me that he was beginning to explore permanent housing for farm workers who no longer wanted to be migrants. I figure that I should stop in and see him because he might offer me some insight into the ways a house could offer stability to the chronically rootless.

Bell doesn't look as if he would know anything about the needs of impoverished farm workers or that stability should be in his bag of tricks. At age forty-three, he still appears impossibly young and untroubled, handsome in a guileless, straightforward way. We have lunch at a surprisingly chic little restaurant hidden away up a flight of stairs on a street that seems to be Raleigh's nightlife district. His mission, he tells me, is "bridging the void between good design and the low end." Me, too, I say. I am beginning to notice that that particular form of bridge-building might be a generational mission, something a particular breed of younger architect has adopted in reaction to the current housing market and the technologically intensive way architecture was taught in the 1990s.

Somehow Bryan Bell arrived here, in this exceptionally populist niche, after getting his undergraduate degree in architectural history at Princeton. "It was the Michael Graves days. You had to be a Michael Graves. I wasn't," Bell tells me. He worked for a time in London with Richard Rodgers, the architect responsible for the Pompidou Center in Paris.

Bell eventually found his way to Samuel Mockbee's door, before there was such a thing as Rural Studio. He worked for Sambo in Jackson, Mississippi, on houses made of corrugated metal before corrugated came back into fashion. The job paid $4 an hour, but the experience was invaluable. Mockbee approached everything with the energy and enthusiasm of a big dog, rambunctious and troublemaking. "He was something else in those days."

Bell graduated from the architecture program at Yale and got a job with the architect Steven Holl, whose work is arid and intellectual compared to Mockbee's, and whose personality is at the chilly end of the spectrum. Bell was troubled, in particular, by Holl's relationships with his clients: "They were millionaires but they were nice people. He just bashed them."

But more than that, Bell's stint with Mockbee had taught him that there were other ways to approach the profession. "In New York I felt redundant. I wanted to go someplace where there were no other architects. My sister was in Gettysburg, inspecting migrant housing for violations." He visited her there and found the perfect place, a spot in the heart of Pennsylvania's apple country, a spot that had some 12,000 migrant workers but no architects, that thought it had no use for architects. Bell fell in with a nonprofit called Rural Opportunities and got a $2,500 grant from the American Institute of Architects (AIA) to develop a little manufactured housing unit for the migrants. Eventually the nonprofit hired him as a housing developer and, Bell says, "It's basically what I still am."

His job, he explains, "involved identifying a need, surveying workers, finding funding sources, constructing housing, getting it rented up, and finding a manager. At that point, I felt like I left architecture. But now this is my definition of architecture and design. When I say I go to projects with no other architects, I go to projects where they don't even know there's a project."

Bell remained with Rural Opportunites for five years and then began to work as a consultant to other nonprofits, designing housing for migrant workers and getting farmers to contribute to its construction.

"We bring in 50 percent of the construction cost. The grower puts up 50 percent and the land." Design Corps's half of the money "is not a gift, it's a loan." The farmer pays it back by complying with a set of rules for twenty years. "They can't throw you out whenever they want to. They can't use bunk beds. Can't charge too much rent. Have to maintain upkeep."

We finish lunch. I want to pay, to support Bell's good works, but he insists: "We had a good week last week. Lots of grants came in."

We drive across town to the Design Corps office, a couple of rooms that Bell shares with his wife, Victoria, also an architect, in a suburban-style generic office building. In a small conference room, Bell spreads out photos of his "migrant camp," a 728-square-foot mobile-home-shaped unit with a single four-man bedroom, a kitchen, a bathroom, and a screened porch. Like many of the architects I've met along the way, Bell has come up with a strategy for working with existing manufactured home companies to get them to do what he wants: "You've got to know what you can ask for and what you can't ask for."

Bell has worked out designs for single men and for families and he's moved on to helping migrant families who want to build a permanent home. He's set up a situation in which thirteen farm worker families in the Gettysburg area helped build one another's houses with financial help from the USDA Rural Development program. It's a community-minded program that, in the current political climate, seems remarkably idealistic: "No one can move in until they're all done."

They are conventionally framed, stick-built houses, because it seemed faster and simpler to stay with ordinary building methods. The overall shape of the house was also dictated by expediency: "We learned a square house gives the most volume for your price. It minimizes the size of the foundation and the roof."

Although the envelope was a given, each family was involved in the customizing of its own house. One required a quiet homework area. Another wanted a landing with a seating area on the stairs. A Muslim family needed its house to face east. "Sometimes I call it an ounce of design. It's only an ounce but it's dealing with this specific family."

The result of Bell's work around Gettysburg is a cluster of simple, decent-looking houses. Each is about 1,100 square feet and costs $85,000. They are not the kind of houses that I dream of, but they are also not bad. I begin to see Bell as a secular version of the Habitat for Humanity ethos. His ounce of design is the bridge between Rural Studio's architecture-intensive charity houses and Habitat's generic homes.

After Raleigh I take a little vacation. I drive to Cape Hatteras in part because I feel the need for a couple more days of beach, in part because my road trip is nearing its conclusion and I am not ready for it to be over. I pick out the Falcon Motel in a town called Buxton on the skinny, one-highway strip of barrier island. A hurricane is threatening but it isn't due in for another few days. And all I can think is that if the hurricane hits with any force, this whole place is going to get washed into the ocean. It is chocka-block with recent vintage waterfront condos, from under which the beach is already eroding. I have never been in a beach town that I liked less.

Cape Hatteras depresses me, but my stop in Charlottesville, Virginia, cheers me up again. I have agreed to do a radio piece about architecture and democracy for the public radio show *Studio 360,* so I stop in Charlottesville to interview the town's mayor about Thomas Jefferson.

First I revisit Monticello. I'd first gone there in the late 1980s when my career as a design critic was just beginning and I've always remembered Jefferson's home as the only colonial-era house in which I've ever felt comfortable. At the time, I couldn't articulate exactly why, so I return, take the tour, and realize that Jefferson used daylight in a very modern way, installing skylights in his bedroom and in the dining room, perhaps a first in America. And the house is all full of oversized windows, which give its rooms an open feeling uncommon in eighteenth-century American homes.

My real task, however, is to spend time with the mayor, Maurice Cox, and have him show me around the campus Jefferson designed for the University of Virginia, his "academical village," a place I've never before visited.

Cox is a very Jeffersonian character, a practicing architect as well as a professor at the university. When he talks about the campus and what it means, he sounds very much like the hybrid he is:

"Clearly this was Jefferson's crowning achievement and his last great work. . . . It synthesizes a lot of his thoughts on what it would take for this experiment in democracy to work. He believed that order, symmetry, and hierarchy and very definite limits to space were part of creating a humane environment, an intellectual community."

We stand on the steps of the rotunda, a half-sized brick remake of the Roman Pantheon, under whose unornamented dome the university's original library was housed. The building sits at the crest of a gentle slope. To our left and right, a row of little temples extends from either side of the steps surrounding a long, green lawn. The classical temples were built as undergrad housing and are still used as dorm rooms, except that now you have to be a very special student to live in one.

"Jefferson, in choosing a village as the model for a public institution, was ultimately suggesting that the ideal democratic society is a communal one, that it's a collective," Cox says, "a place where people learn good citizenship."

Near the north end of the mall, hidden on a small plaza surrounded by shrubbery, there's a statue of a seated Jefferson. It is not a triumphant statue like the one that dominates the streetside steps of the Rotunda. Here, he seems simply to have sat down to enjoy the quiet pleasures of this place that he built.

At the base of the statue is this inscription: "I am closing the last scene of my life by fashioning and fostering an establishment for the instruction of those who come after us. I hope that its influence on their virtue, freedom, fame and happiness will be salutary and permanent."

Virtue, freedom, fame, and happiness. Once again I find myself thinking about Jefferson's most famous expression, "the pursuit of happiness." It's a brilliant expression, wonderfully optimistic, but it gets misread and abused. People think this country is about happiness, which plays out in places like Buxton, North Carolina, as easy gratification, consequences be damned. Charlottesville, on the other hand, feels more like it's about the pursuit.

Charlottesville turns out to be the last stop on my swing through the South, and it's the best place, the most complete place, I have visited on this leg of the trip. I eat dinner two nights in a row at the sidewalk café of a French diner on the downtown mall, where everybody in the area seems to congregate in the evening. And I drive north thinking that the whole business of democracy cuts two ways when it comes to architecture. Jefferson, who was gifted at using architecture as a symbol of democracy, was actually very undemocratic in his methodology. The university campus is as tightly structured as it's possible for a place to be. And that is what gives it its beauty. On the other hand, the architecture of Cape Hatteras is truly democratic in that it seems unrestricted and free but it speaks poorly of who we are and what we prioritize.

The eternal A-frame

Bill of Troy

15

September 21, 2003   Bovina Center, New York

What I'm reminded of is how much I love this part of New York State, especially the view from Susan Y.'s backyard. And there is something appealing about having a little retreat up here. My own back porch, my own view.

Architect Bill Massie, no surprise, needs to postpone our appointment. He's a hard guy to catch up with and always has been. And so, instead of Troy, New York, a played-out industrial city north of Albany where Massie is currently based, I'm in the much smaller town of Bovina Center.

Because Massie is my official last stop on the trip, his postponement leads me to change course ever so slightly and drive instead to the western Catskills, where my friend Victoria is borrowing a house that belongs to a couple we know, Susan and Mike. It's a house that I've visited before. From the front, it looks like nothing, its low facade standing quite close to the two-lane road that wanders through Bovina Center, once a prosperous dairy town and now another outpost for weary urbanites. But it's a beautiful part of the Catskills, where the land just rolls, where hilly meadows surround picturesque little clusters of buildings. I like it here. I like it a lot.

I sit on the back deck of the house staring dreamily at the pasture that used to be full of dairy cows and is now home to a few horses. And I think that, for all the miles I've driven, some 14,320 to date, there is no place in America that I like better than right here. What pleases me most is that my friends are here, and after my lonely odyssey, I feel as though having congenial neighbors counts for a lot.

On Saturday afternoon Victoria, her pal Trevor, and I drive with the top down along roads that smell sweetly of late summer. We hopscotch from town to town, marveling at villages that have been largely untouched by major development schemes, hamlets where smallness has been preserved in large part by the rules enforced by New York City's water department, administrator of the city's vast watershed. We find a store called Bibliobarn, a commodious barn stuffed with books, where we browse for an hour. Victoria starts talking with the proprietor, an amiable old hippie, about *her* hunt for a house to buy. He tells her about a church he used to own in a town called Stamford, how he sold it for $40,000 to the Episcopalians, who are now trying to unload it. A very nice building, he says, except that the basement is flooded.

So we find the church and discover that the basement is, indeed, full of water. We make swimming pool jokes, and Victoria spins elaborate fantasies about the parties she would throw if she lived in a little church in the Catskills.

We both have it, I realize: a bad case of the real estate bug. It's been going around. And when I finally depart for Troy, I take the long way around, stopping in Delhi, one of the larger towns in the area, to look at the pictures in the windows of the real estate agencies along the main street. And I notice that there are parcels of land for sale around Bovina, five acres for $20,000. So, as I meander my way north, stopping at a roadside stand for a hot dog and arriving in Troy's Best Western in late afternoon, I construct an elaborate fantasy about building a house in the Catskills, one that seems entirely plausible. If a place feels like home, I tell myself, it must *be* home.

Troy is not quite the postindustrial wasteland that Massie had described when I last saw him. I had originally met him almost a year earlier in Bozeman, Montana, where he had been teaching for several years, but I'd been hearing about him for a lot longer. He had devised a method of hooking a sophisticated computer-drafting program to a machine that fabricates molds based on computer-generated specifications. This would enable him, in theory, to build houses from poured concrete forms made from the molds he'd manufactured. It was a way, he claimed, to skip the construction drawings that architects generally supply to contractors and—wishful thinking—skip the contractors themselves.

Massie was the first architect I'd heard of who seemed to truly understand the potential of the computer for changing architecture. To him, the technology wasn't about making possible the sort of flourishes that famous architects like Frank Gehry could produce, but how it could be used to make great architecture for regular people. "Modernism has become this bourgeois condition that costs a huge amount of money," Massie complained to a reporter back in 2002.

Formerly an architect at the New York firm of James Stewart Polshek, Massie took a teaching position in 1996 at the University of Montana in Bozeman and, in the relatively unregulated terrain surrounding the Continental Divide, was able to set up a prototype house factory in a garage and build a couple of homes. One, a 2,000-square-foot elliptical tower that he built for an English couple who settled on a ranchette outside Townsend, Montana, cost something in the neighborhood of $145,000. And he was always at work on his own house outside Bozeman, nicknamed the Big Belt. He claims it is an experiment in "visual rhyming," establishing harmony between the house and the landscape, reflected in the long windows framing the endless views and in the rippled terrain of the poured concrete sinks that seem to mimic the landforms outside.

I came to Bozeman to speak at a conference of the Montana AIA in late 2002 and wound up spending a lot of time talking with Massie about his ideas and his work. By that time he had already accepted a new teaching post at Rensselaer Polytech in Troy and was as enthused about the possibilities of the faded industrial landscape of that old Hudson River town as he had been about the mountain terrain of Bozeman. He'd bought a huge old industrial building for $20,000 and was ready to set up an even better house factory. He was, however, beginning to recognize the limitations on his high-tech/low-tech approach. Sure, he was using a state-of-the-art computerized laser cutter to fashion plywood panels and other building components but he always wound up trucking building parts to the site in his own pickup truck. Increasingly he was obligated to be everywhere at once: teaching, building his clients' houses, and running off to do high-profile special projects in China or in Long Island City, New York . . . He was, quite literally, all over the map.

In Bozeman Massie showed me a house that architect Richard Neutra had designed on the outskirts of town. Here the LA-based modernist had built his one and only log cabin, perhaps the only modernist log cabin anywhere, with a sod-covered roof, back in the 1950s. But the highlight of my trip was a hike Massie led through the snowy woods to a frozen waterfall, where rock climbers equipped with ice picks and pitons inched their way up the icy rock face. Somewhere along the way we began talking about A-frame houses, how efficient it was to build a house in which the walls and the roof were one and the same, how it was a shame that they'd gone out of fashion. Massie began speculating, as we walked through snow so powdery that it hardly felt cold, about how he could use his set-up to fabricate a twenty-first-century A-frame. I was hooked. I knew that even though I was still in a difficult transitional moment—I'd quit my job but hadn't really gotten my freelance career back on track yet—I wanted Massie to build me a twenty-first-century A-frame.

The Best Western "continental breakfast." View out double glass doors of Uncle Sam Lanes. The only available yogurt here is Trix-flavored Yoplait. I wonder how that plays on the continent. Troy is a surprisingly handsome city but more than a little dull. It's like a very solid but unknown section of Brooklyn. I am thinking very seriously about land in Delaware County.

I check out of the Best Western and drive down Second Street, out of the center of town and into a neighborhood that gets more desolate the farther I go. Lots of old warehouses and factories, few signs of life.

When I arrive at Massie's building, a two-story former bell foundry, I wander into an unrenovated warehouse space full of mysterious building components. The only human inhabitants are a couple of scruffy guys in their twenties working in one corner, a sort of enclosed courtyard where a laser device hooked up to a computer was cutting primal house shapes—pitched roof, straight walls—out of sheets of cardboard. It turns out that they are building a doghouse for a charity auction, benefiting an organization called Puppies Behind Bars, which allows prisoners to train Seeing Eye dogs. *Funny,* I think, *that all of Massie's technological prowess was being devoted to fashioning the most low-tech house imaginable, the kind a kindergartner would draw with his fat crayons.*

Massie, of course, is nowhere to be found; he is running late. Go back downtown and get some coffee, suggests one of the guys.

I remember the first time we met, back in Bozeman. A local architect had arranged to show another conference speaker and me the town. Massie was going to join us. We all met up by the architecture building of the school, and Massie made an entrance wearing a duster, a long coat that billowed in the wind, and a porkpie hat. He had just flown in from someplace or other, and was about to fly out to someplace else. It was fun, like spending a day with liquid mercury. Now that I'm in Troy actually waiting for mercury, it's less fun.

I drive downtown, pick up a coffee, drive back, and hang out on the second floor of the factory, the so-called office, which contains two computer stations and not much else. Nothing seems exactly weatherproof. There are gaping holes in the floor and in the walls, and maybe in the roof, too. I'm not sure. It's a little like finally catching up with Rocio Romero and realizing that her high-tech-looking LV house is just a lot of pieces of wood. Massie's house factory is here, in a way, but it's far from being all here. After I finish the coffee I'd brought back from town, I learn that they haven't put in a bathroom yet. Definitely a work in progress.

Eventually, Massie appears. He'd been at home in Warwick, New York, near the New Jersey border, where he lives with his wife, an interior designer, and two kids and has been sick for days. He wasn't going to even show up today, but because he is behind on everything he decided to come.

And now that he is here, his motor turns over and begins to rev. Massie talks and talks, faster and faster. First Puppies Behind Bars. Then houses, one he's building in Red Hook, New York. One he might be building on the Palisades. A possible subdivision.

I begin to see that Massie is about houses the way a certain kind of guy is about cars. He sees them less as discrete architectural objects than as a collection of components. He's the guy with a half dozen old cars parked in the yard in different states of repair, constantly transplanting parts from one to another. We sit down by one of the two computers upstairs, a little oasis of technology surrounded by hundreds of square feet of splintery wood, and he shows me the digital renderings of the house he's designing for a man named Greg Wooten. "This wall," he says, pointing to a long, curving expanse on the computer screen, "this wall is downstairs."

And that's what it's like in Massie's world. The elegant computer renderings are fed into the $100,000 laser cutter and spit out as slices of wood, moving from virtual to real, piece by piece by piece. It's mind-boggling.

What Massie is doing in his abandoned foundry is reinventing the construction industry—at least, that's his aim. The balloon-frame house—the thing that is everywhere, that is made from 2×4s, 2×6s, plywood, and Sheetrock—is actually a collection of prefabricated components that architects and contractors have been working with since World War II. The main thing that the computer changed in this conventional set-up is how building materials are ordered and how construction is staged.

Massie, in contrast to other architects, is using the computer to manufacture a new set of building components and so inventing a whole new system. It's as if everyone else were playing with a traditional set of blocks while Massie has Tinkertoys, which is to say that what Massie is doing is very hard. It might even be impossible.

For Wooten's 2,000-square-foot house, which Massie describes as a "long one-story bungalow with a 34-foot-tall snorkel shower," he's anticipating a cost of $160,000 to $170,000. The idea is that the extra-tall shower will give Wooten a bit of architectural drama, an element reminiscent of the tower house in Montana. Inside the shower will be a mirror angled at 45 degrees, so that the whole enclosure will act like a periscope, offering a view of the Catskills across the Hudson River.

Another design Massie has stored on his computer is one for a million-dollar home on the Palisades overlooking the Hudson. He sees the large budget as an opportunity for him to "experiment with everything I can experiment with," including architectural form and materials. But this dramatic vertical project for a wealthy client doesn't interest me as much as the eleven-house experimental subdivision that Massie is planning with a developer for an upstate New York town called Eagle Mills. The idea is to create a year-round community for urbanites, a suburb for artists outside what

Massie describes as a "sleepy colonial town." Each residential unit will come with eleven acres of land, and like a cohousing project, the houses will be small, and there will be some shared space in common buildings. The eleven houses will all be a little distinct from one another. Massie compares them to the follies that architect Bernard Tschumi designed for Parc de la Villette in Paris—they share a language, but each one says a slightly different thing. Best of all, the houses with the land will be designed to sell for from $200,000 to $250,000. It's the sort of deal that might sidetrack me from my quest.

He sees the subdivision as a culmination of all the work he's done to date: "It comes from every project I'm doing now. Every single one." But he worries about what might happen if he gets sucked into a development project—that he'll lose control of the designs or that the developer will lose his nerve.

Eventually our conversation leads us downstairs, where we wander among the building components waiting to be shipped somewhere and assembled. Here, as promised, is Greg Wooten's wall, a big, semicircular slice of a house made of sixty laser-cut sections nailed together, very high-tech and very low-tech all at the same time. If you picture the computers tethered to old-fashioned manual typewriter keyboards in Terry Gilliam's *Brazil,* you've got the idea. There is a concrete drain board for a kitchen sink, and there is the whole facade of a house, a "plywood and acrylic curtain wall." A big, oriented strand board (wood that looks like a Presto Log or luncheon meat) box is destined to become the shower tower. Showers, it turns out, are something about which the chronically overbooked, behind-schedule Massie is passionate. "I think the shower is this incredibly quiet moment," he reflects, "the separation between sleeping and the car." Another Massie bathroom features a dimple in the wall, sized to accommodate the homeowner's body, so he can recline into the wall as he showers.

Massie shows me two interlocking pieces of steel that look a bit like the French curves that used to come in your back-to-school pencil case. They are designed to be part of a new truss system he is inventing. "We've more than anecdotally studied this," he says, as he hands me one of the pieces. "It shows you how nerdy I am about this shit."

Because he can't process the steel himself with his own laser device, it's farmed out to a company outside Schenectady that uses precision water jets. It's a very clear example of a building component that has gone almost directly from being a computer rendering to a physical object.

As we meander through his collection of house parts—the feel is random, more like a junkyard than a lumberyard—Massie admits, "The more we're doing, the less I can distinguish one building from the next."

It takes all morning for us to get around to the subject of my own house, my theoretical $100,000 A-frame. But eventually, after we find our way back upstairs and sit in an open window frame—no glass, no sill, no plastic sheeting—looking out over the low, eerily quiet, postindustrial landscape and at a pile of stress skin panels directly below that are destined to become the walls of someone's house, Massie says the words I'm longing to hear: "I would be able to build a beautiful $100,000 house if it was an A-frame. I would so love to do that, you wouldn't believe it."

I feel as though he's just proposed marriage. And I react exactly as I would if he had: I share the part that scares me. My greatest fear about A-frames is that the sloping walls won't accommodate my bookshelves. But Massie already has an answer: hanging bookshelves that act as part of the structural system, pulling down on the slopes of the A, anchoring the walls.

But just then Massie can no longer ignore his cell phone, which has been ringing at ten-minute intervals all morning. He has to get over to the school for a meeting, and I need to go check out the state capital campus in Albany for my architecture and democracy essay. We don't really get a chance to finish the conversation, but I promise to come visit him again in a couple of months.

A couple of months—between Massie's schedule and mine—turns into a couple of years. We talk on the phone occasionally, but I don't see him again until July of 2005.

I am spending the month of July 2005 in a one-room house, formerly the tractor shed of a farm, in Bridgehampton, New York. I can't help but notice that the little house is a Primal Shed, with a sleeping loft built into the steep angle of the roof. The main floor has a bed, a desk, a couple of IKEA easy chairs, and a pretty decent kitchen. Out back is a picnic table under a trellis covered with grape vines, and there are berry bushes all around. It is an unpretentious place, an unforced amalgam of rustic and modern. I am supremely happy here.

I am, however, in the Hamptons, the official summer playground of moneyed and fashionable New Yorkers. I am surrounded on all sides by shingled mansions, huge houses with lawns that go on forever, and hedges that are so closely and symmetrically trimmed that they look like Marines newly arrived at Camp Pendleton. I go on architectural surveillance rides on my bicycle, past the 100,000-square-foot house that a wealthy industrialist built in the middle of Sagaponack's cornfields, past the exquisite modernist houses that architect Norman Jaffee designed in the 1970s, and past a collection of multimillion-dollar homes currently under construction on the wrong side of the tracks in Sagaponack, miles from the ocean, designed by today's most famous architects. And, of course, all of it is totally out of my reach. The land alone that my one-room house sits on is probably worth a million or two. The idea of a perfect $100,000 house has never seemed crazier.

Massie and I agree to meet after the Fourth of July weekend, when the traffic has thinned a bit. That date gets pushed back once or twice because Massie is on a construction site upstate; the dregs of a hurricane are coming, and his crew is scrambling to get the roof finished before the deluge hits.

On the morning of July 7, the date we finally settle on, I wake up early to news from London. As I get in my car to drive to Troy, they are still saying that a calamity on the London subways was probably a short in the electrical system. But by the time I get to Port Jefferson, a town on Long Island Sound, to catch a ferry to Connecticut—a shortcut to upstate New York—it's clear that terrorists have struck.

This is life's soundtrack, I think. Our lives used to play out to the sound of, say, Diana Ross singing "Stop! In the Name of Love" and they are now lived to the sounds of hate, death, and loss. People are being murdered on their way to work, and I am driving along rain-soaked Connecticut roads on my way to see an architect.

I make my way into Troy, navigating by memory. I know that Massie's building is on the south end of town and I'm able to find it with only a few wrong turns. I get out of my car and take note of the blue sign with the address painted in such big numbers that they can be read from blocks away. I walk through the unlocked front door and into a room that is stuffed with identical building components, like a kit of parts for a smallish town. Now I'm impressed. Massie has finally got himself a house factory.

A young guy appears from somewhere in the back, and I prepare myself for his telling me that Bill is late or missing or couldn't show. Instead, he runs upstairs to get Massie, who's actually here. At the appointed time. Bill appears in a T-shirt and shorts, looking as relaxed as I've ever seen him. He's tan from time spent on the roof and he's got a sparkle in his blue eyes that I find alluring. It's not romance that I see there but mania.

He invites me upstairs, and I am amazed at how much work he's done on the place since my last visit. The windows are enclosed. The holes in the floors have been patched up. There's a row of desks with computers, all unoccupied; a giant room-length whiteboard; and plunked down on one side of the floor, perpendicular to the south wall, a freestanding module shaped like a giant loaf of Wonder Bread.

"Was my office built the last time you were here?" Massie asks.

The loaf turns out to be a tube of panels interlocked like puzzle pieces, plywood on the outside, with glass at either end. The far end of the office module protrudes through the exterior wall of the factory. Inside the loaf-shaped office, an air conditioner is roaring. The interior walls are all cork-board except where there's whiteboard, so every surface is covered with important pieces of paper pushpinned to the wall. Even the flat computer screen is surrounded by a frame made of whiteboard, on which notes are scribbled all around the display. On one wall are bookshelves. One shelf is about a foot wide, the size and shape of a little shrine. I read the titles: *Twin Towers Remembered,* by Camilo Vergara. *Earth Moves: The Furnishing of Territories,* by Bernard Cache. *Bauhaus,* by Frank Whitford. *City of Glass: Douglas Coupland's Vancouver. New Elementary Algebra,* by Charles Davies. *Chaos,* by James Gleick. *Madness and Civilization,* by Michel Foucault.

It is a parade of architecture, urbanism, math, and theory, ending with the Thypin catalog of stainless and carbon steel. Standing inside the office, I feel as if I'm right inside Massie's head, and this shelf represents the chunk of his brain, probably the right side, that does all the intuitive, creative thinking.

He pulls a book of sixteenth-century Japanese carpentry off his desk, full of detail shots of complex wooden joints, and hands me a corrugated card-board reproduction of one of them, the precise pieces having been cut by a computer-driven laser. "It's a compound scarf joint," Massie tells me. The name doesn't mean anything to me, but the concept—that you could use digital data to mimic this ancient form of carpentry, one that uses tremendous discipline and skill to join pieces of wood without nails—just knocks me out.

I'm standing here, thinking that Massie has finally gotten it together, that he has put his world in order, and it's a very cool, well-constructed world, when Massie informs me that he's moving. This office and everything in it are about to disappear. Poof. He's taken a new job running the architecture department at Cranbrook, the famously adventurous arts school located in suburban Detroit's Bloomfield Hills. It's a step up, a more prestigious gig. He'll continue teaching at Rensselaer Polytech in Troy—always in two places at once—but he's going to sell this building and buy one in Michigan. A friend of his will come and photograph it to document it, but then, in a matter of weeks, everything will be packed up to go. I wish I could take his office just as it is and put it in a museum.

Needless to say, I find Massie fascinating and could hang out all day talking about Japanese carpentry, but I have an agenda, a mission to complete. I want to talk about my twenty-first-century A-frame. So we relocate to a sofa that's sitting out in the middle of the unair-conditioned floor. I've brought show-and-tell, a book called *A-frame* by architectural historian Chad Randl, published in 2004. It makes the argument that "the A-frame was the right shape at the right time." It became a symbol of postwar prosperity, when a middle-class family could expect to own two of everything—TVs, cars, bathrooms—including a second home. Inexpensive A-frames, often sold as kits, became very popular from the 1950s until the 1970s.

"I bought the same thing at Borders," Massie tells me when I pull the book out of my bag. "I saw it and bought it and it's fabulous."

And so we sit here, on this battered sofa in the middle of perhaps 10,000 square feet of old bell foundry attic, poring over the A-frame book like two little kids going page by page through the Sears catalog.

"Yeah," I say. "If you get away from the Swiss chalet thing and just think about it structurally, it's so simple."

"It's so simple," Massie echoes. He thumbs through the book, pausing to point out especially good pictures. There are black-and-white shots of surprisingly chic California A-frames, diagrams showing how the houses can be prefabricated, and lots of reproductions of old magazine ads. "There's some incredible things in here and they're so beautiful," Massie gushes. "It's just so smart. Someone has to revisit it, and I'd love to do it."

He leafs to the back of the book, where Randl has reprinted the plans for a "Leisure-time" A-frame beach cabin, a sweet little building with a substantial deck and a sheet-metal fireplace. The very sight of construction drawings makes Massie start talking faster:

"But it is such a beautiful architectural figure, and the thing I'm thinking, of course, is that with structural insulated panels, SIPs, like the ones outside there . . . 24 feet long is the maximum length, and they're 8 feet wide."

And faster:

"Subsequently, if you look and analyze the drawings in all those books, they're approximately 24 feet. When you look at a right triangle, it works out to be a nice 400- or 500-square-foot bungalow, and those panels are already prefabricated, meant to be in a horizontal or a vertical direction, but they could work that way perfectly."

I want to ask whether that 400 or 500 square feet is just the first floor but it's hard to break in.

"I would love to do it, and that, I think, could be done very inexpensively," he concludes.

There's a pause.

Then before I can get him to clarify the question of square footage and to talk about how inexpensive he really means, we change subjects.

Earlier I'd told him about a trip I made in June to San Francisco. There, I went to visit the Anderson brothers in the South of Market office where they're spending most of their time lately. They showed me their latest efforts: a house in New Mexico with chicken-wire-enclosed porches to keep the small farm animals safe from predators and a massive house in Colorado with its own landing strip. The brothers Anderson seemed to have no shortage of interesting, lucrative projects. But we also continued our discussions about the problems with the current prefab movement, how it mostly tackles the parts of the building process that are not necessarily the most costly.

It was a Friday evening in San Francisco, so the Andersons and I decided to go have a drink at an outdoor bar called The Ramp. We drove to the seedy, disused south end of the waterfront, which is quickly being transformed by a massive redevelopment project called Mission Bay. As we followed the shoreline I saw something that looked a lot like a house sitting up on blocks like a car that's been stripped. Basically it was a box with boarded-up windows. It looked modernist in intention but not very well executed. "What was that?" I asked Mark and Peter.

They told me that it was the one prototype eked out by a company called Clever Homes, a local startup with a slick Web site that was promising to deliver prefab houses the way Kozmo.com once delivered pints of Häagen-Dazs. The company, last I checked, still exists, but the prototype was a monument to the fact that it's easier to build a Web site than a house.

Massie picked up that earlier thread: "A good friend from Detroit called me and said, 'Would you collaborate on a building project with me, because I want to prefabricate it?' I said, 'Sure.' He's a good friend. He, of course, thought like so many people think, that prefabrication is like a magic bullet, you know?"

Yeah, I know. I tell him a little about the Andersons' economic analysis and about Peter's fear that the whole prefab thing was just another bubble. And I conclude with the thing Mark had said to me two years earlier, a sentence that continues to resonate: "The least expensive way of building is the most conventional."

"The reason no one's saving money with modular," I note, "is that systems for building houses, as old-fashioned as they are, are pretty efficient already."

"They're exquisite," Massie agrees. "Stick-building is totally this incredibly exquisite thing. It's like the equipment to make a building all supports stick frames; all of the codes and inspection processes all support this. Everything is funneled toward the making of buildings, at least residential buildings, within the stick-frame world. And the reason is that when you get the economy and the policy pushing at both ends, that happens. And there's no policy or economy pushing in terms of prefabrication."

Massie then explains that he doesn't use prefabrication because it offers an economic advantage. It doesn't—not exactly. What it does allow him to do is offer oddball architecture at an affordable price—for, say, $300,000 instead of a million. It allows him to build unusual houses for a somewhat younger, somewhat less affluent clientele. But he's not attempting to build "affordable" housing per se, not the kind the federal government might subsidize. And he even questions whether the Rural Studio approach, which has inspired so many imitators, is a reasonable one.

Massie's take, of course, is that eccentric architecture better serves people who actually want it, who sign up for it. In other words, his clientele.

"If you're going to do an eccentric building, whatever that is, then prefabrication has justification," Massie explains. "I'm not going to build a volume that cantilevers eight feet off the side of a building because I want it to catch light in a certain way by talking to a series of local carpenters. That's not going to happen. So if the local carpenters, the local framers, can't build the building, then the cost of the building quadruples.

"I've said this before," he continues. "I don't think I can reduce the cost of building a conventional building, but I think I can meet the cost of conventional building and make a more extraordinary thing. And that's as much as I can do."

"It sounds like you've gone from a fantasy about mass production to a more realistic idea about doing customization," I point out.

Actually, it's taken him a long time to figure this out. I remember a conversation over dinner in Bozeman long ago, when Massie, elated at having been named one of 2002's best and brightest by *Esquire*, was ready to turn the homebuilding industry in this country upside down. But he's since learned that there are limits to what he can do. On the one hand, he does have the house factory that he was dreaming about back then. But all those prefabricated wall sections downstairs, they have nothing to do with homebuilding in this country. They are going to be shipped to Mustique to be the guest cottages at a resort there. Massie hadn't found a way to radicalize homebuilding in America but he'd been able to compensate for a labor shortage in Mustique.

We talk and talk, about prefab, about architectural innovation, about the politics of cheap houses. Eventually we navigate our way to the end of the story about Massie's friend in Detroit.

"I got to the point where I bid this thing," Massie recalls. "And he said, 'That's way more than I think it will cost if we stick-build it.' And I said, 'Well, I know. The building is not so unconventional, but, you see, if it were a more unconventional building, it would be approximately the same cost relative to the techniques I'm talking about.' He said, 'Right, it's not so unconventional, and so we can probably stick-build, but I really love the idea of prefab. I want to do prefab . . .'"

"That's the fashion talking," I interject.

"Exactly. So he said, 'There's got to be someone out there that I can get to prefab it.' I said, 'Keith, you know what? If you can find a company to prefab what you've designed right there and give it to you at the same cost as stick-built, call me up, and I'll drive to Detroit and pay for the trip for us to drive there and do it.'

"He said, 'Of course I can find someone. Everyone's doing prefab. Everyone's talking about prefab.' He and three people in his office have spent two months solid. I said, 'Where is there a company that I can contact that will prefabricate my work in a bidded process right now? Where is one? Because if there is one, I'll do it. I mean, I'm not even joking.'"

Massie's take on prefab is full of built-in contradictions, but the upshot is that although he is personally prefabricating building components, he no longer sees it as a solution to a broader problem. Rather, it's a solution to his own problem. He wants to be able to closely supervise how his designs are built but he doesn't want to travel to do that. Prefabrication, in theory, permits Massie to supervise construction without actually being on-site. (Of course, our appointment was postponed by a day or two because he was on-site putting a roof on a house.)

But there's something more. Prefab, for Massie, is an art form. Using computer-driven tools to translate digital information into physical objects is his particular means of expression. The fact that he does it doesn't mean that it's practical or feasible for less obsessive architects or builders. Actually, although Massie has developed a high-tech system for building, there's something decidedly low-tech and anti-systematic about what he does. There is, in truth, something wacko about Massie's whole approach to building, which is what I like about him.

Or, as he puts it, "Who was it, Dennis Rodman, who said, 'I'm no role model'?"

At some point we get up off the sofa and tour the giant room, pausing to inspect models of houses under construction and models of houses that will, for one reason or another, never get built. Since my last visit a number of projects, including the subdivision and the million-dollar house on the Palisades, have fallen by the wayside. We look at the way the plywood panels of Massie's office interlock. And he talks for a while about his obsession with puzzle-piece-style connections. And, again, I could do this all day, but I'm afraid that if I don't get the conversation back on track his cell phone will ring and he'll vanish.

"Back to the A-frame," I say. "You did drawings?"

"I did a couple of drawings. I don't know if I have the sketches here."

"Are there things you think would set a twenty-first-century A-frame apart from the 1970s version?" I ask.

"The one thing about the A-frame, it obviously gets its strength out of making a panel out of joists, long joists, and then the skin gives it lateral strength. It's an ideal condition, an A, but the side of the A becomes rigid. Well, you never see that skin fucked around with. And the reason you don't is that there's a rhythm of the joists that you can produce efficiently. Of course, that's where the fun part really is, in that those walls . . . they were always opaque."

Okay, I follow. A twenty-first-century A-frame differs from a twentieth-century A-frame in that the skin is "fucked around with." I like an architect who doesn't resort to jargon.

"There's the other thing. These were companies that produced these and not individual architects."

"Right," I say. "They were guys on the highway in New Jersey."

"Absolutely. I've just been analyzing the efficiency of these things, and the major thing you can tell by looking at this book. . . . I looked at all the material lists, and looked at the framing lumber, and analyzed that, and said, 'What would that cost now?' If the 2×6, which is the dominant structure, costs $31 for that length, it's more expensive than a SIPs panel, but this is the big thing. All of the lateral strength comes from sheeting it this way, and so you get virtually no transparency on those elevations. It's a tube."

Now, admittedly, I am a little lost.

"That's the A-frame," Massie says pointing at a section diagram, "and the transparency is this direction, like that." Now he's indicating the windowed area on the front of the building. "If it were a panel, then there'd be the ability to poke holes in it . . ."

"And not compromise the strength?" I ask.

"Perforate it," he continues, lost in schematics, "almost like shoot it with a shotgun of rectangular apertures to be able to have this incredible . . ."

"So it's a screen?"

"Yeah. An aperture that's got a filter of light. So that's what I'm thinking."

Okay, I like the idea of an A-frame with a roof that is somehow translucent instead of opaque. But, as Massie talks, questions occur to me. For instance, SIPs panels are sandwiches, typically a layer of rigid foam insulation squeezed between layers of Sheetrock covered with oriented strand board. How can you perforate a sandwich? But Massie's in overdrive, now. There's no real way to form my unease into a sentence and inject it into the flow.

"Like, that is amazing to me," he says, returning to the picture portion of the book. This ranch house with an A-frame carport. It is such a fundamental and elemental building shape. It's beautiful but, of course, made by sticks. The shape has nothing to do with its technology. You know what I mean? Like you could take a piece of cardboard and do that, and you can test that. So stress skin panels are more elemental."

Stress skin panels are the same as SIPs panels, another name for a structural sandwich with a foam filling. In truth, it's a very old-fashioned form of prefab construction. But he's still talking about perforating the roof:

"If the shape is maintained and there are these apertures, and it becomes a screen, it could be a truly amazing building. I really want to do one."

He pauses. He is, suddenly, talking more slowly. He has my full attention.

"If you want to say—and you don't have to pay me in any way—if you just say, maybe . . . I'll just try and figure one out. And give me until next year at this time, and call me once every two months to prod me, I'll do it. I'd love to just . . ."

Here's where I should ask, "How on earth do you perforate a Styrofoam-filled sandwich?" Here's where I should ask, "How many square feet? How much will it cost? How can you possibly find time to do it? Do you really mean it?" I should be asking any number of questions.

What I actually say is this:

"Okay."

"I will," he continues. "But it . . . and then if . . . I really think . . ."

And that's it. I've got it on tape. Those are the words that I've traveled 14,000-plus miles to hear. "But it . . . and then if . . . I really think . . ."

So, we haven't agreed to a price, and I haven't bought the land yet, but for the first time in the whole adventure, I can visualize it: the translucent A-frame in the western Catskills, or maybe in the Hudson River Valley, north of the two-hour-drive-from-New-York-City mark.

And I even pick one out of the A-frame book that I think will work. The page is marked by a Post-it that says, "This one!" In 1962 it was the most popular A-frame in America. Oddly the floor plan reminds me of my Yester-morrow house. It's got 815 square feet on the main floor and 319 square feet upstairs. It's got a living room, kitchen, bathroom, and bedroom on the main floor. Upstairs is a second bedroom at the rear of the house and a balcony bedroom overlooking the living room. The balcony bedroom is, of course, my office. The house has a front deck and a rear balcony on the second floor, accessible from the back bedroom. The 1962 version is covered with wooden shakes and is dark and rustic. It looks as if it belongs in Yosemite. But if you took the overall design and changed the palette of materials, if you "fucked with it," as Massie suggests, it could be a lovely house.

As I'm getting ready to leave Troy, it occurs to me that I've never actually seen anything Massie has built, not in person anyway. I've looked at pictures. I've observed the component parts but I've never seen them assembled. So he gives me directions to two houses under construction off the Taconic Parkway, a highway that runs north-south through a particularly beautiful slice of upstate New York halfway between the Hudson River and the Massachusetts and Connecticut borders. They're both on my way back to the Bridgeport–Port Jefferson Ferry.

Massie also suggests that the area surrounding one of the houses might be a good spot for me to look for land. Indeed, the Sternall house, a long, simple rectangle made of oriented strand board panels and concrete blocks covered with pieces of store-bought interlocking Styrofoam insulation, sits at the high end of a large meadow. Massie thinks of it as the "Hay House," because that's what will surround it, acres of tall grass. It's $210,000 worth of house sitting on $50,000 worth of property. The surrounding country-side is lovely, and the home prices in the real estate brochure that I pick up at the local diner are surprisingly low. I am now well north of the New York City weekend home zone.

I continue down the Taconic feeling equal parts elated and spooked. One part of my brain is dreaming of translucent A-frames and the other part is listening to the London bombing news on the radio. One part of me is argu-ing for permanence and the other part is arguing that there's no such thing.

Following Massie's directions, I drive another 30 miles south, exit, and follow a series of winding roads. At the crest of a particular hill, I'm sup-posed to look left to see the Wooten house, the one with the curved wall and the 34-foot-tall shower, but the hill keeps cresting, and every time I look left I see some unremarkable country house or a gate that says "Beware of Dog." Finally, I drive much farther than the directions indicate, and the hill crests one more time. I look left, and there it is. What I see is the curved wall, a patchwork of concrete panels, that I'd first seen two years earlier at Massie's place in Troy. Now, here it is looking like a component of a particu-larly diabolical skateboard park. The concave curve is facing me, and the wall is surrounded by construction-site detritus. It's dusk, no one else is on this wooded lot, just me and this wonderfully odd little house. The Sternall house was pretty standard issue, a modern house as drawn by that hypo-thetical kindergarten student. This one is different. It's modest in scale, but hugely ambitious. It is Massie's fastest talking successfully translated into wood, Sheetrock, and concrete.

Once again, I flash on the childhood thrill of sneaking into houses under construction. Sometimes it just amazes me that as an adult this is something I'm allowed to do, that I'm supposed to do. Still, I look around to see if anyone's here. There's a trailer parked beside the house, but no one appears to be inside.

First I inspect the curved wall from every angle. I love that when you're inside, the wall curves inward, making it seem as though the house was built up against a giant water main. And viewed from the edge, the wall reveals itself as a bravado feat of engineering, a wall that stands despite the fact that it's C-shaped instead of straight.

I poke around the still mostly unenclosed interior until I find the bathroom. As instructed, I step into the shower enclosure and look up. Above me is a tall, chimney-shaped superstructure with a rectangle of daylight at the top. I lean back and gaze at the periscope mirror that reflects not the surrounding landscape but the branches of the tree that is currently blocking the view of the Hudson and the Catskills beyond. "That tree will be gone," Massie avowed as I left his office. But I don't mind that it's there.

I stand in the unfinished shower, looking up at the reflection of a tree and laughing. I am delighted that Massie has actually succeeded in building a periscope shower. It suggests to me that anything—even a twenty-first-century A-frame—is possible. I linger for a while and as I watch what's left of daylight disappear in the angled mirror, I decide that my road trip is officially over.

Jacobs family home circa 1961,
Palisades Park, New Jersey

Conclusion

Except that the road trip is never over. Not really.

Not long ago I headed out on a mini road trip to Pittsburgh to visit the Warhol Museum and to make a pilgrimage to Falling Water, the famous Frank Lloyd Wright house. And while I thought Falling Water was wonderful, a monument to the beauty of the cantilever, it wasn't the house that made the biggest impression on me. En route to Pennsylvania, I stopped in my old New Jersey hometown.

When I turned onto the street where I grew up, everything looked wrong. My house, the "minimal traditional" with the yellow aluminum siding, the granite front facade, the slate walkway, the towering blue spruce, and the lawn that never grew anything but crabgrass was gone, replaced by a bigger house made of brown, white, and red brick. (Talk about compromise style.) The new building is three stories tall, with bay windows on the two main floors—a sort of mock-historical touch—and a matched pair of two-car garages consuming the bottom level.

I stood there in the street staring, dumbfounded. Even though I knew that this was exactly the kind of house that is now typically built in my hometown, I was still shocked by it. What I got out of the experience, besides a rush of an emotion that was somewhere between self-righteous indignation and rage, was a very clear confirmation of the power of the idea of home. Even though I hadn't actually lived here since I was seventeen, even though my mother had sold the house more than a decade ago, it still felt as if something that was part of me had been destroyed.

As I write this it is November 2005. In the past months I've been to the Mississippi Gulf Coast, where I spent a few days at a planning session about rebuilding in the aftermath of Hurricane Katrina; on a road trip around Florida, visiting New Urbanist or neo-traditional developments all over the state; and back to a couple of my stops on the road trip I did for this book, including Marfa, Texas, and Prospect, Colorado. And I flew out to San Francisco and spent an afternoon driving around the subdivisions in the dusty brown hills east of the city.

Every time I tell someone where I've been lately they say, "Oh, you're still working on the book." And I explain, "No I'm not. I'm done with that." In truth, I'm not done. Done doesn't figure into this.

Then comes the inevitable next question: Did you find your house? And the nearly inevitable addendum: Given the way prices have shot up, aren't you going to change the name of the book?

And short answers are as follows:

Yes, there's a house I believe I'm going to build . . . although committing to it means forgoing all those other houses that have so much allure, so much potential. I am not—have I mentioned this?—so good at commitment. This is the exact reason that I am not, at this very moment, married. But I recognize that a house is different. When you stop loving it, you can sell it. And it's legal to have more than one.

And no, while the real estate market has everything to do with the fact that in the middle of writing this book I bought a studio apartment in Brooklyn (as opposed to a one-bedroom apartment in Manhattan), it has very little to do with what this book is about. Not that the architects that I met on my journey are immune to the temptations and nightmares of the real estate bubble, but the state of the marketplace doesn't affect my attitudes about what houses are, how they should be built, and how much they should cost.

The longer answer goes like this:

Since my 2003 road trip, I've continued to think about houses—how they're made, how they look—and to enjoy an ongoing conversation with many of the architects I encountered along the way. And I've continued driving, meeting with other architects, and looking at other houses. What the architects with whom I'd most like to work on my $100,000 house have in common is the view that such a house wouldn't be an ordinary commission, a custom design for one person, unique from all the other individual custom designs they create. Rather, it would be the beginning of an enterprise, a prototype for a house they could build over and over, either on-site or in kit form. Rocio Romero's LV Home was originally constructed for her mother on a piece of property in Chile. She then took that house as a model, studied it, and figured out how to turn it into a kit. Likewise, if I were to work with Peter and Mark Anderson on a house, they would do it only if it made sense as a prototype for a house they could build again and again. Bill Massie's interest in building me a twenty-first-century A-frame has less to do with me and more to do with, as he puts it, "the politics of taking on a type."

In one respect, I failed in my quest, because I learned that the Perfect $100,000 House doesn't exist in the wild. It is not exactly a normal product of the marketplace. It's not something obtainable from America's top five homebuilders, who collectively crank out something like 180,000 houses a year. But it is something that can and even does exist where there are architects, builders, and buyers looking to change the way home design and construction in this country works. If what I get out of this endeavor is a house, I will have succeeded in a small way. If, in making this journey and writing this book, I encourage the nascent renegade housing movement, if my Perfect $100,000 House spawns a cascade of Perfect $100,000 Houses, I will regard my trip as having been an unqualified success.

I'm grateful that I began my travels at what was originally intended to be their endpoint. I had hoped to start driving in the spring of 2003 and to follow a clockwise path around the country, heading south from New York. My last stop was supposed to be Yestermorrow in Vermont in July, which I had decided on as something of an insurance policy. If I couldn't find the right architect and the right situation, I would simply build my own house. As it happened, my agent sent out my proposal for this book at the exact moment the Iraq war began, and no one was then much interested in a project about houses. It took a few months to find a publisher, and I couldn't really begin my trip without one for reasons of both budget and pride. So, by the time I had a deal, my only choice was to go directly to housebuilding camp and to begin my trip along a northerly route, making a counterclockwise loop.

What I learned at the beginning of my trip, besides how to read simple construction drawings well enough to notice a missing 2×4, is how complex a product a house is. Even the simple shed we were building for our class project was surprisingly nuanced. While the Vermont sawmill lumber we were using was more lumpy and irregular than the wood a commercial homebuilder would have at the ready, the tools and methods involved were pretty standard. My two weeks at design/build school made me appreciate the incredible skill level of the carpenters who build houses day in and day out.

In the time that's passed since my trip, the idea of prefab housing has grown increasingly fashionable, and any number of architects and builders claim to be able to deliver a house in kit form. My time at Yestermorrow also equipped me to look at the Web sites of many of the start-up prefab firms with a degree of skepticism. The most striking thing about many of the prefab houses they offer is their price tag. Several of them sell for upwards of $500,000, which, admittedly, is not a lot for an architect-designed modernist house. But then, many of the architects who've plunged into prefab are not necessarily the ones I'd choose if I were searching for the perfect $500,000 house.

Over the past couple of years, I've had numerous discussions about the prefab movement: whether it is saving homebuyers money, whether it represents real change or is simply a buzzword. "Most of the prefabricated building systems focus on the framing and the basic structure of the building," Peter Anderson recently told me. "We've been doing a lot of studying. Where do costs go in building construction? The things that are getting prefabricated are a very small slice of the pie in terms of time, money, and complexity. They're not really solving a lot of the bigger problems.

"The part that has to be solved is not just how you do the wall panels but getting things connected to the site and appropriate to the site," Peter continued. "Foundations, utilities, are there any ways to modularize the processes and techniques, even the approvals process? The surface is just being scratched."

Peter and I concur that the one thing truly innovative and exciting in today's prefab movement is that it has become a way for architects to retail their services. In other words, today's prefab fad doesn't represent a significant technological breakthrough but it does change the way architectural services are marketed. And the person who really figured this out first was Rocio Romero. Even as competitors and imitators spring up, Rocio is the one who really took on the problem of prefabricating a simple, attractive, low-cost modern house and solved it as well as any small-scale entrepreneur could. I still have endless admiration for her design skill and her straightforward approach.

Two years after I visited her little office in the lumberyard while she was waiting for her first wall panels to be delivered, she was shipping about three houses a month. And she was expanding her line to include a larger version of the LV Home, versions that were configured to sit on top of basements (instead of concrete slabs), an LV garage, and a line of small Fish Camp houses that are meant to be assembled by do-it-yourselfers instead of contractors. The Fish Camp houses come with pre-drilled holes in all the panels, just like an IKEA bookcase.

But her sleek, prefab, Galvalume-sided houses are, despite appearances, not the least bit high-tech. "The wall panels are traditional," Rocio tells me. "And that is probably the most attractive thing about my product. Anywhere in America every single general contractor is going to have the tools and the knowledge of how to put these together."

Rocio's operation fits in with my theory about the twenty-first century: namely, that it's less like one of those seamless science fiction places, where everything is smooth and technologically advanced, and more like a cut-and-paste job, with the new tightly tethered to the old. By my standards, Rocio is the ultimate twenty-first-century architect, doing something new by using old technologies and systems. But somehow I don't think that the LV Home is my Perfect $100,000 House. Why? In part, its flat roof may not be quite strong enough for a part of the country with heavy snowfall, like the Catskills. It's better suited to temperate Northern California. But I'm not sure that's the whole answer.

The LV Home is such a strong design that it's iconic; it is, as Rocio says, a product. That's what it's supposed to be, and the packaged nature of the house is the key to its success. But I'm something of an iconoclast. I avoid buying things that are too identifiable as design objects: I own no Eames or Mies chairs, no Tizio lamp or Juicy Salif lemon squeezer. I like buying things for their design, not their status as design icons. Similarly, I own a Volkswagen Cabrio rather than a New Beetle because the Beetle is such a fetish object. And, honestly, because I believe that the LV Home will be a classic design, something about which preservationists and cognoscenti will hold conferences fifty years hence, this perversely makes me less likely to want one. On the other hand, Rocio's Base Camp—a larger, more sophisticated version of the Fish Camp—with its shed roof, its long deck, and its sliding glass doors and movable interior walls—looks pretty perfect to me. The only problem is that at 450 square feet it's small . . . even by my standards. But then, I could have two of them back-to-back or side by side.

While it's not easy to build good, inexpensive houses, it's even harder to continue building them once you've done so successfully. It is a rule that the better a firm is at designing and building low-cost housing, the more attractive it will become to wealthier clients. People with a lot of money often have an aversion to spending it or, at least, are as interested in getting a good deal as anyone else. When I stop by the Andersons' San Francisco office in the spring of 2005 they show me a project they're building for a client in Colorado who needs his own airstrip, and a house in New Mexico that will incorporate indoor rooms for the couple's livestock. Back in Austin, Chris Krager of KRDB told me that they were always getting inquiries from potential clients "with obvious resources and savvy."

"We're catching some flack in the design and building community," he explained. Apparently, the other firm's clients kept asking, "Why is my house $250 a square foot when these guys are building for $125?"

Still, Chris Krager continues to design and build low-cost developments, small subdivisions in and around Austin that feature his firm's signature window treatments and simple shed roofs. Because it's an architecture firm with a genuine commitment to inexpensive housing, and because it's one that promises to someday do it on a large enough scale to make a difference, KRDB is worth keeping an eye on. But the firm is largely a local phenomenon, one that works its magic in the Austin area. Part of the KRDB formula that isn't necessarily transferable to other parts of the country is the low Texas labor cost. Krager tells me, "If you are looking for a skilled carpenter here you will pay at least $20 per hour. If you just want someone who won't hurt themselves with power tools, you can get away with $12 to $15 per hour. Texas is a 'right to work' state (right to work for little or nothing)." And while Krager continues to meet with manufactured home companies, searching for a relationship that will enable him to produce houses for a wider geographical area, he hasn't cracked that nut yet. If I want a KRDB house, I'd have to move to Austin. And as much as I enjoyed my visit, as much as I'd like to go back to watch the bats emerge from under the bridge at sunset, I'm pretty sure I don't want to live there.

A year after I stopped in Houston on my road trip, Brett Zamore completed the Shot-Trot. He began e-mailing me photos, which was like getting a good friend's baby pictures; I was both pleased and proud. The interiors are clean and open, with storage built into the walls that nominally divide the rooms. It's actually startling how much the interior resembles the inside of the genuine shotgun house Brett renovated for his thesis project, but at the same time there's nothing faux or overly cute about the house. Looking at the pictures now, I am once more reminded of what I like about Brett: it's that wonderful mix of pragmatism and sensibility. I feel a twinge of regret about my decision to build the twenty-first-century A-frame. It's not, I suppose, too late to change my mind.

When I last spoke to Brett, he was hard at work developing a Shot-Trot kit. In his usual methodical way, he was talking to manufactured home builders and companies that supply trusses and panels. He doesn't want to do what Rocio Romero's been doing, making the components in a single location and shipping them by truck or rail container (although given the competitive labor costs in Texas, it's something he might consider). Rather, he thinks that it should be possible to put together a national network of suppliers who can spit out the pieces locally. He is, in other words, thinking big. "I want to have a system where—boom!—they can just knock it out like an IKEA kit," he tells me. If it were anyone but Brett, I'd believe that it was just another case of an architect imagining that a house was no different than a computer rendering of a house. But Brett knows his way around the guts of a house, and I'm betting that sooner or later—ten years, twenty years—he will emerge as the Starbucks of housing, the guy who takes something ordinary and makes it better in a way that affects how people live nationwide.

He tells me that he imagines that his kit—which, like Rocio's, will not include plumbing or wiring—will sell for $50,000 or $60,000, and that the final cost for a 1,250-square-foot house will be somewhere between $80 and $90 a square foot, or $100,000 to $112,500. Perfect, except for one detail: the kit version of the Shot-Trot doesn't exist yet.

One of the things I've learned along the way is that I'm not quite the modernist I thought I was. Of my favorite houses, the ones I might truly want to build, none of them has a flat roof. Even the Andersons' Fox Island house has a rolling roof. And the two that I'm most likely to build, the A-frame and the Shot-Trot, have roofs that are so sharply pitched that they are almost like parodies of traditional architecture. Maybe this makes me a postmodernist, or maybe this is just more pragmatism.

The fact that I've acknowledged the value of the pitched roof does not, however, mean that I'm about to embrace traditions. In fact, what I found when I spent several days among the neo-traditional architects of the New Urbanist movement was a renewed respect for modernism.

Some six weeks after Hurricane Katrina hit, I went to Biloxi to report on a gathering of New Urbanist architects and planners who were spending a week working on rebuilding schemes for the Gulf Coast. As part of the event I went on a tour of a town called Bay Saint Louis, Mississippi, which sits at the spot where Katrina made her second landfall (after slamming Louisiana). What I saw there was mile after mile of waterfront neighborhoods where not a single house remained standing. Homes, some that had been weathering hurricanes since before the Civil War, had been ripped from their foundations by a record storm surge and reduced to smelly piles of pulp. I'd never experienced anything like it; no one with whom I was traveling had. Comparisons to Hiroshima and Dresden kept coming up, because no one knew how else to describe the devastation.

Back in Biloxi I spent days wandering around a giant hotel ballroom that had been converted into a studio where over a hundred architects and planners were drawing up schemes for a more pedestrian-oriented, greener, happier Gulf Coast. One architecture team had drawn up buildings that were mostly what you'd expect from the New Urbanists, famous for their love of historical architecture. There were little replicas of shotgun houses designed to be erected quickly as temporary housing and casino complexes that looked as if they might have been around for the French Revolution. In the middle of all this, I noticed two architects, a man and a woman, sitting at different tables, who had drawn a similar style of angular live-work buildings. It turned out that they were a married couple, John and Allison Anderson—another matched set of Anderson architects—and that a month before Katrina hit, they had moved into a home of their own design. I was about to offer my condolences, but they told me it was still standing.

The Anderson residence on Citizen Street in Bay Saint Louis is a relatively unexceptional modernist building located about 1,000 feet from the beach. The 3,000-square-foot house is divided into a connected pair of two-story, slanted-roof sheds clad in gray cement board, with corrugated metal under the eaves. It's a nice enough house, not so different from the sort of thing KRDB does in Austin. What's remarkable about it is that it withstood Hurricane Katrina's 130-mile-an-hour winds and the storm surge, a fast-moving wall of water that roared in and out in the space of an hour, destroying most everything within a quarter to a half mile of the shoreline. Pre-Katrina, this house did not have a water view. But, as Allison Anderson told me when I called to find out about it, "Now there are no houses standing between us and the beach. You can see the sunrise over the rubble."

John was quick to add, "I wouldn't go so far as to say that the fact that our house survived is due to the contemporary style, but more to a contemporary quality of construction."

Maybe so. Houses that survived Katrina tended to be either very old, dense masonry structures or houses new enough to be built to the standards of the International Building Code. "That means," Allison explained, "very heavy duty clips from the slab to the wall studs, to the floor joists, to the second floor wall studs, to the rafters all the way up." But despite John's demurral, I do believe the Andersons' house survived because of the couple's modernist approach.

"It was designed to be an environmental demonstration house," Allison explained. "We were using some principles that we were trying to get our clients to do down here, that they have been a little bit suspicious of." As it turns out, the environmentally driven design decisions, particularly the use of highly durable, low-maintenance materials, helped mitigate the disaster. "We used a lot of things that would limit redundancy," Allison explained. "This is a slab-on-grade house, so we did a polished concrete slab floor. It's a very accessible kind of thing. . . . It cleaned up pretty well, too.

"And we also have a green roof," Allison continued. Just before Katrina, the Andersons had seeded the roof with grass. "It hadn't come up, really, before the hurricane," Allison laughed, "and it came up afterward." The weight of the sod, they believe, helped hold the roof in place during the storm.

When they realized that they couldn't afford to make the front walls entirely of glass, they used plywood instead. Because they felt the need to beef up the structure and also because they'd made a philosophical choice to have structural materials double as finish materials whenever possible, they added a second, interior layer of birch plywood. They believe this second layer braced the facade against the hurricane-force winds and the seven feet of water that rolled through the ground floor of their home. So while modernist style didn't save the Andersons' house, a modernist way of thinking surely helped.

And the Andersons' brand of modernism is precisely the thing I originally went on the road to find. For one thing, they built their house for about $106 a square foot, which means it's in my price range . . . or it would be if it were a lot smaller. But to me it's emblematic of an approach to modernism that is less about surface and more about strategy. The story of the Andersons' house reinforced my belief that architectural style isn't just style, that design decisions can have consequences. I can add the Andersons of Mississippi to my growing list of New Pragmatists.

So, yes, I did find my house. In fact, I found several. I could have an LV Home; I could probably persuade the (Seattle) Andersons to work with me on a new low-priced prototype. I could have an Earthship outside Taos. I could live in a spiffed-up manufactured house in Austin, Topeka, or—the way things are going—New Orleans. I could eventually have the Shot-Trot in kit form.

I figure the odds are about 50-50 that by the time you read this, I will have embarked on the next phase of the project, that I will be shopping for land, leaving increasingly desperate voice-mail messages for Bill Massie or some other architect, and having tense conversations with the building departments of small Catskills towns. Although—who knows?—maybe by the time you reach the end of this book, I will be knee deep in SIPs panels, silica dust, and spackle. Maybe I will even be living happily ever after in a sweet little twenty-first-century A-frame . . . although it's also quite possible that I will still be driving.

Bibliography

INTRODUCTION

Gropius, Walter. "Principles of Bauhaus Production," a 1926 essay reprinted in Ulrich Conrads, *Programs and Manifestoes on 20ᵗʰ-Century Architecture.* Cambridge, MA: MIT Press, 1971.

CHAPTER 1

Connell, John. *Homing Instinct: Using Your Lifestyle to Design and Build Your Home.* New York: McGraw-Hill, 1999.
Piedmont-Palladino, Susan, and Mark Alden Branch. *Devil's Workshop: 25 Years of Jersey Devil Architecture.* New York: Princeton Architectural Press, 1997.

CHAPTER 2

Giedion, Siegfried. *Mechanization Takes Command.* London: Oxford University Press, 1948.
Hagerty, James R., and Kemba J. Dunham. "How Big U.S. Home Builders Plan to Ride Out a Downturn." *Wall Street Journal,* November 20, 2005.
Kalkin, Adam. *The Butler Variations.* Bernardsville, NJ: Nice Nietzsche Press, 2001.
McAlester, Virginia and Lee. *A Field Guide to American Houses.* New York: Knopf, 1984.

CHAPTER 3

Venturi, Robert, Denise Scott Brown, and Steve Izenour. *Learning from Las Vegas.* Cambridge, MA: MIT Press, 1991 (revised edition).

CHAPTER 4

Wanzel, Grant, Brian Carter, and Juhani Pallasmaa. *Designing and Building: Rockhill and Associates.* Halifax, Nova Scotia: Tuns Press, 2005.

CHAPTER 5

Buchanan, Wyatt. "Affordable Yankton: South Dakota's Housing Prices Worlds Away from Palo Alto's." *San Francisco Chronicle,* January 2, 2003.

CHAPTER 6

Anderson, Mark and Peter. *Anderson Anderson: Architecture and Construction.* New York: Princeton Architectural Press, 2001.
———. *Prefab Prototypes: Site-Specific Design for Offsite Construction.* New York: Princeton Architectural Press, 2006.
Zeiger, Mimi. "Some Assembly Required." *Dwell,* April 2001.

CHAPTER 7

Eyraud, Cole. "The Legend of Cabot Yerxa." http://www.cabotsmuseum.org/archive/legend.htm.

CHAPTER 8

Jacobs, Karrie. "Something Happened." *Dwell,* April 2002.

CHAPTER 9

Porche, Verandah. "Folk Rock: Back in the Sticks with Jack." Unpublished. Vermont, 1990.

Reynolds, Mike. *Earthship, Volume I: How to Build Your Own.* Taos, NM: Solar Survival Press, 1990.

CHAPTER 11

Browning, Dominique. "What I Admire I Must Possess." *Texas Monthly,* April 1983.

Choay, Françoise. *Le Corbusier.* New York: George Braziller, Inc., 1960.

Fox, Stephen. "Houston 2000: Looking Back." *Livable Houston,* 2000.

Jimenez, Carlos. "Some Reflections on Architecture and Houston." *Livable Houston,* 2000.

Le Corbusier. *The Modulor.* Cambridge, MA: MIT Press, 1968 (first English-language edition, 1954).

Upton, Dell, and John Michael Vlach. *Common Places: Readings in American Vernacular Architecture.* Athens: University of Georgia Press, 1986.

Vlach, John Michael. *Back of the Big House: The Architecture of Plantation Slavery.* Chapel Hill: University of North Carolina Press, 1993.

CHAPTER 12

Agee, James, and Walker Evans. *Let Us Now Praise Famous Men.* New York: Ballantine, 1939.

Dean, Andrea Oppenheimer, and Timothy Hursley. *Rural Studio: Samuel Mockbee and an Architecture of Decency.* New York: Princeton Architectural Press, 2002.

CHAPTER 15

Hay, David. "How to Build a House for $145,000." *Dwell,* August 2002.

Kroloff, Reed. "Yes, he creates amazing-looking structures. But he's also out to revolutionize the industry. If all goes according to plan, William Massie will be the Frank Gehry of prefab housing." *Esquire,* December 2002.

Randl, Chad. *A-frame.* New York: Princeton Architectural Press, 2004.

Web Sites

C H A P T E R   1

Yestermorrow Design/Build School, Warren, Vermont
http://www.yestermorrow.org

Jersey Devil
http://www.jerseydevildesignbuild.com

Forest Moon: Phil and Cindy Blood's environmental homestead for cancer
survivors
http://www.forestmoon.org

C H A P T E R   2

Adam Kalkin, Bernardsville, New Jersey
http://www.architectureandhygiene.com

Ply Architecture, Ann Arbor, Michigan
http://www.plyarch.com

CHAPTER 3

Rocio Romero, Perryville, Missouri
http://www.rocioromero.com

CHAPTER 4

Studio 804, Lawrence, Kansas
http://www.studio804.com

El Dorado, Inc., Kansas City, Missouri
http://www.eldoradoarchitects.com

CHAPTER 6

AndersonAnderson, Seattle, Washington, and San Francisco, California
http://www.andersonanderson.com

CHAPTER 7

Michael Rotondi, Los Angeles and Desert Hot Springs, California
http://www.rotoark.com

Andrea Zittel, Joshua Tree, California
http://www.zittel.org

CHAPTER 8

Prospect, Colorado
http://www.prospectnewtown.com

Arapahoe Acres, Colorado
http://www.arapahoeacres.org

CHAPTER 9

Mike Reynolds, Taos, New Mexico
http://www.earthship.org

The Chinati Foundation, Marfa, Texas
http://www.chinati.org

CHAPTER 10

Chris Krager/KRDB, Austin, Texas
http://www.lividpencil.com

CHAPTER 11

Brett Zamore, Houston, Texas
http://www.brettzamoredesign.com

CHAPTER 12

Dan Camp, Starkville, Mississippi
http://www.thecottondistrict.net

Rural Studio, Newbern, Alabama
http://www.ruralstudio.com

CHAPTER 13

Bill Carpenter, Decatur, Georgia
http://www.lightroom.tv

CHAPTER 14

Habitat for Humanity's Global Village and Discovery Center
http://www.habitat.org/gvdc

Bryan Bell, Raleigh, North Carolina
http://www.designcorps.org

CHAPTER 15

Bill Massie, Troy, New York, and Bloomfield Hills, Michigan
http://www.massiearchitecture.com

Index

Page numbers in *italics* refer to illustrations.